COLLEGE ACCOUNTING

Twelfth Edition

PART 2

Arthur E. Carlson, PhD
Professor of Accounting
School of Business Administration
Washington University, St. Louis

James A. Heintz, DBA, CPA
Professor of Accounting
Indiana University
Bloomington, Indiana

A82

Published by
SOUTH-WESTERN PUBLISHING CO.

CINCINNATI   WEST CHICAGO, IL   DALLAS   PELHAM MANOR, NY   LIVERMORE, CA

ISBN: 0-538-01820-8

Library of Congress Catalog Card Number: 85-62381

2 3 4 5 6 K 0 9 8 7

Printed in the United States of America

PREFACE

College Accounting is designed for students of accounting, business administration, computer science, and secretarial science. An understanding of the principles of business accounting is essential for anyone who desires a successful career in business, in many of the professions, and in many branches of government. Those who manage or operate a business, its owners, its prospective owners, its present and prospective creditors, governmental taxing authorities, and other government agencies have need for various types of information. Accounting systems are designed to fill such needs. The particular practices followed are tailored to meet the requirements and the circumstances in each case. However, the same accounting principles underlie all of the practices—just as the same principles of structural engineering apply to the construction of a single-car frame garage and of a fifty-floor steel and concrete office building.

This twelfth edition of College Accounting continues the pattern of earlier editions—explanations of principles with examples of practices. Numerous forms and documents are illustrated. Because the terminology of accounting is undergoing gradual change, the currently preferred terms are used throughout the textbook. Diagrams, flow-charts, and color are used both to facilitate understanding and, in the case of many of the color illustrations, to conform to practice. This twelfth edition continues to include "Chapter Objectives" at the beginning of each chapter, "Building Your Accounting Knowledge" review questions at the end of each chapter section (there are one or more sections per chapter), and "Expanding Your Business Vocabulary" terms at the end of each chapter. In addition, a feature entitled "Applying Accounting Concepts" has been added at the end of each chapter section to provide immediate learning reinforcement.

Chapter 13 introduces ACRS (Accelerated Cost Recovery System) depreciation and expands the discussion of like-kind and unlike-kind exchanges of assets. In addition, the corporation section of Chapter 16 has been streamlined to deal primarily with transaction analysis.

The textbook is organized to facilitate the use of various supplementary learning aids. A workbook containing study assignments correlated with the chapter sections is available. Each workbook study assignment (called a report) includes an exercise on principles and one or more problems bearing on the material discussed in the related section of the textbook. A compilation of check figures for selected workbook problems is available for distribution to students. Additional accounting problems to be used for either supplementary or remedial work are included following Chapters 15 and 20. A revised practice set is available which involves the accounting records of a wholesale and retail bakery business (the partnership of Spinner & Thomas). The set provides realistic work designed to test the student's ability to apply the knowledge of accounting principles which has been gained from studying the textbook and from completing the workbook assignments. Upon completion of the practice set, a test is provided to determine the student's ability to interpret intelligently the records and financial statements of the enterprise. A comprehensive periodic testing program is provided. Tests are available for use following completion of Chapters 12, 15, 17, and 20.

The authors acknowledge their indebtedness and express their appreciation to the considerable number of accounting instructors, business executives, accountants, and other professional people whose suggestions contributed to the preparation of this textbook.

A. E. Carlson
J. A. Heintz

CONTENTS

PART 2 — CHAPTERS 11-20

CHAPTER 11

Accounting for Notes and Interest

CHAPTER OBJECTIVES

Careful study of this chapter should enable you to:

- Describe and explain the nature and use of promissory notes and compute any related interest on such notes.
- Describe and process transactions that involve notes receivable and to prepare a notes receivable register.
- Describe and process transactions that involve notes payable and to prepare a notes payable register.
- Explain and process end-of-period adjustments for:
  1. Interest earned but not yet collected, and
  2. Interest incurred but not yet paid.
- Describe and illustrate the various types of indorsement on notes.

A major characteristic of modern business is the extensive use of credit. Each day hundreds of millions of transactions involve the sale of goods or services in return for promises to pay at a later date. Sales of this type are said to be "on credit" or "on account," and are often described as charge sales. As mentioned in Chapter 7, to facilitate such transactions, the use of credit cards has become commonplace. When opening a credit card account, a form or document is signed that obligates the customer to pay for all purchases within a specific number of days after a bill for the purchases is received from the business. When making a purchase, the buyer then merely signs a sales slip or sales ticket that acknowledges the receipt of the merchandise or service.

This chapter deals with credit transactions that are both less common and more formal than such "open account" or credit card sales transactions. Specifically, the use of and accounting for promissory notes are explained.

The Promissory Note

A promise to repay a borrowed sum of money nearly always takes the form of a promissory note (usually just called a note). The extension of credit for periods of more than 60 days, or for large amounts of money, may result in the use of notes. Such notes have certain legal characteristics that cause them to be negotiable commercial paper. In order to be considered negotiable commercial paper, a promissory note must:

1. Be in writing and signed by the person or persons agreeing to make payment;
2. Be an unconditional promise to pay a certain amount of money;
3. Be payable either on demand or at a definite future time;
4. Be payable to the order of a specified person or firm, or to the bearer.

The following is a promissory note which has all the characteristics of a negotiable commercial paper. William Alverson is known as the maker of the note because he promises to pay a certain amount of money ($1,542.50) at a definite future time (90 days after June 9). Susan Lavin is called the payee of the note because she is the one who is to receive the specified amount of money. Notice that to William Alverson it is a note payable while to Susan Lavin it is a note receivable.

Notes may be interest-bearing or non-interest-bearing. The note illustrated is interest-bearing, with interest at 9% per year. Sometimes no rate of interest is specified on the note; however, the transaction will result in some interest. For example, a borrower might give a $1,000 non-interest-bearing note, payable in 60 days to a bank in return for a loan of $985. The $15 difference between the amount received ($985) and the amount that must be repaid ($1,000) when the note matures (is due) will truly become interest expense at maturity. Interest accrues gradually as time passes. Accounting for this type of transaction is explained on page 352.

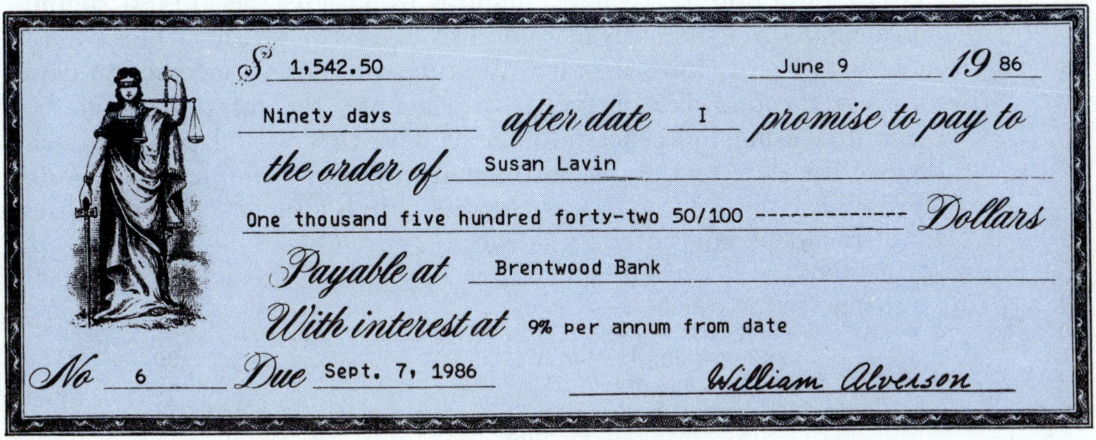
$ 1,542.50 June 9 19 86

Ninety days after date I promise to pay to

the order of Susan Lavin

One thousand five hundred forty-two 50/100 ------------ Dollars

Payable at Brentwood Bank

With interest at 9% per annum from date

No 6 Due Sept. 7, 1986 William Alverson

Promissory Note

Calculating Interest

In calculating interest on notes, it is necessary to take the following factors into consideration:

1. The principal of the note.
2. The rate of interest.
3. The period of time involved.

The principal of the note is the face amount of the note that the maker promises to pay at maturity separate from any specified interest. The principal is the base on which the interest is calculated.

The rate of interest usually is expressed in the form of a percentage, such as 8% or 10%. Ordinarily the rate is an annual percentage rate, but in some cases the rate is quoted on a monthly basis, such as 1 1/2% a month. A rate of 1 1/2% a month is equivalent to a rate of 18% a year payable monthly (1 1/2% × 12 = 18%). When a note is interest-bearing but the rate is not specified on the face of the note, it is subject to the legal rate, which varies under the laws of the different states.

The time of the note consists of the days or months from the date of issue of a note to the date of its maturity (or the interest payment date if it comes earlier). When the time is specified in months, the interest is calculated on the basis of months rather than days. For example, if a note is payable 3 months from date, the interest should be calculated on the basis of 3 months or 1/4 of a year (3 mos. ÷ 12 mos. = 1/4 yr.). However, when the time of a note is specified in days or when the due date is specified in a note, the interest should be computed using the exact number of days that will elapse from the date of the note to the date of its maturity. For example, if a $1,000, 9% note is dated March 1, and the due date is specified as June 1, the time should be computed as shown:

Days in March	31
Deduct date of note, March 1	1
Days remaining in March	30
Add: Days in April	30
Days in May	31
Note matures on June	1
Total time in days	92

Notice that in this computation the date of maturity was counted but the date of the note was not counted. If the note had specified "3 months after date" instead of June 1, the interest should be computed on the basis of 90 days instead of 92 days since a month, when specified as such, is assumed to have 30 days.

In computing interest, it is customary to consider 360 days as a year. Most banks and business firms follow this practice, though some banks and government agencies use 365 days as the base in computing daily interest. In any case, the formula for computing interest is:

I = **PRT**, where:
- **I** = amount of interest
- **P** = amount of principal
- **R** = rate of interest
- **T** = time (usually a fraction of a 360-day year)

Thus, for the $1,000, 9% note described above, interest on the due date would be $23 ($1,000 × 9% × 92/360). The gradual accumulation of interest on the note to a maturity value of $1,023 is shown by the following time line:

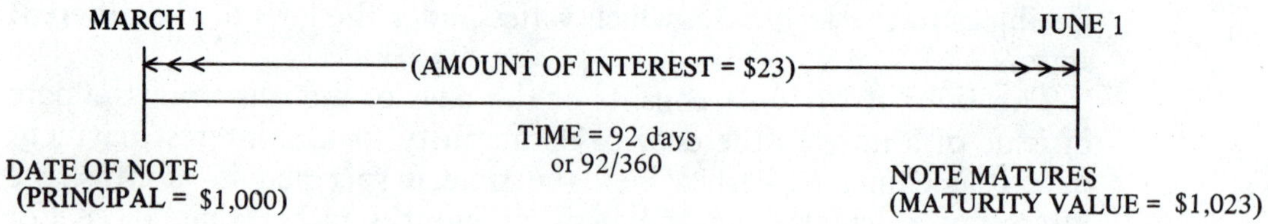

In the case of long-term notes, the interest may be payable periodically, such as semiannually or annually.

The 30-Day, 12% Method. There are short cuts that may be used in computing interest on the basis of a 360-day year. The interest on any amount for 30 days at 12% can be determined simply by moving the decimal point in the amount two places to the left. The reason for this is that 30 days is 1/12 of a year, and interest on any amount at 12% for 1/12 of a year is the same as the interest at 1% for a full year. Thus, the interest on $650 for 30 days at 12% is $6.50.

The 30-day, 12% method may be used to advantage in many cases even though the actual time may be other than 30 days and the actual rate other than 12%. The following examples will serve to illustrate this fact.

Factors

1. Principal of note, $3,000
2. Time, 30 days
3. Rate of interest, 8%

Calculation

Interest at 12% for 30 days = $30
Interest at 8% = 8/12 × $30 = $20

Factors

1. Principal of note, $4,000
2. Time, 90 days
3. Rate of interest, 10%

Calculation

Interest at 12% for 30 days = $40
Interest at 12% for 90 days = $120
Interest at 10% = 10/12 × $120 = $100

Sometimes it is helpful to determine the interest for 3 days at 12% and then use the result as the basis for calculating the actual interest. Since the interest on any sum for 3 days at 12% may be determined simply by moving the decimal point three places to the left, the interest on $1,000 at 12% for 3 days is $1. If the actual time is 24 days instead of 3 days, the interest will be eight times $1 or $8. This method differs from the 30-day, 12% method only in that 3 days and 12% are used in the basic computation instead of 30 days and 12%.

Published tables are available for reference in determining the amount of interest on stated sums at different rates for any length of time. These tables are widely used by financial institutions and by other business firms.

Accounting for Notes Receivable Transactions

Businesses other than lending institutions such as commercial banks and savings and loan associations generally encounter four types of transactions involving notes receivable:

1. Note received from customer to obtain an extension of time for payment of an obligation.
2. Note collected at maturity.
3. Note renewed at maturity.
4. Note dishonored.

Note Received from Customer to Obtain an Extension of Time for Payment. To obtain an extension of time for the payment of an account, a customer may issue a note for all or part of the amount due. A merchant may be willing to accept the note because it is a written acknowledgment of the debt and undoubtedly will bear interest.

Assume that Chris McLean owes the Lehman Hardware Co. $862.31 on open account. The account is past due and Lehman insists upon a settlement. McLean offers to give a 60-day, 9% note dated May 12, and Lehman accepts McLean's offer. The note is entered in the books of the Lehman Hardware Co. in two-column journal form as follows:

May 12	Notes Receivable	862.31	
	Accounts Receivable		862.31
	Received a note from Chris McLean.		

If instead of giving a note for the full amount, McLean gives a check for $62.31 and a note for the $800 balance, the transaction would be entered in Lehman's books in two-column journal form as follows:

May 12	Cash	62.31	
	Notes Receivable	800.00	
	Accounts Receivable		862.31
	Received check and note from Chris McLean.		

The foregoing entry can be entered in a combination journal, cash receipts journal, or any other appropriate book of original entry. This observation applies to all illustrations of entries involving the receipt of cash.

Note Collected at Maturity. When a note receivable matures, it may be collected by the holder or it may be left at a bank for collection. If the maker of the note resides in another locality, the note may be forwarded to a bank in that locality for collection. Usually the maker is notified a few days before the maturity of a note so that the maker may be reminded of the due date, the amount that must be paid, and where the amount is to be paid. When the bank makes the collection, it notifies the holder, on a form similar to the following credit advice, that the net amount has been credited to the holder's account.

ADVICE OF CREDIT — **CENTERRE BANK**, Bonne Terre, Missouri

TO Lehman Hardware Co.
Account No. 315 30959

July 11 1986

WE CREDIT YOUR ACCOUNT AS FOLLOWS:

Chris McLean's note	$862.31	
Interest for 60 days at 9%	12.93	
	$875.24	
Less collection charge	10.00	$ 865.24

OFFSETTING DR.

APPROVED R. Shaw

Credit Advice

To illustrate the necessary accounting procedure, assume that Lehman left McLean's 60-day, 9% note for $862.31 at Centerre Bank for collection, and on July 11 received notice that the note had been collected including the accrued interest of $12.93. The bank fee for collecting the note amounted to $10.

The transaction is entered in Lehman's books as follows:

July 11	Cash	865.24	
	Collection Expense	10.00	
	Notes Receivable		862.31
	Interest Revenue		12.93
	Received credit for the proceeds of Chris McLean's note collected by the bank.		

Note Renewed at Maturity. If the maker of a note is unable to pay the amount due at maturity, it may be possible to renew all or part of the note. If, instead of paying the note for $862.31 at maturity, McLean is allowed to pay only the interest, $12.93, and give another note for 60 days at the same rate of interest, the transaction is entered in the books of the Lehman Hardware Co. in two-column journal form as follows:

July 11	Cash	12.93	
	Notes Receivable (new note)	862.31	
	Notes Receivable (old note)		862.31
	Interest Revenue		12.93
	Received a new note for $862.31 from Chris McLean in renewal of his note due today and $12.93 in cash for the interest on the old note.		

Note Dishonored. If the maker of a note refuses or is unable to pay or renew it at maturity, the note is said to be dishonored. It thereby loses the quality of negotiability which means that it loses its legal status as a note receivable. Usually the amount is transferred from the notes receivable account to the accounts receivable account pending final disposition of the obligation involved. For example, if Lehman is unable to collect the interest-bearing note for $862.31 received 60 days before from McLean, the following two-column journal entry is made in the books of the Lehman Hardware Co.:

July 11	Accounts Receivable	875.24	
	Notes Receivable		862.31
	Interest Revenue		12.93
	Chris McLean's note dishonored.		

If the claim against McLean should turn out to be completely worthless, the $875.24 will be removed from the accounts receivable account and recognized as an uncollectible account expense. The manner of accounting for this type of transaction was discussed in Chapter 8.

Notes Receivable Register

When many notes are received in the usual course of business, it may be advisable to keep an auxiliary record. An auxiliary record of notes receivable that provides more detailed information than a ledger account is usually known as a notes receivable register. One form of a notes receivable register is reproduced at the top of pages 350 and 351. The notes shown in the illustration were those received by the V. J. Nooney Co. during the period indicated by the record. The information contained in the register is obtained directly from the notes received. The notes are numbered consecutively as they are entered in the register. (This number should not be confused with the maker's number in the lower left-hand corner of the note, as shown in the illustration on page 343.) The due date of each note is determined and entered in the proper When Due column. The interest to maturity is calculated and entered in the Interest Amount column. When a remittance or a new note is received in settlement of a note, the date is entered in the Date Paid column.

Notes Receivable Account

The information contained in the notes receivable account should agree with that entered in the notes receivable register. The following account contains a record of the notes that were entered in the notes receivable register of the V. J. Nooney Co. Notice that each note is

ACCOUNT *Notes Receivable* ACCOUNT NO. *121*

DATE		ITEM	POST. REF.	DEBIT	CREDIT	BALANCE DEBIT	BALANCE CREDIT
1986 Apr.	4	No. 1	CR3	468 12		468 12	
	21	No. 2	CR3	600 00		1 068 12	
May	2	No. 3	CR4	757 20		1 825 32	
	19	No. 4	CR4	820 00		2 645 32	
June	1	No. 3	CR5		757 20	1 888 12	
	3	No. 1	CR5		468 12	1 420 00	
	20	No. 2	CR5		600 00	820 00	
	20	No. 5	CR5	500 00		1 320 00	

identified by the number assigned to the note. If the notes are not numbered, each note should be identified by writing the name of the maker in the Item column of the account.

Proving The Notes Receivable Account

Periodically (usually at the end of each month) the notes receivable account is proved by comparing the balance of the account with the total of the notes owned as shown by the notes receivable register. Note that the following schedule of notes owned on June 30 has the same total as the balance in the notes receivable account illustration.

Schedule of Notes Owned

No. 4	$ 820
No. 5	500
	$1,320

PAGE 2 NOTES RECEIVABLE REGISTER

DATE RECEIVED		No.	BY WHOM PAYABLE	WHERE PAYABLE: BANK OR FIRM	WHERE PAYABLE: ADDRESS	DATE MADE: MO.	DAY	YEAR
1986 Apr.	4	1	L.A. Peters	First State Bank	Eureka	Apr.	4	'86
	21	2	J.M. Slawski	Commerce Bank	University City	Apr.	21	'86
May	2	3	S.M. Alpart	Farmers' Bank	Kirksville	May	2	'86
	19	4	L.L. Sheinbein	Central Trust	Jefferson City	May	19	'86
June	20	5	J.M. Slawski	Commerce Bank	University City	June	20	'86

Notes Receivable Register (Left Page)

Accrued Interest Receivable

While interest on a note literally accrues day by day, it is impractical to keep a daily record of such accruals. If the life of a note receivable is within the accounting period, no entry is made for the interest until the amount is received.

If, however, the business owns some interest-bearing notes receivable at the end of the accounting period, neither the net income for the period nor the assets at the end of the period will be correctly stated unless the interest accrued on notes receivable is taken into consideration. The amount of the accrued interest may be computed by reference to the notes themselves or to the data provided by a notes receivable register. The accounts are then adjusted by debiting Accrued Interest Receivable and by crediting Interest Revenue for the amount of interest that has accrued to the end of the period. Assume that at the end of a fiscal year ending June 30, a business owns four interest-bearing notes as shown in the following schedule:

Schedule of Accrued Interest on Notes Receivable

Principal	Date of Issue	Rate of Interest	Days From Issue Date to June 30	Accrued Interest June 30
$800.00	April 15	9%	76	$15.20
500.00	May 5	10%	56	7.78
545.80	May 29	9%	32	4.37
700.00	June 12	9%	18	3.15
Total accrued interest on notes receivable				$30.50

When the amount involved is so small, some accountants would ignore it on the ground of immateriality, but technical accuracy requires the following two-column journal entry as of June 30:

NOTES RECEIVABLE REGISTER PAGE 2

TIME	WHEN DUE J	J	J	A	D	AMOUNT	INTEREST RATE	INTEREST AMT.	DISCOUNTED BANK	DISCOUNTED DATE	DATE PAID	REMARKS
60 da.		3				468 12	8%	6 24			June 3	
60 da.		20				600 00	9%	9 00			June 20	Renewal for $500
30 da.		1				757 20	9%	5 68			June 1	Sent for coll. 5/30
90 da.				17		820 00	9%	18 45				
60 da.				19		500 00	9%	7 50				Renewal of Note No. 2

Notes Receivable Register (Right Page)

June 30	Accrued Interest Receivable........................	30.50	
	Interest Revenue		30.50
	Interest accrued on notes receivable as of June 30.		

In preparing the financial statements at the end of the year, the balance of the interest revenue account (which will include the $30.50 earned but not yet received) will be reported in the income statement, while the balance of the account, Accrued Interest Receivable, will be reported in the balance sheet as a current asset.

Accounting for Notes Payable Transactions

There are generally four types of transactions involving notes payable:

1. Note issued to a supplier to obtain an extension of time for payment of an obligation.
2. Note issued as security for cash loan.
3. Note paid at maturity.
4. Note renewed at maturity.

Note Issued to a Supplier to Obtain an Extension of Time for Payment. When a firm wishes to obtain an extension of time for the payment of an account, a note for all or part of the amount due may be acceptable to the supplier. Assume that Lehman Hardware Co. owes Wigington & Co. $654.70. By agreement, on June 11 Lehman issues to Wigington a check on the Centerre Bank for $54.70 and a 90-day, 10% interest-bearing note for $600. This transaction is entered in the books of the Lehman Hardware Co. in two-column journal form as follows:

June 11	Accounts Payable	654.70	
	Cash		54.70
	Notes Payable		600.00
	Issued check for $54.70 and note for $600 to Wigington & Co.		

Note Issued as Security for Cash Loan. Many firms experience brief periods during the year in which receipts from customers are not adequate to finance their operations. During such periods, business firms commonly borrow money from banks on short-term notes to help finance their business operations. Assume that on June 16, Lehman borrows $6,000 from the Centerre Bank on a 60-day, 10 1/2% interest-bearing note. The transaction is entered in two-column journal form as follows:

June 16	Cash	6,000	
	Notes Payable		6,000
	Borrowed $6,000 at the bank on a 60-day, 10 1/2% note.		

Commercial banks often deduct interest in advance, and this procedure is known as **discounting**. For example, instead of the transaction previously described, suppose that Lehman borrowed on a $6,000, 60-day, non-interest-bearing note which the bank discounted at 10 1/2%. The bank would calculate the implied interest on the note to maturity, known as **bank discount**, and deduct this amount from the $6,000 face of the note. This transaction may be illustrated in time-line form as follows:

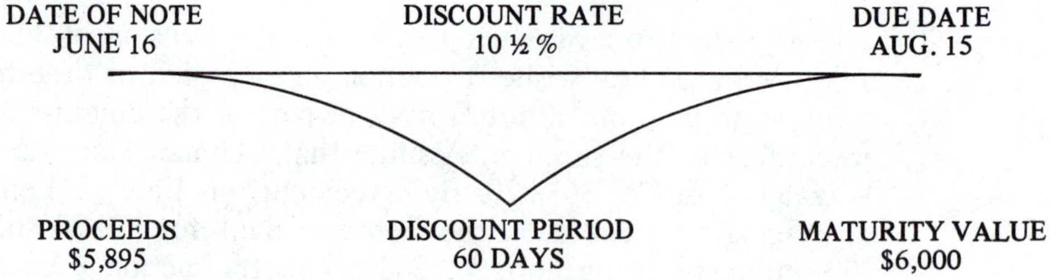

The formulas for determining how much cash the Lehman Hardware Co. would receive on June 16 are as follows:

1. **Face + Interest = Maturity Value**

Face		Interest		Maturity Value
$6,000	+	0	=	$6,000

2. **Maturity Value × Discount Rate × Discount Period = Discount Amount**

Maturity Value		Discount Rate		Discount Period		Discount Amount
$6,000	×	10 1/2%	×	60/360	=	$105

3. **Maturity Value − Discount Amount = Proceeds**

Maturity Value		Discount Amount		Proceeds
$6,000	−	$105	=	$5,895

Thus, Lehman Hardware Co. would receive only $5,895 proceeds ($6,000 − $105), and the transaction would be entered as follows:

June 16	Cash	5,895	
	Discount on Notes Payable	105	
	Notes Payable		6,000
	Discounted at 10 1/2%, a $6,000, 60-day, non-interest-bearing note.		

The $105 debit to the discount on notes payable account represents an offset to the $6,000 note payable. Lehman's liability at this time is only $5,895, which is the net amount or proceeds received from the bank. Discount on Notes Payable is a contra-liability account. The $105 discount becomes interest expense gradually each day. It is recognized in full when the note matures on August 15, and the $6,000 principal amount of the note is repaid. Accordingly, Lehman Hardware Co. will enter the payment of the note at maturity in two-column journal form as follows:

Aug. 15	Notes Payable	6,000	
	Interest Expense	105	
	Cash		6,000
	Discount on Notes Payable		105
	Paid 60-day, non-interest-bearing note due today, and recognized interest expense at 10 1/2%.		

Note that, even though the stated rate of interest was 10 1/2% in both cases, the money received was less in amount and therefore more expensive in the second case. In the first case, $6,000 was obtained for 60 days at a cost of $105—exactly 10 1/2% ($105 ÷ $6,000 = 1.75% for 60 days; 10.5% for 360 days). In the second case, $105 was paid for the use of $5,895 for 60 days—a rate of nearly 10.7%, which is known as the effective rate of interest ($105 ÷ $5,895 = 1.781% for 60 days; 10.687% for 360 days). (While notes receivable may also be discounted, small businesses deal with notes payable transactions much more frequently than with notes receivable transactions.)

Note Paid at Maturity. A note made payable to a bank for a loan commonly is paid at that bank upon maturity. When notes made payable to other payees mature, payment may be made directly to the holder or to a bank where the note was left for collection. The maker knows who the payee is but may not know who the holder is at maturity because the payee may have transferred the note to another party. When a note is left with a bank for collection, it is customary for the bank to mail the maker a notice of maturity. For example, assume that Wigington & Co. forwards the 90-day, 10% note for $600 received from Lehman on June 11 to the Centerre Bank for collection. The bank would notify Lehman before the maturity date by sending a notice similar to the following illustration:

CENTERRE BANK
Bonne Terre, Missouri

Your note described below will be due

MAKER-COSIGNER-COLLATERAL	NUMBER	DATE DUE	PRINCIPAL	INTEREST	TOTAL
A. M. Lehman Lehman Hardware Co.	19360	9/9/86	$600.00	$15.00	$615.00

ENDORSER

TO

A. M. Lehman
Lehman Hardware Co.
Box 362
Bonne Terre, MO 63628-5544

Note: Please bring this notice with you. PAYABLE AT Centerre Bank

Notice of Maturity of Note

Upon receiving this notice, Lehman issues a check to the bank for $615 in payment of the note and interest. The transaction is entered in the books of the Lehman Hardware Co. in two-column journal form as follows:

Sept. 9	Notes Payable	600	
	Interest Expense	15	
	Cash		615
	Paid note issued June 11 to Wigington & Co., plus interest.		

Note Renewed at Maturity. If the maker is unable to pay a note in full at maturity, it may be possible to renew all or a part of the note. For example, on September 9, Lehman might pay the $15 interest and $100 on the principal of the note ($600, issued to Wigington & Co. on June 11), and give a new 60-day, 10% note for $500. This transaction should be entered in two-column journal form as follows:

Sept. 9	Notes Payable (old note)	600	
	Interest Expense	15	
	Cash		115
	Notes Payable (new note)		500
	Issued a check for $115 and a note for $500 to Wigington & Co. in settlement of a note for $600 plus interest.		

Notes Payable Register

When many notes are issued in the usual course of business, it may be advisable to keep an auxiliary record. An auxiliary record of notes payable that provides more detailed information than a ledger account is usually known as a **notes payable register**. One form of such a register is reproduced on pages 356 and 357. The notes shown in the illustration were those issued by the V. J. Nooney Co. during the period indicated by the record.

The information contained in the register may be obtained directly from the note before it is mailed or given to the payee, or from a note stub. Blank notes are usually made up in pads with stubs attached on which spaces are provided for entering such essential information as amount, payee, where payable, date, time, rate of interest, and number. The due date of each note is determined and entered in the proper When Due column of the register. The interest at maturity is also calculated and entered in the Interest Amount column. When a note is paid, the date is entered in the Date Paid column.

PAGE 1

NOTES PAYABLE REGISTER

DATE ISSUED		No.	TO WHOM PAYABLE	WHERE PAYABLE		DATE MADE		
				BANK OR FIRM	ADDRESS	MO.	DAY	YEAR
1986 Apr.	14	1	J.L. Knoop	First State Bank	Eureka	Apr.	14	'86
May	13	2	Commerce Bank	Commerce Bank	Univ. City	May	13	'86
June	2	3	Bloodgood Brothers	Commerce Bank	Univ. City	June	2	'86

Notes Payable Register (Left Page)

Notes Payable Account

The information contained in the notes payable account should agree with that entered in the notes payable register. The following account contains a record of the notes that were entered in the notes payable register of the V. J. Nooney Co.

ACCOUNT *Notes Payable* ACCOUNT NO. *216*

DATE		ITEM	POST. REF.	DEBIT	CREDIT	BALANCE DEBIT	BALANCE CREDIT
1986 Apr.	14	No. 1	CP3		2 149 61		2 149 61
May	13	No. 2	CP4		8 000 00		10 149 61
June	2	No. 3	CP5		1 357 35		11 506 96
	13	No. 1	CP5	2 149 61			9 357 35

Proving the Notes Payable Account

Periodically (usually at the end of each month), the notes payable account is proved by comparing the balance of the account with the total notes outstanding as shown by the notes payable register. Note that the following schedule of the notes outstanding on June 30 has the same total as the balance in the notes payable account illustration.

NOTES PAYABLE REGISTER PAGE *1*

TIME	WHEN DUE J	F	M	A	M	J	J	A	S	O	N	D	AMOUNT	INTEREST RATE	INTEREST AMOUNT	DATE PAID	REMARKS
60 da.						*13*							*2149 61*	*9%*	*32 24*	*June13*	*Settlement of Feb. 14 inv.*
90 da.								*11*					*8000 00*	*10%*	*200 00*		
30 da.							*2*						*1357 35*	*11%*	*12 44*		*Settlement of Apr. 2 inv.*

Notes Payable Register (Right Page)

Schedule of Notes Outstanding

No. 2	$8,000.00
No. 3	1,357.35
	$9,357.35

Accrued Interest Payable

Neither the expenses for a period nor the liabilities at the end of the period will be correctly stated unless the interest accrued on notes payable is taken into consideration. The mechanics of calculating the amount of interest accrued on notes payable are the same as in the case of notes receivable. If a notes payable register is kept, it should provide the information needed in computing the amount of interest accrued on notes payable. If the total amount of such accrued interest was calculated to be $269.12, and the fiscal period ended June 30, the proper adjusting entry may be made as follows:

June 30	Interest Expense	269.12	
	Accrued Interest Payable		269.12
	Interest accrued on notes payable as of June 30.		

In preparing the financial statements at the end of the year, the balance of the interest expense account, which will include the $269.12 incurred but not yet paid, will be reported in the income statement, while the balance of the account, Accrued Interest Payable, will be reported in the balance sheet as a current liability.

Indorsement of Notes

A promissory note is usually made payable to a specified person or firm, though some notes are made payable to "Bearer." If the note is payable to the order of a specified party, that party must indorse the note to transfer the promise to pay to another party. To indorse means to sign one's name as payee on the back of a note.

The two major types of indorsements are (1) the blank indorsement and (2) the special indorsement. The indorsement is called a blank indorsement when only the payee's name is signed on the left end of the back of the note. The indorsement is called a special indorsement if the words "Pay to the order of" followed by the name of a specified party and the payee's signature appear on the back of the note. The legal effect of both types of indorsement is much the same. However, a blank indorsement makes a note payable to the bearer, while a special indorsement identifies the party to whose order payment is made.

Under certain circumstances, the maker of a note may arrange for an additional party to join in the promise to pay, either as a cosigner or as an indorser of the note. A cosigner signs below the maker's signature on the face of the note. If the other party makes a blank indorsement on the back of the note, it is called an accommodation indorsement. In either event, the payee of the note has an additional person responsible for payment, which is intended to add security to the note.

If a partial payment is made on a note, it is common practice to record the date of the payment and the amount paid on the back of the note, which is called indorsing the payment.

Shown on page 359 is a reproduction of the promissory note originally made payable to the order of Susan Lavin. (See illustration of note on page 343.) The maker of the note, William Alverson, had Darlene Gubuan become an accommodation indorser. Later, the payee, Lavin, transferred the note to T. L. Fischer by a special indorsement. On July 9, $500 was paid on the note.

BUILDING YOUR ACCOUNTING KNOWLEDGE

1. What form does a promise to repay a borrowed sum of money nearly always take?

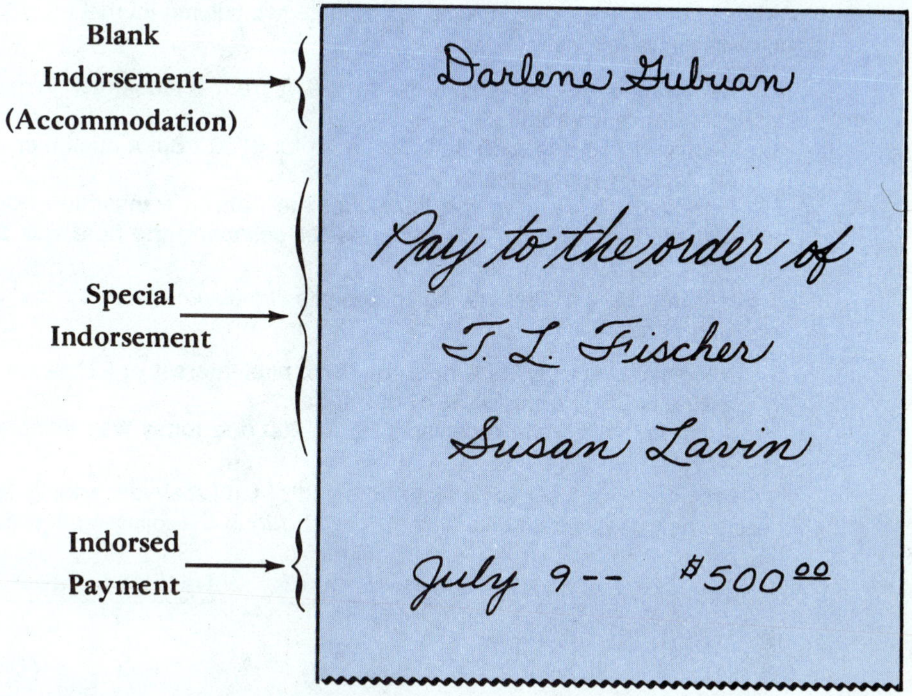

Indorsements on Note

2. What are the four characteristics that a promissory note must evidence in order to be considered negotiable commercial paper?
3. What three factors must be taken into consideration in calculating interest on notes?
4. In computing the exact number of days of interest on a note, what date is counted? What date is not counted?
5. What number of days is considered as a year by most banks and business firms in computing interest?
6. What generally are the four types of transactions involving notes receivable and how do they differ from one another?
7. What generally are the four types of transactions involving notes payable and how do they differ from one another?
8. How are accrued interest receivable and accrued interest payable reported on the balance sheet?

APPLYING ACCOUNTING CONCEPTS

(Use a 360-day year in all of these exercises.)

Exercise 11-1. Compute the amount of interest on each of the following notes.

1. \$1,000, 60 days, 11%. 1000 X 11% X 60 ÷ 360
2. \$800, 90 days, 13%.
3. \$1,200, 120 days, 10%.

Exercise 11-2. Prepare the appropriate two-column journal entry for each of the following transactions.

1. **Received a 90-day, 10% note for $912 from a customer in payment of an account receivable.**
2. **Received $73 and a 60-day, 11% note for $700 from a customer in payment of an account receivable.**
3. **Received notice from the bank that the note in transaction number (2) was collected at maturity. The bank fee for collecting the note was $11.**

Exercise 11-3. Prepare the appropriate two-column journal entry for each of the following transactions.

1. **Received a 60-day, 11% note for $875, plus interest of $21.88, in settlement of a 90-day, 10% note for $875 due today.**
2. **A 60-day, 12% note receivable for $1,200 due today was dishonored.**

Exercise 11-4. Assume that at the end of the fiscal year ending July 31, a business owns three interest-bearing notes as shown in the following schedule.

Principal	Date of Issue	Rate of Interest
$1,000.00	May 15	12%
1,200.00	May 30	11%
900.00	June 25	12%

Prepare the adjusting entry at July 31 to recognize the accrued interest receivable on these notes.

Exercise 11-5. Prepare the appropriate two-column journal entry for each of the following transactions.

1. **Issued a check for $29.25 and a 60-day, 12% note for $400 to a supplier in payment of an account.**
2. **Paid the $400 note in transaction number (1) at maturity.**

Exercise 11-6. Prepare the appropriate two-column journal entry for each of the following transactions.

1. **Borrowed $8,000 from the bank on a 90-day, 13% note.**
2. **Borrowed money from the bank on a $4,000, 90-day, non-interest-bearing note which the bank discounted at 12%. (You must compute the proceeds of this note.)**
3. **Issued a check for $260 and a note for $8,000 at 13.5% in settlement of the note in transaction number (1).**
4. **Paid the $4,000 non-interest-bearing note in transaction number (2) at maturity.**

Exercise 11-7. Assume that the total amount of accrued interest on notes payable at the fiscal year end is $81.65. Prepare the adjusting entry at the fiscal year end to recognize the accrued interest payable on these notes payable.

Report No. 11-1

Complete Report No. 11-1 in the study assignments and submit your working papers to the instructor for approval. Then proceed with the textbook discussion in Chapter 12 until Report No. 12-1 is required.

EXPANDING YOUR BUSINESS VOCABULARY

What is the meaning of each of the following terms?

accommodation indorsement **(p. 358)**
bank discount **(p. 352)**
blank indorsement **(p. 358)**
contra-liability **(p. 353)**
cosigner **(p. 358)**
credit advice **(p. 347)**
discount amount **(p. 353)**
discounting **(p. 352)**
dishonored **(p. 348)**
effective rate **(p. 354)**
indorse **(p. 358)**
indorsing the payment **(p. 358)**
maker of the note **(p. 342)**
maturity value **(p. 353)**
negotiable commercial paper **(p. 342)**
notes payable register **(p. 355)**
notes receivable register **(p. 348)**
notice of maturity **(p. 354)**
payee of the note **(p. 342)**
principal of the note **(p. 343)**
proceeds **(p. 353)**
promissory note **(p. 342)**
rate of interest **(p. 343)**
special indorsement **(p. 358)**
time of the note **(p. 343)**

CHAPTER 12

Accounting for Inventory and Prepaid Expenses

CHAPTER OBJECTIVES

Careful study of this chapter should enable you to:

- Describe and contrast the two principal systems of accounting for inventory—the periodic system and the perpetual system.
- Explain the procedures involved in determining the end-of-period physical quantity of goods on hand, and to prepare an inventory sheet.
- Explain and contrast the specific identification, fifo, weighted average, and lifo methods of cost assignment to inventory; and to use the lower of cost or market rule in connection with the specific identification, fifo, and weighted average methods.
- Explain the gross margin and simplified retail methods of estimating the amount to be assigned to the end-of-period inventory.
- Explain and contrast the asset method and the expense method of accounting for supplies and prepayments.

Merchandise inventory and prepaid expenses have an important characteristic in common: both represent costs incurred in one accounting period that are expected in part to benefit the following period. Because the benefit is expected to be realized within a relatively short time, these assets are considered to be current rather than long-term. In most cases, the dollar amount of merchandise inventory is much larger than that for prepaid expenses. For this reason, accounting for merchandise inventory poses a much greater problem and receives much more attention.

MERCHANDISE INVENTORY

One of the major reasons for processing accounting information is to determine the net income (or net loss) of a business on a periodic basis. If the business purchases and sells merchandise, it is essential that the cost of all merchandise available for sale during the accounting period (goods on hand at the start of the period plus net purchases) be apportioned in a reasonable manner between the expense called cost of goods sold (merchandise inventory expense) and the asset commonly called merchandise inventory. The routine involved in accounting for merchandise, using accounts for purchases, purchases returns and allowances, purchases discount, and merchandise inventory, has been discussed and illustrated in preceding chapters. The problem of determining the quantity of goods on hand at the end of the period and of assigning cost to these goods remains to be considered.

Types of Inventory Systems

There are two principal systems of accounting for inventory — (1) the periodic system and (2) the perpetual system. In the periodic system, the merchandise inventory account balance is merely a record of the most recent physical inventory count, usually made only once a year when the stock is low or business is slow. As discussed in Chapter 6, the purchases account is debited with the cost of all goods bought at their respective invoice prices. As discussed in Chapter 7, the sales account is credited with the respective selling prices of all goods sold. The cost of goods sold is not determined until the end of the accounting period, at which time the following formula is applied:

Beginning Inventory	+	**Net Purchases**	−	**Ending Inventory**	=	**Cost of Goods Sold**
(last year's physical count)		(account balance at end of this year)		(this year's physical count)		(for entire period)

Purchases returns and allowances and purchases discounts are subtracted from the purchases account to arrive at net purchases.

In the perpetual system, the merchandise inventory account is an active account. It is debited with the cost of all goods bought at their respective invoice prices, and credited with the assumed cost of all goods sold, as well as the cost of any inventory returns, allowances, or discounts. Thus, the balance of the account represents the cost of goods on hand at all times. No purchases or contra purchases accounts are kept. A cost of goods sold account is kept, and when goods are sold, it is debited for the same amount that Merchandise Inventory is credited. At the same time, Accounts Receivable (or Cash) is debited and Sales is credited for the selling prices of all goods sold. Thus, *two* entries are required for each sale as follows:

1. Accounts Receivable (or Cash)	XXXX	
Sales		XXXX
2. Cost of Goods Sold	XXXX	
Merchandise Inventory		XXXX

Taking a Physical Inventory

Under the periodic inventory system, businesses do not maintain a record that shows the quantity and the cost of the merchandise on hand. Lacking such a record, the first step in attempting to apportion merchandise costs between sold and unsold goods consists of counting or measuring the goods that are on hand at the end of the period. This process is called **taking a physical inventory**.

Taking a physical inventory of a stock of merchandise can be a sizable task. Frequently, it is done after regular business hours. Some firms cease operations for a few days to take inventory. The ideal time to count the goods is when the quantity on hand is at its lowest level. If a fiscal year is selected so as to start and end at the time that the stock of goods is normally at its lowest level, it is known as a **natural business year**. Such a year is used by many businesses for accounting purposes.

It is desirable for all goods on hand to be inventoried in as short a time as possible. Extra help may be employed in order to take the inventory. Even if this is done, however, the taking of an inventory may require several days. If regular business is carried on during this time, special records must be kept of additions to and subtractions from the stock during the inventory-taking period. In this way, the quantities of goods that are on hand at the end of the last day of the fiscal period can be determined.

Various procedures are followed in taking an inventory so as to be sure that no items are missed, and that no items are included more than once. Frequently, persons taking inventory work in pairs; one counts the items and calls out the information to the other who records it. Usually this information is entered on a special form. This form, known as an inventory sheet, is arranged with columns to show the description of each type of item, the quantity on hand, the cost per unit, and the extension — the amount that results from multiplying the quantity by the unit cost. (The cost per unit usually is determined and the extensions completed after the count is finished.) Inventory sheets commonly provide spaces for (1) the date of the inventory count, (2) the location of the items listed, and (3) the names or initials of the persons who did the calling, recorded the quantities, entered the unit costs, made the extensions, and verified the information. The following is a reproduction of part of an inventory sheet of a furniture store. Two extension columns are provided so that subtotals may be separated from extensions.

INVENTORY *Aug. 31* 19 *86* Page *1*

Sheet No. *1* | Costed by *V.E.R.*
Called by *W.L.M.* | Department *A* | Extended by *V.E.R.*
Entered by *K.N.* | Location *Storeroom* | Examined by *C.J.C.*

Description	Quantity	Unit	Unit Cost	Extensions	
Table lamp	*20*	*ea.*	*52.80*	*1,056.00*	
Wall rack	*18*	*ea.*	*9.70*	*174.60*	
Bookcase	*7*	*ea.*	*88.10*	*616.70*	
End table	*13*	*ea.*	*33.20*	*431.60*	
Desk	*6*	*ea.*	*108.30*	*649.80*	
Total					*4,465.10*

Inventory Sheet

In taking a physical inventory, it is very important to be sure that only the goods that are the property of the firm are included. The two main problems in determining the items to be included in physical inventory are (1) goods acquired and later sold on consignment and (2) goods in transit. The important thing to remember about goods on consignment is that they remain the property of the shipper (consignor) and should not be included in the inventory of the company holding the goods (consignee). Thus, if a company has acquired goods on consignment, they should not be included in that company's inventory. If a company has shipped goods on consignment for later sale, they should be included in that company's inventory.

In determining whether goods in transit at year end should be included in inventory, it is necessary to know the FOB terms. If goods are shipped FOB shipping point, the goods are the property of the buying company as soon as they are shipped. If goods are shipped FOB destination, the goods are the property of the selling company until they are received by the buying company.

Assigning Cost to the Inventory

After the quantities of goods owned have been determined at the end of the accounting period, the next step is to decide how much cost should be assigned to each unit. This might seem to be an easy, though perhaps a time-consuming job. If all purchases of the same article were made at the same price per unit, the unit cost times the number of units in the inventory would give the total cost to be assigned to those units. Frequently, however, identical articles are purchased at different times at different costs per unit. The question then arises as to which unit costs should be assigned to the goods in the inventory. If it is possible to separately identify and price items on hand when they are sold, this approach to cost assignment is preferred, and is known as specific identification costing. Often there is no way of knowing exactly which price was paid for the specific goods that are on hand. If so, one of three other methods of cost apportionment normally is adopted. These methods are (1) first-in, first-out costing, (2) weighted average costing, and (3) last-in, first-out costing.

Specific Identification Costing. A method of assigning merchandise cost which requires that each item that is sold and each item remaining in inventory be separately identified with respect to its purchase cost is called the specific identification method. This method is practical only for businesses in which sales volume is relatively low, inventory unit value is relatively high, and items can be distinguished easily from each other. Otherwise, record keeping becomes expensive and time consuming, if not impractical.

To illustrate how this method works, assume the following data for a particular item of merchandise:

	Units	Unit Price	Total Cost
On hand at start of period	400	$5.15	$ 2,060
Purchased during period:			
1st purchase	300	5.35	1,605
2nd purchase	700	5.75	4,025
3rd purchase	600	5.95	3,570
Number of units available for sale	2,000		$11,260
On hand at end of period	500		
Number of units sold during period	1,500		

Of the 1,500 units sold during the period, it is known for certain that 300 were from the beginning inventory, 200 were from the first purchase, 500 were from the second purchase, and 500 were from the last purchase. The cost of goods sold and the value of inventory at the end of the period are determined as follows:

	Cost of Goods Sold		Value of Ending Inventory	
Beginning inventory	300 units @ $5.15 =	$1,545	100 units @ $5.15 =	$ 515
From 1st purchase	200 units @ 5.35 =	1,070	100 units @ 5.35 =	535
From 2nd purchase	500 units @ 5.75 =	2,875	200 units @ 5.75 =	1,150
From 3rd purchase	500 units @ 5.95 =	2,975	100 units @ 5.95 =	595
Total	1,500 units	$8,465	500 units	$2,795

First-In, First-Out Costing. Another widely used method of allocating merchandise cost is called the **first-in, first-out** or **fifo** method. This costing method assumes that the first goods bought were the first goods sold and that, therefore, the latest goods bought remain in inventory. Applying this method to the data given at the top of the page, the cost of goods sold and the value of inventory at the end of the period are determined as follows:

	Cost of Goods Sold		Value of Ending Inventory	
Beginning inventory	400 units @ $5.15 =	$2,060	-0-	
From 1st purchase	300 units @ 5.35 =	1,605	-0-	
From 2nd purchase	700 units @ 5.75 =	4,025	-0-	
From 3rd purchase	100 units @ 5.95 =	595	500 units @ $5.95 =	$2,975
Total	1,500 units	$8,285	500 units	$2,975

Note that the 500 items on hand at the end of the period are considered to be those most recently purchased. The term "fifo" relates to the goods *sold* during the accounting period and *not* to the goods in inventory at the end of the period.

First in, first out costing is widely used because of two features: (1) Whenever the flow of merchandise can be controlled, the business will see to it that the older goods are moved out first. Thus fifo costing is often in harmony with the actual physical movement of the goods. (2) Fifo costing assigns the most recent purchase costs to the ending inventory shown in the balance sheet. This satisfies those accountants who contend that inventory should be shown on the balance sheet at the most current cost possible.

Another reason for the continuing widespread use of fifo costing is that firms have used this method for a long time. Accountants are reluctant to change a long-followed method of accounting when such a change would affect the comparability of their income calculations over a period of years. Consistency based on comparability is important in accounting.

Weighted Average Costing. Another method of allocating merchandise cost is called the weighted average cost method, also known as the average cost method. This costing method is based on the average cost of identical units.

Using the data shown on page 367, the average cost of identical units is determined by dividing the total cost of units available for sale ($11,260) by the total number of units available for sale (2,000).

$$\frac{\$11{,}260 \text{ (cost of units available for sale)}}{2{,}000 \text{ (units available for sale)}} = \$5.63 \text{ weighted average cost per unit}$$

The cost of goods sold and the value of the end-of-period inventory are calculated as follows:

Cost of goods sold	1,500	units @	$5.63	=	$ 8,445
Value of ending inventory	500	units @	5.63	=	2,815
Total	2,000	units			$11,260

There is a logical appeal to the use of the weighted average basis to allocate cost between goods sold and goods on hand. In this example, one fourth (500) of the total units available (2,000) were unsold. The average cost basis assigns one fourth ($2,815) of the total cost ($11,260) to these goods.

Last-In, First-Out Costing. A fourth method of allocating merchandise cost is called the last-in, first-out or lifo method. It assumes that all of the sales in the period were made from the most recently purchased goods and that, therefore, the earliest goods bought remain in inventory. Applying this method to the data given on page 367, the cost of goods sold and the value of inventory at the end of the period are determined as follows:

	Cost of Goods Sold		Value of Ending Inventory	
Beginning inventory	-0-		400 units @ $5.15 =	$2,060
From 1st purchase	200 units @ $5.35 =	$1,070	100 units @ 5.35 =	535
From 2d purchase	700 units @ 5.75 =	4,025	-0-	
From 3d purchase	600 units @ 5.95 =	3,570	-0-	
Total	1,500 units	$8,665	500 units	$2,595

Note that the 500 units on hand at the end of the period are considered to be the 400 units that were on hand at the start of the period plus 100 of the units from the first purchase. The term "lifo" relates to the goods *sold* during the accounting period and *not* to the goods in inventory at the end of the period.

Sometimes the lifo method has been justified on the grounds that the physical movement of goods in some businesses is actually last-in, first-out. This is rarely the case, but the method has become popular for other reasons. One persuasive argument for the use of the lifo method is that it matches the most current cost of items purchased against the current sales revenue. In many cases in which the lifo method is used, the calculated amount for inventory that has been sold, called cost of goods sold, is really the cost to replace the goods sold. When this amount is subtracted from sales revenue, the resulting gross margin figure is neither inflated nor deflated by gain or loss due merely to price changes. In the opinion of many accountants, this is proper and desirable.

Probably, the major reason for the growing popularity of the lifo method is the fact that when prices are rising, net income calculated by using the lifo method is smaller than the amount determined from using either the fifo or the weighted average method. As a result, the related income tax is smaller. The reverse would be true if prices were falling, but periods of falling prices have been few and brief in the past two centuries.

The lifo method is used by firms in many industries. In fact, procedures have been developed to apply the lifo principle to situations in which the goods sold are not literally replaced. High-fashion merchandise is an example. Suitable adjustments are made to state costs on a lifo basis.

Opponents of the lifo method contend that its use causes old, out-of-date inventory costs to be shown in the balance sheet. The theoretical and practical merits of fifo and lifo are the subject of much professional debate.

Physical Flows and Cost Flows. It is important to recognize that of the four inventory costing methods described, only the specific identification costing method will necessarily reflect cost flows that match physical flows of goods. Each of the other three methods—fifo, weighted average, and lifo—is based on assumed cost flows which are not required to reflect the actual physical movement of goods within the company. Any one of the three assumed cost flow methods may be used under any set of physical flow conditions.

Comparison of Methods. To compare the results obtained by the use of the four cost assignment methods discussed, assume that the 1,500 units were sold for $12,000. The following tabulation contrasts the cost assigned to the ending inventory and cost of goods sold, and the resultant gross margin under each of the four methods. It must be remembered, however, that the example relates to a period in which costs and prices were rising.

	Specific Identification	Fifo	Weighted Average	Lifo
Sales	$12,000	$12,000	$12,000	$12,000
Cost of goods sold:				
Beginning inventory	$ 2,060	$ 2,060	$ 2,060	$ 2,060
Purchases	9,200	9,200	9,200	9,200
Merchandise available for sale	$11,260	$11,260	$11,260	$11,260
Less ending inventory	2,795	2,975	2,815	2,595
Cost of goods sold	$ 8,465	$ 8,285	$ 8,445	$ 8,665
Gross margin	$ 3,535	$ 3,715	$ 3,555	$ 3,335

Note that in all cases, the total cost of merchandise available for sale ($11,260) is the same. It is the apportionment between goods sold and goods on hand at the end of the period that differs. For example, under fifo costing, $8,285 is apportioned to cost of goods sold and $2,975 to ending inventory. Under conditions of rising prices, the gross margin is lowest if lifo is used because the most recent, and therefore the highest purchase costs are matched against sales revenue. Under conditions of falling prices, the gross margin would be lowest if fifo were used because the earliest and therefore the highest purchase costs would be matched against sales revenue.

It is common practice to describe the methods that have been discussed as methods of inventory valuation. It should be apparent, however, that this process also values the cost of goods sold. The term "valuation" is somewhat misleading, since what is involved is really **cost apportionment**.

Lower of Cost or Market Method of Inventory Valuation

It is a well-established tradition in accounting that unrealized gains should not be recognized except in very unusual cases. If the value of an asset increases while it is being held, no formal entry of the gain is made on the books because it has not been actually realized. On the other hand, if the value or usefulness of an asset declines while it is being held, it is generally considered proper to recognize and enter the loss, even though it has not yet been realized. This is in keeping with the convention of conservatism, which states that gains should not be anticipated, but that all potential losses should be recognized.

The assignment of the lower of cost or market to the items that comprise the inventory of merchandise at the end of an accounting period is an important application of the convention of conservatism. Cost in this usage means the amount calculated using either the specific identification, fifo, or weighted average method. In determining the cost to be assigned to goods in an inventory, it is proper to assign to the goods on hand a fair share of any transportation costs that were incurred when the goods were purchased. In other words, cost means cost at the buyer's place of business, not cost at the supplier's shipping point. In some cases, transportation charges are an important part of the total cost of merchandise acquired. In addition, costs should be reduced by the amount of any purchases returns, allowances, or discounts taken.

Market in this usage means the cost to replace. It is the prevailing price in the market in which goods are purchased—not the prevailing price in the market in which they are normally sold—that is involved. An improved statement of the practice is the lower of cost or cost to replace. Accountants have assigned upper and lower limits to the market value that may be used in particular cases. The meaning and calculation of these limits is a topic for a more advanced course. Suffice it to say that market may neither exceed the calculated upper limit nor be less than the calculated lower limit.

To illustrate the application of the lower of cost or market rule, assume the following end-of-period data with respect to an inventory consisting of three items:

Item	Recorded Purchase Cost	End-of-Period Market Value	Lower of Cost or Market
1	$ 8,000	$ 7,000	$ 7,000
2	9,000	10,000	9,000
3	7,000	6,500	6,500
	$24,000	$23,500	$22,500

The illustration demonstrates two possible ways of making the lower of cost or market calculation. First, the lower of cost or market rule can be applied to the total inventory. In the foregoing illustration, this would involve comparing the $24,000 total cost with the $23,500 total market value. Under the second approach, the rule is applied to each item in inventory. In the foregoing illustration, this would involve comparing $24,000 total cost with $22,500 lower of cost or market value determined by comparing cost with market for each item. The approach chosen should be applied consistently between periods. The difference between the cost and market value is considered a loss due to holding inventory and typically is included in cost of goods sold on the income statement.

The Gross Margin Method of Inventory Estimation

Taking a physical inventory often is such a sizable task that it is attempted only once a year. If interim income statements and balance sheets are to be prepared, the portions of the cost of goods available for sale during the interim period to be allocated to goods sold during the period and to goods on hand at the end of the period must be estimated. One way of doing this is to apply the gross margin method, in which the amount of sales during the period is reduced by the normal percentage of gross margin (gross profit) to determine the estimated cost of goods sold. Deducting this amount from the total cost of goods available for sale gives the estimated amount of the ending inventory.

To illustrate, assume the following data with respect to a particular firm, which must be available if the method is to be usable:

1. Net sales, first month	$110,000
2. Normal gross margin as a percentage of sales	40%
3. Inventory, start of period	$ 80,000
4. Net purchases, first month	70,000

The estimated cost of goods sold during the month and the estimated merchandise inventory at the end of the month would be determined as shown at the top of page 373.

This computation is applicable only if the normal gross margin on sales has prevailed during the immediate past period and is expected to prevail during the following periods when the goods in the inventory will be sold. This type of calculation also can be used to evaluate the reasonableness of the amount of an inventory that was computed on the basis of a physical count. Any sizable difference in the two

1. Estimated cost of goods sold:	
Net sales	$110,000
Normal gross margin ($110,000 × 40%)	44,000
Estimated cost of goods sold	$ 66,000
2. Cost of goods available for sale:	
Inventory, start of period	$ 80,000
Net purchases, first month	70,000
Cost of goods available for sale	$150,000
3. Estimated inventory at end of month:	
Cost of goods available for sale	$150,000
Less estimated cost of goods sold	66,000
Estimated end-of-month inventory	$ 84,000

calculations might indicate a possible mistake in the count, in costing the items, or a marked change in the realized rate of gross margin. The gross margin procedure also can be used to estimate the cost of an inventory that may have been destroyed by fire or other casualty. Such a calculation might be useful in negotiating an insurance settlement.

The Retail Method of Inventory Estimation

Many retail merchants use a variation of the gross margin method to calculate cost of goods sold and ending inventory for interim-statement purposes. The procedure employed, called the retail method of inventory, requires keeping records of the selling prices of all goods purchased. This information, together with the record of the cost of goods purchased, makes it possible to compute the ratio between cost and retail prices. When the amount of retail sales is subtracted from the retail value of all goods available for sale, the result is the estimated retail value of the ending inventory. Multiplying this amount by the ratio of cost to selling price gives the estimated cost of the ending inventory.

Following is an example of the calculation of the estimated cost of an inventory of merchandise by the retail method:

	Cost	Retail
Inventory, start of period	$ 60,000	$ 85,000
Net purchases during period	126,000	163,000
Merchandise available for sale	$186,000	$248,000
Less sales for period		180,000
Inventory, end of period, at retail		$ 68,000
Ratio of cost to retail prices of merchandise available for sale ($186,000 ÷ $248,000)		75%
Estimated inventory, end of period, at cost (75% of $68,000)	$ 51,000	

The foregoing example was simplified by assuming that there were no changes in the prices at which the goods were marked to sell. In practice, such changes as additional markups, markup cancellations, and markdowns are commonplace and the calculation must take such adjustments into consideration.

In addition to using the retail method in estimating the cost of inventory for interim-statement purposes, the cost-retail ratio that is developed can be used to convert the amount of a physical inventory which originally has been priced at retail to its approximate cost.

Perpetual Inventory Records

Firms that deal in certain types of merchandise sometimes find it feasible to keep up-to-date records continuously of the quantities and costs of goods on hand, known as perpetual inventory records. The general ledger account for Merchandise Inventory under such a system is somewhat like the account for Cash; a chronological record of each addition (purchase) and subtraction (sale) is maintained. The balance of the account at any time shows the cost of goods that should be on hand.

When perpetual inventory records are kept, the merchandise inventory account in the general ledger is usually a control account. A subsidiary ledger with an account for each type of goods is maintained. These accounts are often in the form of cards or computer disks which are formatted to handle additions, subtractions, and the balance after each change. Goods sold can be assigned cost on either a specific identification, fifo, weighted average, or lifo basis.

Assume that 1,000 units of NELZA were acquired by a firm on August 12 for a total of $2,000, and that the entire quantity was sold on September 9 for $2,750. The necessary entries under a perpetual inventory system would appear in two-column journal form as follows:

1. At time of purchase:

Aug. 12 Merchandise Inventory	2,000	
Accounts Payable or Cash		2,000
Bought 1,000 units of NELZA @ $2.		

2. At time of sale:

Sept. 9	Accounts Receivable or Cash	2,750	
	Sales		2,750
	Sold 1,000 units of NELZA @ $2.75.		
9	Cost of Goods Sold	2,000	
	Merchandise Inventory		2,000
	Cost of 1,000 units of NELZA sold today.		

Perpetual inventories do not eliminate the need for taking periodic physical inventories. The records must be examined from time to time to discover and correct any errors. However, it is not always necessary to count everything at the same time. The stock can be counted and the records verified by groups of items, by departments, or by sections as time permits, so long as the inventory is completely verified within a single accounting period.

A business that sells a wide selection of comparatively low-cost goods (such as a limited-price variety store) may not find it practical to keep a perpetual inventory. In contrast, a business that sells a relatively few high-cost items (an automobile dealer, for example) can maintain such a record without incurring excessive processing cost. The increasing use of the microcomputer and "point-of-sale" recording probably will cause more of the former types of businesses to switch from periodic to perpetual inventories.

Many types of businesses often keep supplementary or auxiliary records of inventory items in terms of quantities only, called **stock records**. Stock records serve as a guide in purchasing operations, may help to reveal any shortages, and may provide information as to the goods on hand as a basis for assigning merchandise cost for interim-statement purposes.

BUILDING YOUR ACCOUNTING KNOWLEDGE

1. What are the fundamental differences between the periodic system of accounting for inventory and the perpetual system of accounting for inventory?

2. What is the first step in attempting to apportion merchandise costs between sold and unsold goods?
3. If it is assumed that the first units purchased were the first ones sold, what is assumed about the source of the units left at the end of the accounting period?
4. What two factors are taken into account by the weighted average costing method of merchandise cost allocation?
5. If it is assumed that all sales in the accounting period were of the goods most recently purchased, what is assumed about the source of the units left at the end of the accounting period?
6. When "lower of cost or market" is assigned to the items that comprise the ending merchandise inventory, what does "cost" mean? What does "market" mean?
7. For what two major purposes is the gross margin method of inventory estimation utilized?
8. For what two major purposes is the retail method of inventory estimation utilized?

APPLYING ACCOUNTING CONCEPTS

Exercise 12-1. Assume the following data for a single item of merchandise sold by Posh Company.

	Units	Unit Price	Total Cost
On hand at start of period	500	$4.00	$2,000
Purchased during the period:			
1st purchase	400	$4.10	1,640
2nd purchase	700	$4.20	2,940
Number of units available for sale	1,600		$6,580
On hand at end of period	600		
Number of units sold during period	1,000		

Compute the cost of goods sold and ending inventory for Posh Company under each of the following methods.

1. **Specific identification. (Of the 1,000 units sold, 400 were from the beginning inventory, 300 were from the first purchase, and 300 were from the last purchase.)**
2. **First-in, first-out.**
3. **Weighted average.**
4. **Last-in, first-out.**

Exercise 12-2. Assume that Shore Company has three items of inventory with costs and market values at year end as follows.

Item	Cost	Market value
1	$ 6,000	$ 5,000
2	$ 9,000	$10,000
3	$12,000	$11,000

Compute the amount of Shore's inventory at year end using (1) the lower of cost or market rule applied to the total inventory, and (2) the lower of cost or market rule applied to each item in the inventory.

Exercise 12-3. Assume the following data for Gromar Company.

Net sales, January	$120,000
Normal gross margin as a percentage of sales	30%
Inventory, January 1	$ 90,000
Net purchases, January	$ 80,000

Use the gross margin method to estimate the cost of goods sold for January and the inventory at January 31.

Exercise 12-4. Assume the following data for Remet Company.

	Cost	Retail
Inventory, April 1	$ 50,000	$ 70,000
Net purchases, April	104,000	150,000
Merchandise available for sale	$154,000	$220,000
Less sales, April		170,000
Inventory, April 30, at retail		$ 50,000

Use the retail method to estimate the inventory at April 30.

Exercise 12-5. On August 15, Perle Company sold inventory with a cost of $700 for $1,050 cash. Prepare the necessary entries for this sale under a perpetual inventory system.

Report No. 12-1

Complete Report No. 12-1 in the study assignments and submit your working papers to the instructor for approval. Then continue with the following textbook discussion until Report No. 12-2 is required.

PREPAID EXPENSES

Office supplies, store supplies, advertising supplies, and other purchased supplies may not be wholly consumed in the period in which they are acquired. The premiums on insurance policies covering merchandise, equipment, and buildings are often prepaid, but the terms of the policies may extend beyond the current accounting period. Rent and interest may be paid in advance, but the expenses may not be wholly incurred in the same accounting period. The cost of unused supplies on hand at the close of the accounting period and the portion of prepayments such as insurance, rent and interest that will benefit future periods are known as prepaid expenses. Prepaid expenses should be treated as current assets because the benefits will be realized within a comparatively short time.

When accounts are kept on the accrual basis, it is necessary to adjust certain of them at the close of each accounting period for the following:

1. Supplies or services purchased during the period that were entered as **assets** at time of purchase and a portion of which was consumed or used during the period.
2. Supplies or services purchased during the period that were entered as **expenses** at time of purchase and a portion of which was not consumed or used during the period.

Asset Method of Accounting for Prepaid Expenses

Supplies and services that may not be wholly consumed in the period in which they are purchased may be entered as assets at the time of purchase. Under the asset method of accounting, it is necessary to adjust the accounts at the end of each accounting period in order that the used portions may be recorded as expenses. A delay in the recognition of an expense already paid (or of revenue already received) is known as a deferral. On the other hand, as mentioned previously, recognition of an expense that is owed at the end of an accounting period but has not yet been paid (or revenue that is earned but has not yet been received) is known as an accrual.

Supplies. Supplies such as office supplies, store supplies, advertising supplies, fuel, and postage, which may not be wholly consumed in the accounting period in which they are acquired, are usually entered as assets at the time of purchase. Office supplies include letterheads, envelopes, pencils, adding machine and computer tape, notebooks, computer diskettes, typewriter ribbons, and other miscellaneous supplies that are normally consumed in the operation of an office. Transactions arising from the purchase of supplies on account are entered in a multi-column purchases journal with one debit column for entering merchandise purchases and a second debit column for entering purchases of supplies. When supplies are purchased for cash, the transactions are entered in the cash payments journal. In either case, the purchases are posted to the office supplies account in the general ledger.

At the end of each accounting period, an inventory of the office supplies on hand is taken, and an adjusting entry is made for the amount of the office supplies consumed during the period. For example, if at the end of the accounting period, the office supplies account shows a debit balance of $984.26 and a physical inventory count reveals that the cost of supplies on hand amounts to $540, it is assumed that the supplies expense during the period is $444.26 ($984.26 – $540). The adjusting entry is as follows:

Office Supplies Expense	444.26	
Office Supplies		444.26
Office supplies consumed during period.		

After this entry is posted, the office supplies account will have a debit balance of $540, which is reported in the balance sheet as a current asset. The office supplies expense account will have a debit balance of $444.26, which is reported in the income statement as an operating expense. To illustrate, using T accounts:

Office Supplies

Debit	Credit
984.26	444.26
Bal. 540.00	

Office Supplies Expense

Debit	Credit
444.26	

Store supplies include wrapping paper, twine, cellophane tape, corrugated board, paper bags, containers, cleaning supplies, and other miscellaneous supplies that are normally consumed in the operation of a store. Advertising supplies include catalogs, circulars, price lists, order blanks, and other miscellaneous supplies that are normally consumed in an advertising program. Transactions arising from the purchase of such supplies should be entered in the same manner as transactions arising from the purchase of office supplies. The end-of-period adjusting process and resulting treatment of asset and expense elements on the financial statements are similar.

Postage. The cost of postage purchased is usually treated as a current asset and entered by debiting Postage and by crediting the cash account. Some of the postage may be used on packages, and some on ordinary mail. If postage used on packages is billed to the customer, the entry for the sale will include a credit to the postage account. Usually no entry is made when postage is used on ordinary mail each day, but periodically the postage on hand is counted (or valued, if a postage meter is used). The difference between the amount of the unused postage on hand and the debit balance of the postage account represents the amount of postage used and not billed to customers. This requires an adjusting entry to the postage account.

If the account for postage is debited (1) for the amount of postage on hand at the beginning of the month, $76, and (2) for the amount of postage purchased during the month, $261.80, and is credited (3) for the amount of postage used on packages during the month, $95, the account will have a debit balance of $242.80 at the end of the month. If at that time, the actual amount of postage on hand is found to be $62.40, the difference of $180.40 represents the amount of postage that appears to have been used and not billed to customers during the month. The following adjusting entry will be made:

Postage Expense....................................	180.40	
Postage		180.40
Amount of postage used on ordinary mail.		

After this is posted, the postage account will have a debit balance of $62.40, which is reported in the balance sheet as a current asset. The postage expense account will have a debit balance of $180.40, which is reported as an operating expense in the income statement. To illustrate, using T accounts:

Postage

Debit	Credit
76.00	95.00
261.80	180.40
Bal. 62.40	

Postage Expense

Debit	Credit
180.40	

A business may meet its postage requirements by (1) buying postage stamps, (2) making a deposit under the postal permit system for a certain amount of postage, or (3) using a postage meter. In the third case, a certain amount of postage is paid for, and the meter is set so that the postage may be used as needed. Regardless of how postage is purchased, the accounting procedure can be the same. The prepaid postage is charged to the postage account and the amount of stamps used or postage consumed is charged to the proper expense account.

Insurance. A variety of risks are assumed in the operation of a business. Property such as buildings, furniture, machinery, supplies, and merchandise inventory may be damaged or destroyed by fire, water, earthquake, windstorm, or other natural disaster. Many types of property, especially money, may be stolen by burglars and sometimes by employees. State laws impose liability on the part of an employer to employees for injury or death arising out of the employees' work. The hazards connected with the ownership and operation of motor vehicles are well known. Accidents to persons unconnected with the business but occurring on business premises pose the threat of lawsuits and possibly large settlements. Loss of income as a result of the interruption of business operations because of a fire or a flood is a possibility.

It is possible to obtain insurance against these types of losses and certain others not mentioned. A separate insurance policy relating to each type of risk can be obtained, but in recent years, the practice of obtaining one policy covering most or all of the risks has become commonplace. Such contracts are described as "package," "blanket," or "multi-peril" policies. In total, the cost of such types of insurance is lower than a collection of policies for separate individual risks.

A contract under which an insurance company (the insurer) agrees to protect the business (the insured) from loss is known as an **insurance policy**. The amount that the insured is required to pay for insurance protection is known as the **premium**. The premium is usually stated as a specified rate per $1,000 of insurance for one or more years. Rates for workers' compensation insurance and automobile insurance are subject to change each year even though the coverage is part of a policy that includes other matters. The rate for the other features may be for a 3-year period. The premium for a 3-year coverage is usually less than 3 times the 1-year rate, which is a type of quantity discount. Since insurance is usually purchased for a period of one or more years and the premium is paid in advance by the insured, the amount paid is usually charged to a prepaid insurance account. This account is classified as a current asset.

Expired Insurance. The prepaid insurance account gradually decreases in value as the life of the insurance policy grows shorter. It is customary to enter at the close of each accounting period the total amount of prepayment that expired during the period just ended. The expired amount is entered as an expense. If the management of the business does not see a need for any breakdown of the insurance expense, an end-of-year adjusting entry such as the following would suffice:

Insurance Expense	xxx	
Prepaid Insurance		xxx
Insurance expired during the year.		

The amount in the foregoing entry may be determined by referring to the policy (or policies) and calculating the portion of the premium that relates to the year just ended. The amount of the premium for each major type of coverage is shown on the face of the policy. If more detail about the insurance expense is wanted, it would be possible to analyze the total and to classify it into, perhaps, delivery equipment insurance expense, fire insurance expense (with subclassifications relating to building, to furniture and fixtures, and to merchandise), workers' compensation insurance expense, and public liability insurance expense. Separate accounts can be established to provide as much detail as needed.

If a business has several insurance policies, it may be useful to maintain an auxiliary record known as an Insurance Policy Register. This record provides spaces to show the date and number of each policy, name of the insurer, type and amount of coverage, total term, expiration date, total premium, and columns to show the premium applicable to each month. Usually, a separate page is used for each year.

Canceled Insurance. The insurance company or the insured may cancel an insurance policy at any time before the expiration of the policy. If a policy is canceled, the insured is entitled to receive a refund of that part of the premium applicable to the unexpired period. The amount of the refund will depend upon whether the policy is canceled by direct action of the insurance company or at the request of the insured. When the policy is canceled directly by the insurance company, the premium for the expired period is computed on a pro rata basis. When the policy is canceled at the request of the insured, the premium for the expired period is usually computed on a short-term rate basis, which means that the insurance company's refund to the insured is less than the amount of the unexpired premium. The amount refunded is entered by debiting the cash account and by crediting the prepaid insurance account. The remaining unexpired premium, if any, is then debited to Insurance Expense and credited to Prepaid Insurance.

Prepaid Rent. When business property is rented for more than one accounting period on the basis of a lease agreement, and the lease payment is made in advance, it is usual to regard the amount of the lease payment as prepaid rent. Prepaid rent is classified as a current asset.

At the end of the accounting period, the amount of rent expense relating to the period just ended should be determined, and an adjusting entry made to transfer that portion of the lease payment from the prepaid rent account to the rent expense account. For example, assume that on July 1, an office building was leased by the business for a 3-year period, and a lease payment of $36,000 was made in advance. The entry for the lease payment is as follows:

July 1 Prepaid Rent	36,000	
Cash		36,000
Three-year lease of office building.		

On December 31, it was determined that one-sixth of the lease had expired; therefore, the following adjusting entry was made:

Dec. 31 Rent Expense	6,000	
Prepaid Rent		6,000
Prepaid rent transferred to rent expense.		

After the foregoing entry is posted, the prepaid rent account will have a debit balance of $30,000, which represents 2 1/2 years that the lease will remain active. The $30,000 of prepaid rent is reported in the balance sheet as a current asset. The $6,000 debit balance of the rent expense account is reported in the income statement under the heading of "Operating expenses" (and the subheading of "Administrative expenses" if operating expenses are subclassified).

One advantage of using the asset method of accounting for prepaid expenses is that the adjusting entries required at the end of the period are of the write-off type. Such adjustments do not need to be reversed at the start of the new period.

Expense Method of Accounting for Prepaid Expenses

Supplies and services that may not be wholly consumed in the period in which they are purchased may be entered as expenses at the time of purchase. Under the expense method of accounting, it is necessary to adjust the accounts at the end of each accounting period in order that the unused portions may be entered as assets. For example, if office supplies purchased during an accounting period are charged to the office supplies expense account, it will be necessary to adjust the account at the end of the period for the cost of the supplies on hand. To illustrate, assume that Office Supplies Expense had been charged for a total of $425 during the period and an inventory taken at the end of the period shows that supplies on hand amount to $150. The following adjusting entry is made:

Office Supplies	150	
Office Supplies Expense		150
Office supplies on hand.		

After this entry is posted, the office supplies expense account will have a debit balance of $275, which is reported in the income statement as an operating expense. The office supplies account will have a debit balance of $150, which is reported in the balance sheet as a current asset. To illustrate, using T accounts:

Office Supplies

Debit	Credit
150	

Office Supplies Expense

Debit	Credit
425	150
Bal. 275	

When the expense method of accounting is followed, the adjustments made at the end of the period are called deferral adjustments, because they defer expenses to the next period. Adjustments of this type should be reversed at the start of the new period. In the foregoing example relating to office supplies, the reversing entry would be:

Office Supplies Expense	150	
Office Supplies		150

The effect of the adjusting, closing, and reversing procedure is (1) to remove the unused or unexpired amount from an expense account at the end of the period, (2) to transfer the remaining amount to the expense and revenue summary account, and (3) at the start of the new period, to transfer back to the expense account the amount of expense that previously had been deferred.

The asset and expense methods of accounting for prepaid expenses give the same final result. In the asset method, an amount that will eventually become the expense of current and future periods is first put into an asset account, and at the end of each period, a proper portion is transferred to an expense account. In the expense method, the original amount is first put into an expense account. At the end of each accounting period, the portion that will be an expense of future periods is moved into an asset account and subsequently brought back into the related expense account by a reversing entry at the start of the new period.

BUILDING YOUR ACCOUNTING KNOWLEDGE

1. What are the two methods of entering the amounts of supplies or services purchased when accounts are kept on the accrual basis?
2. How is the value of office supplies, store supplies, advertising supplies, or postage on hand at the end of the accounting period determined?
3. Under what heading should supplies or postage on hand be reported in the balance sheet?
4. Under what heading should supplies or postage expense be reported in the income statement?
5. Why has the practice of obtaining a single "multi-peril" insurance policy become commonplace in recent years?
6. Under what heading should prepaid insurance be reported in the balance sheet? Prepaid rent?
7. What type of end-of-period adjusting entries are required when the asset method of accounting for prepaid expenses is used? Do such adjustments need to be reversed?
8. What type of end-of-period adjusting entries are required when the expense method of accounting for prepaid expenses is used? Do such adjustments need to be reversed?

APPLYING ACCOUNTING CONCEPTS

Exercise 12-6. Use the asset method to account for the following prepaid expenses of Prep Company, which just started in business.

1. **Office supplies were purchased for $850 cash.**
2. **Rent was paid in advance for a two-year period, $20,000.**

At the end of the accounting period, prepare adjusting entries for the following:

3. **Office supplies on hand, $160.**
4. **Six months rent has expired.**

Exercise 12-7. Assume the same events as in Exercise 12-6. Use the expense method to account for the four events of Prep Company.

Report No. 12-2

Complete Report No. 12-2 in the study assignments and submit your working papers to the instructor for approval. Then continue with the textbook discussion in Chapter 13 until Report No. 13-1 is required.

EXPANDING YOUR BUSINESS VOCABULARY

What is the meaning of each of the following terms?

accrual **(p. 378)** asset method **(p. 378)**

average cost (p. 368)
convention of conservatism (p. 371)
consignee (p. 366)
consignment (p. 366)
consignor (p. 366)
cost (p. 371)
cost apportionment (p. 370)
deferral (p. 382)
deferral adjustments (p. 384)
expense method (p. 383)
first-in, first-out (fifo) (p. 367)
gross margin method (p. 372)
insurance policy (p. 381)
in transit (p. 366)
inventory sheet (p. 365)
last-in, first-out (lifo) (p. 368)
lower of cost or cost to replace (p. 371)
lower of cost or market (p. 371)
market (p. 371)
natural business year (p. 364)
periodic system (p. 363)
perpetual inventory records (p. 374)
perpetual system (p. 363)
premium (p. 381)
prepaid expenses (p. 378)
retail method (p. 373)
short-term rate basis (p. 382)
specific identification (p. 366)
stock records (p. 375)
taking a physical inventory (p. 364)
weighted average cost (p. 368)

CHAPTER 13

Accounting for Property, Plant, and Equipment

CHAPTER OBJECTIVES

Careful study of this chapter should enable you to:

- Determine the cost of property, plant, and equipment.
- Explain the nature and purpose of depreciation, the different acceptable depreciation methods and their possible effects on net income.
- Account for the acquisition, disposition, and depreciation of property, plant, and equipment.
- Prepare a property, plant, and equipment record.
- Describe the reporting of depreciation in financial statements.
- Explain the nature of wasting assets and the two different methods of accounting for their depletion.

Many types of business assets, acquired with the expectation that they will remain in service for a number of accounting periods, are called **property, plant, and equipment** or **long-term assets**. The descriptions **fixed assets** and **capital assets** also are used sometimes. Such assets can be classified in various ways. From a legal standpoint, all property is either real property or personal property. **Real property** (realty or real estate) includes land and anything attached to the land. In nearly all cases, any real property owned by a business is considered to be a long-term asset. Real estate acquired as a short-term investment is an exception. **Personal property** includes everything else that can be owned other than real property. Many kinds of personal property also are classified as property, plant, and equipment. Furniture, equipment, motor vehicles, machinery, patents, and copyrights are common examples of personal property that is owned and used by a business for a number of accounting periods.

Another way of classifying long-term assets is on the basis of tangibility. All real property is tangible (has physical substance). The same is true of such personal property as furniture, equipment, and machinery. Major examples of intangible (no physical substance) assets are patents, copyrights, leases, franchises, trademarks, and goodwill. These are considered long-term assets because they are expected to bring future economic benefit for more than one year and, except for goodwill, have a legal status that allows them to be classified as property. The subject of goodwill will be considered in Chapter 16.

Sometimes businesses own interests in other incorporated businesses in the form of capital stock, bonds, or long-term notes. Government bonds or notes are also commonly owned. If these investments are temporary in nature, they are considered marketable securities and should be classified as current assets. If these assets are expected to be owned for a long time, they are considered long-term investments and should be shown in the balance sheet under the heading Investments

For accounting purposes, a common classification of property, plant, and equipment is on the basis of how the original cost of the property is handled in the process of determining net income. The cost of land used only as a site for a store, a factory, a warehouse, or a parking lot is normally left undisturbed in the accounts as long as the land is owned. Because land does not lose its capability to serve these purposes, it does not depreciate. Tangible assets such as buildings, furniture, and equipment are usually called depreciable assets, because they wear out or are used up as time passes. In determining net income, a portion of the cost of such assets is charged off as depreciation expense. In a similar fashion, the cost of such intangible properties as patents, copyrights, and leaseholds is gradually charged off as expense to the periods benefited by the assets. As applied to intangible assets, however, the periodic write-off is termed amortization in contrast to depreciation of certain tangible assets. Actually, the meaning of the word amortization is broad enough to include depreciation, but customarily the write-off of the cost of most tangible long-term assets is called depreciation, while the write-off of the cost of intangible long-term assets is called amortization.

Certain long-term assets whose physical substance is consumed in the operation of a business are called wasting assets Common examples include mines, stands of timber, and oil and gas wells. The cost of such property is allocated to the periods in which its removal or exhaustion occurs. This periodic write-off is called depletion.

For the sake of brevity, land, buildings, and various types of equipment will often be referred to in the following sections simply as long-term assets. It should be understood that these assets are all in the tangible category.

LAND, BUILDINGS, AND EQUIPMENT

In accounting for tangible long-term assets, two major issues need to be addressed: (1) what elements should be included in the cost of a particular asset or group of assets and (2) how the cost should be allocated or apportioned to those future accounting periods that will benefit from the use of such an asset or group of assets.

Cost of Long-Term Assets

Long-term assets may be purchased for cash or on account. The amount at which long-term assets should be entered initially is the total of all outlays needed to put them in use. This total may include the purchase price, transportation charges, installation costs, and any other costs that are incurred up to the point of placing the asset in service. In some cases, interest may be included in the cost. For example, if money is borrowed for the purpose of constructing a building or other facility, it is considered sound accounting to add the interest incurred during the period of construction to the cost of such building or facility. It is important that the total cost of a depreciable asset be properly accounted for, because this cost becomes the basis for the periodic depreciation write-off.

Transactions involving the purchase of property, plant, and equipment may be entered initially in the appropriate book by debiting the proper asset account and by crediting the cash account for the amount paid, or by crediting the proper liability account, such as Accounts Payable, Notes Payable, or Mortgage Payable, for the obligation incurred.

Additions or improvements represent an increase in the value of long-term assets and should be entered by debiting the proper asset account and by crediting the cash account or the proper liability account. For example, if an addition to a building is constructed, the total cost incurred should be debited to the building account. In the same manner, the cost of improvements, such as the installation of partitions, shelving, hardwood or tile floors, sprinkler systems, air conditioning systems, or any other improvements that increase the usefulness of the property, should be entered by debiting the building or building improvement account. The costs of landscaping grounds surrounding an office or factory building represent improvements in the land which enhance its value. Assessments for street improvements, sidewalks, sewers, flood prevention, or parks also represent improvements in, or enhancement of the value of the land. Such costs and assessments should be entered by debiting the land account.

Depreciation of Long-Term Assets

The central task in attempting to determine net income or loss on a periodic basis is to allocate revenue to the period in which it is earned and to assign expenses to the periods that are benefited from the outlays. Long-term assets frequently last for many years and, accordingly, benefit a number of periods. The process of determining and entering the depreciation of most long-term assets is carried on in an effort to assign their cost to the periods that they benefit or serve.

It should be emphasized that depreciation is a process of cost allocation, not a process of valuation. Many factors cause the values of long-term assets to change over time, and the assignment of long-term costs to future accounting periods is very unlikely to produce net amounts in the asset accounts that represent current values. These net amounts (cost less accumulated depreciation) are merely the portions of the original costs which have not yet been allocated to expense.

Causes of Depreciation. Most long-term assets lose their usefulness over time. The allocation of the cost or other recorded value of a long-term asset over those future periods expected to benefit from its use is called depreciation. There are two major types of depreciation: (1) physical and (2) functional.

Physical depreciation refers to the loss of usefulness because of deterioration from age and from wear. It is generally continuous, though not necessarily uniform from period to period. Assets exposed to the elements may wear out at a fairly regular rate. Assets not exposed to the elements may slowly deteriorate whether in use or not, but the speed at which they deteriorate often is related to the extent to which they are used.

Functional depreciation refers to the loss of usefulness because of inadequacy or obsolescence. The growth of a business may result in some of its long-term assets becoming inadequate. The assets remain capable of doing the job for which they were acquired, but the job has become too big for them. Assets may become obsolete because of a change in the demand for products or services, or because of the development of new methods, equipment, or processes which either reduce costs, or increase quality, or both.

Calculating the Amount of Depreciation for a Period. The net cost of an asset should be apportioned over the periods the asset is expected to serve. **Net cost** means original cost less scrap or salvage value. Scrap or salvage value is quite difficult to predict in most cases. Unless such value is expected to be a significant fraction of original cost, it usually is ignored (considered to be zero). Scrap or salvage value normally is a significant amount in the case of automobiles and trucks. Although the estimation of salvage value can be difficult, the major challenge in depreciation accounting is to attempt to foretell either how many periods the assets will serve or how many units of service the asset will provide. If it were possible to know that a machine could operate a total of 100,000 hours, it would be easy to decide that 5% of its net cost should be charged to the first year if during that year the machine operated 5,000 hours. Likewise, a certain knowledge that an asset would last 10 years and equally serve each of those years would solve the problem of how to apportion its cost. Unfortunately, there is no way of knowing exactly how long an asset will last or exactly what its output will be. All that can be done is to make estimates based upon past experience. In attempting to make such estimates, the accountant may be assisted by information relating to assets previously owned by the business or be guided by the experience of others. Statistics supplied by trade associations and government agencies (such as the Internal Revenue Service) may help. Opinions of engineers or appraisal companies may be sought. Past experience with respect to physical depreciation may be a very good guide for the future. Past events, however, are not much help in attempting to predict depreciation caused by inadequacy or obsolescence. Uncertainty surrounds all depreciation calculations.

Methods of Calculating Depreciation. There are several different ways of calculating the amount of depreciation each period. The most commonly used methods are the following:

1. Straight-line method.
2. Declining-balance method.
3. Sum-of-the-years-digits method.
4. Units-of-output method.
5. ACRS depreciation.

Depreciation may be taken into consideration in calculating income subject to federal and state income taxes. A business is not required to calculate depreciation in the same way for both income tax and business accounting purposes. However, because depreciation is only an estimate, many firms adopt depreciation practices for business accounting purposes that are also acceptable for income tax determination purposes. This does not impose severe limitations, since the tax laws generally allow any method that is reasonable and consistently followed, although the first three methods named above are specifically mentioned in the law for depreciable long-term assets acquired prior to 1981.

Straight-Line Method. The depreciation method in which the net cost of an asset is apportioned equally over its estimated useful life in terms of months or years is called the **straight-line method**. For example, assume that a new asset with a cost of $1,000, an expected life of 4 years, and a $100 estimated salvage value at the end of its useful life, is to be depreciated on a straight-line basis. The amount of depreciation each year would be $225, computed as follows:

$$\frac{\$1{,}000\text{ (cost)} - \$100\text{ (salvage value)}}{4\text{ years}} = \$225\text{ annual depreciation}$$

The annual rate of depreciation would be 25% (100% ÷ 4 years).

A month is usually the shortest period that is considered in depreciation accounting. An asset purchased on or before the fifteenth of the month is considered to have been owned for the full month. An asset purchased after the fifteenth of the month is considered to have been acquired the first of the next month.

The difference between the cost of an asset and the total amount charged off as depreciation as of a certain date is its **undepreciated cost** (sometimes called **book value**). In the foregoing illustration, the undepreciated cost of the asset after the first year, assuming it was in use for 12 months, would be $775 [$1,000 (cost) − $225 (depreciation)]. When the straight-line method is used, the undepreciated cost of the asset decreases uniformly period by period. As shown on the following graph, the undepreciated cost over a number of periods is a downward-sloping, but perfectly straight line. That is how the method got its name.

The straight-line method's outstanding advantage is its simplicity. Since depreciation is based upon estimates, many business people and accountants believe that the use of more complicated procedures is not warranted. The calculation of depreciation on a straight-line basis

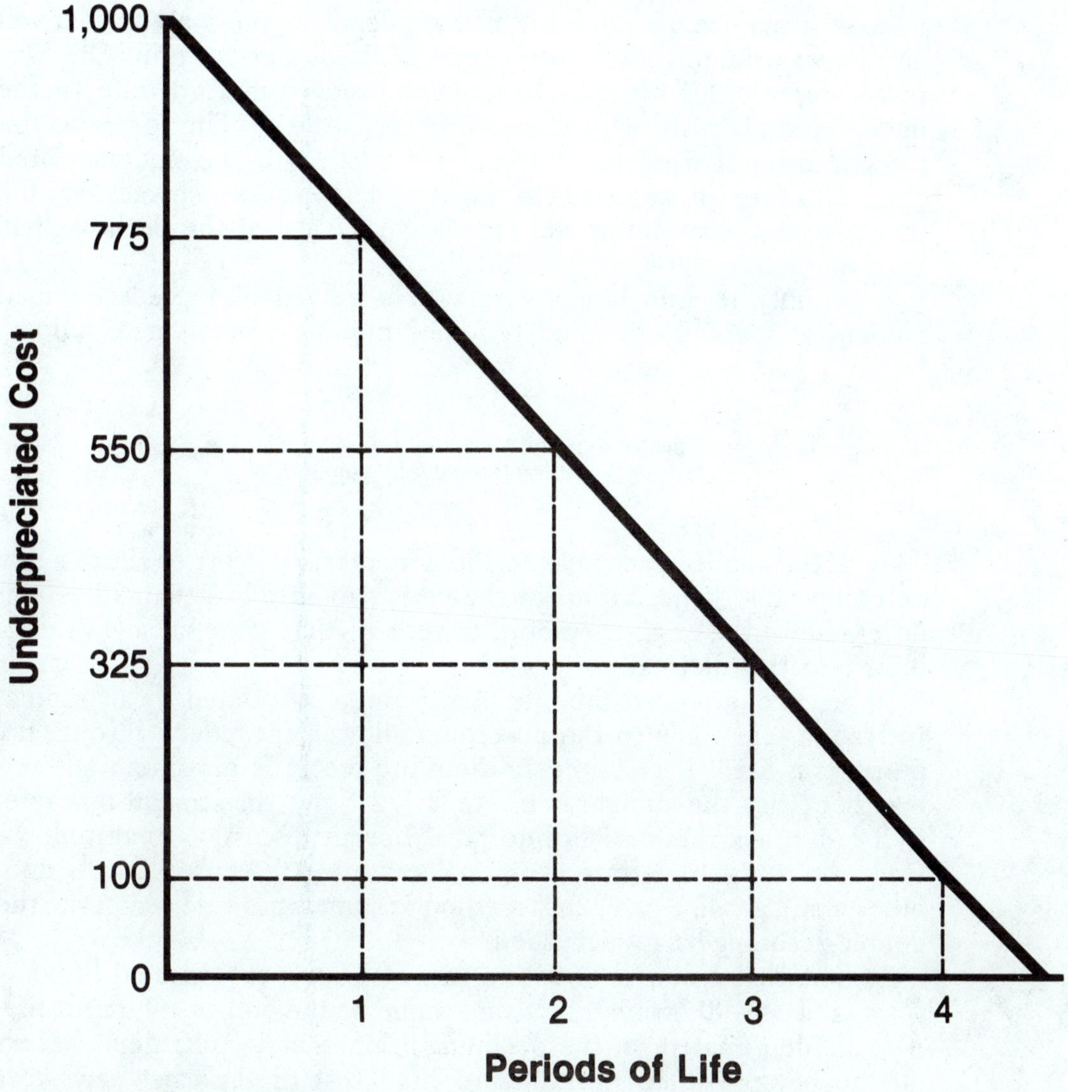

is still a widely followed practice when other methods offer no particular advantage.

Declining-Balance Method. Many long-term assets require repairs and replacement of parts to keep them in service. Such expenses usually increase as the assets grow older. Some accountants believe that depreciation expense should be higher in early years to offset the higher repair and maintenance expenses of the later years. Another reason advanced in support of an accelerated depreciation method is the contention that assets contribute proportionately more to the business during the years that the assets are comparatively new. For these reasons, it may be desirable to calculate depreciation in a way that will give larger write-offs in the early years of the life of the unit. One way to accomplish this result is to apply a fixed or uniform rate to the undepreciated cost of the property each year. The depreciation method using a fixed or uniform rate applied to the undepreciated cost, resulting in successively smaller depreciation charges as the undepreciated cost diminishes year by year is called the declining-balance method.

A formula to calculate a rate which will leave a predetermined amount at the end of a predetermined number of years is as follows:

$$\text{Rate} = 1 - n\sqrt[n]{s \div c}$$

Where n = number of years of estimated life
s = estimated salvage value
c = original cost

This rate is applied each year to the undepreciated cost of the asset to determine the depreciation for the year. Any rate less than 100% will never reduce the original amount to zero, so that some salvage value is built into this method.

In practice, however, the rate used is rarely calculated by a formula. Instead, a rate equal to the maximum allowed for federal income tax purposes is used. If certain conditions are met, the maximum allowed is either twice the straight-line rate, 1-1/2 times the straight-line rate, or 1-1/4 times the straight-line rate. In the discussion that follows, twice the straight-line rate is used. Because a rate is used that is double the straight-line rate, this method is sometimes referred to as the double-declining-balance method.

Assume that a new asset with a cost of $1,000, an expected life of 4 years, and a $100 estimated salvage value at the end of its useful life, is to be depreciated on the declining-balance basis. The depreciation rate to be applied to the undepreciated cost of the asset each year would be 50%, computed as follows:

Straight-line rate = 25% (100% ÷ 4 years)
Declining-balance rate = 50% (2 × 25%)

The undepreciated cost at the end of each year would be as shown at the top of page 395.

As shown on the following graph, the undepreciated cost declines rapidly in the early years and more slowly in the later years of an asset's life.

Note that although salvage value is not considered directly in the determination of the depreciation amount, the asset should not be

Year	Undepreciated Cost Beginning of Year	Rate	Annual Depreciation	Accumulated Depreciation End of Year	Undepreciated Cost End of Year
1	$1,000.00	50%	$500.00	$500.00	$500.00
2	500.00	50	250.00	750.00	250.00
3	250.00	50	125.00	875.00	125.00
4	125.00	50	25.00	900.00	100.00

depreciated below its estimated salvage value. Thus, as shown in the illustration and graph, the amount of depreciation actually recorded in the final year (Year 4) is limited to $25 ($125 − $100).

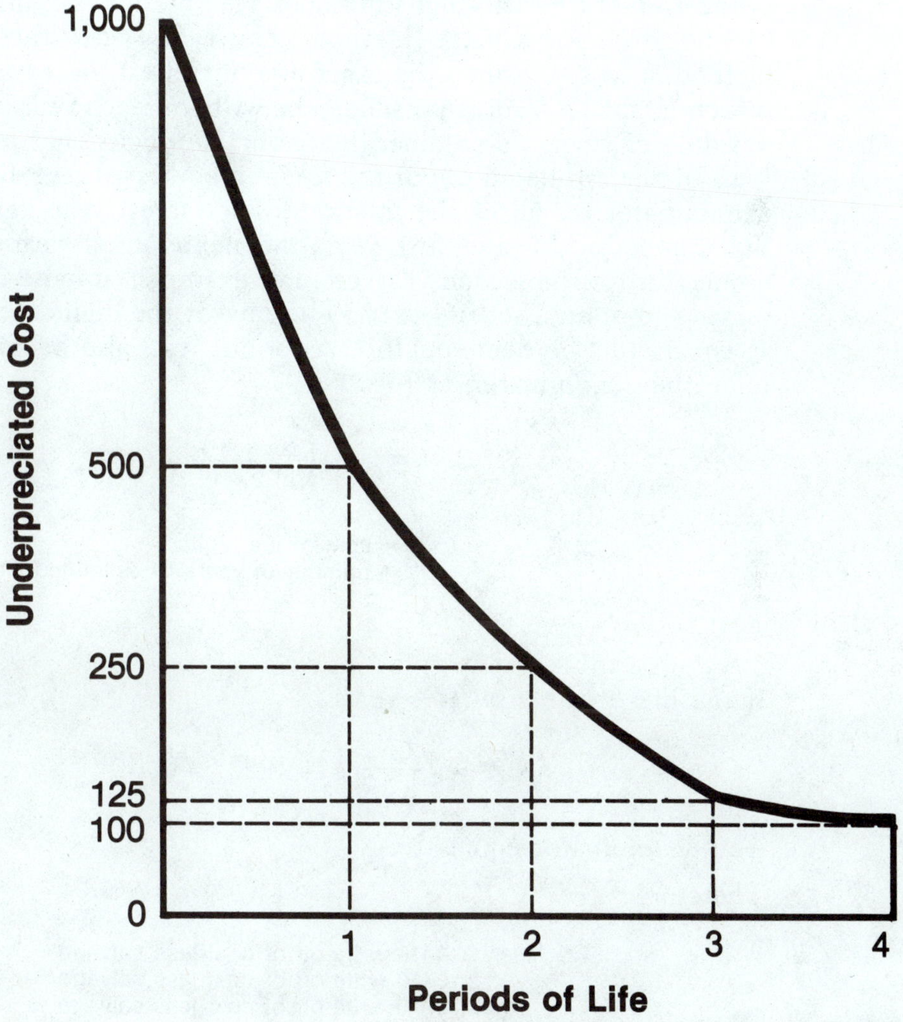

If the business qualifies for the use of declining-balance depreciation for income tax purposes, the declining-balance rate can be abandoned at any time, and the undepreciated cost at that date, less any estimated salvage value, can be written off in equal installments over the estimated remaining life. For example, in the foregoing illustration, suppose that at the end of the second year when the asset had an undepreciated cost of $250, it appeared likely that the salvage value would be zero. Accordingly, $125 ($250 ÷ 2) depreciation could be taken for each of the two remaining years.

Sum-of-the-Years-Digits Method. The depreciation method using a steadily decreasing rate applied to net cost (original cost less salvage value), resulting in successively smaller depreciation charges is known as the **sum-of-the-years-digits method**. This method is similar in effect to the declining-balance method. However, with the years-digits method, a write-down to the exact amount of estimated salvage value (which might be zero) is possible. The write-off each year is based on a schedule of fractions obtained by listing the digits that represent the years of the estimated life of the asset and adding these digits to get a denominator for all of the fractions. The largest year-digit is used as the numerator for the first year, the next largest year-digit as the numerator for the second year, etc. For example, suppose that the estimated life of an asset is 4 years. The sum of the digits (4 + 3 + 2 + 1) equals 10 (the denominator). A formula can also be used to determine the denominator, as follows:

$$S = N\left(\frac{N + 1}{2}\right)$$

S = sum of the digits
N = number of years of estimated life

If the life of the asset is 4 years:

$$S = 4\left(\frac{4 + 1}{2}\right) = 4(2\tfrac{1}{2}) = 10$$

The denominator equals 10.

Therefore:

Year 1: 4/10 write-off of cost less salvage
2: 3/10 write-off of cost less salvage
3: 2/10 write-off of cost less salvage
4: 1/10 write-off of cost less salvage

As applied to an asset costing $1,000, with an estimated salvage value of $100, the results would be as follows:

Year	Net Cost	Rate	Annual Depreciation	Accumulated Depreciation End of Year	Undepreciated Cost End of Year
1	$900	4/10	$360	$360	$640
2	900	3/10	270	630	370
3	900	2/10	180	810	190
4	900	1/10	90	900	100

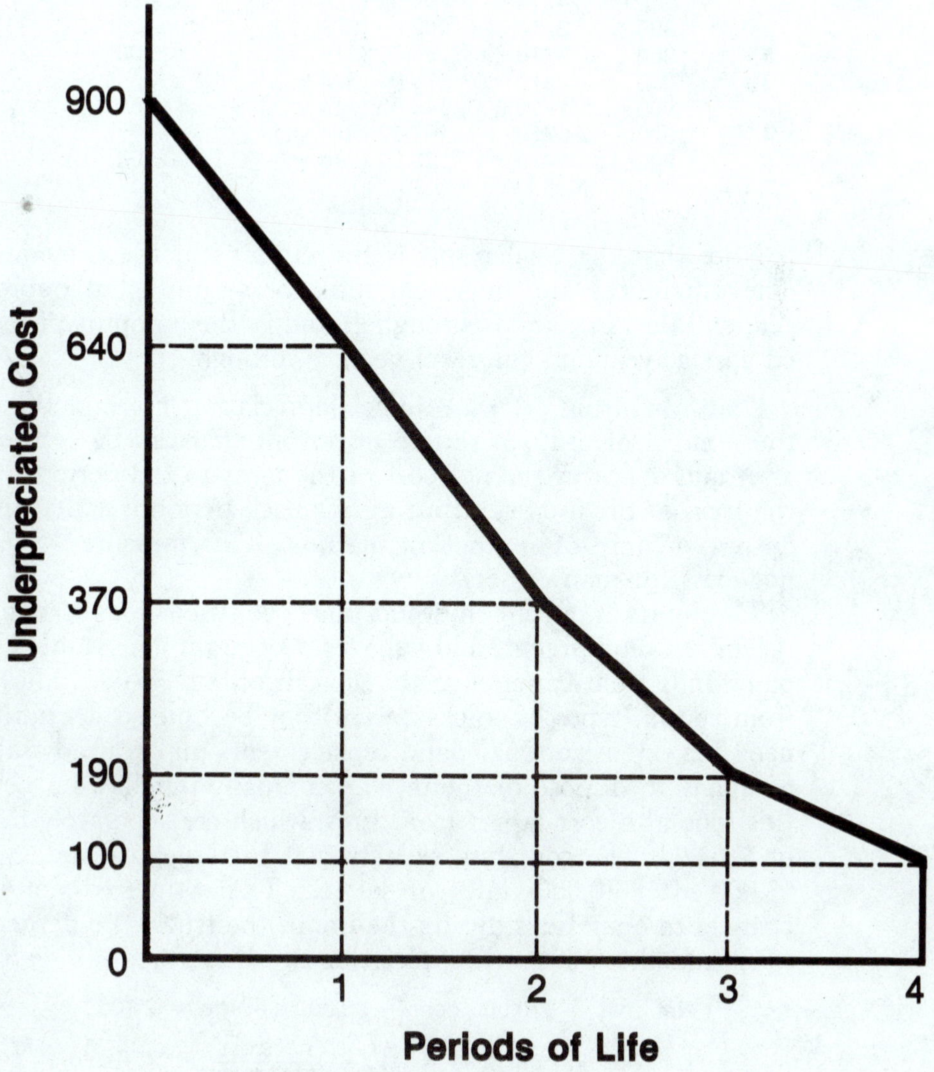

If an asset is acquired during an accounting period, a slight modification of the sum-of-the-years-digits method becomes necessary. Assume that the $1,000 asset described earlier was acquired on April 1 of Year 1. The application of the method would require modification as follows:

Year	Net Cost	Rate	Depreciation	Accumulated Depreciation End of Year	Undepreciated Cost End of Year
1	$900	4/10	$270.00 (3/4 yr.)	$270.00	$730.00
2	900	4/10	90.00 (1/4 yr.)	562.50	437.50
2	900	3/10	202.50 (3/4 yr.)		
3	900	3/10	67.50 (1/4 yr.)	765.00	235.00
3	900	2/10	135.00 (3/4 yr.)		
4	900	2/10	45.00 (1/4 yr.)	877.50	122.50
4	900	1/10	67.50 (3/4 yr.)		
5	900	1/10	22.50 (1/4 yr.)	900.00	100.00

Note that the final result is the same as in the previous example. The differences are in the amounts of accumulated depreciation at year-end (less in years 1 through 4) and in the amounts of undepreciated cost at year-end (more in years 1 through 4).

Units-of-Output Method. The depreciation method that estimates the number of units of service or output that can be secured from an asset and allocates the net cost of the asset to the periods it serves on the basis of the use or output during each period is called the **units-of-output** or **units-of-production method**. This measure of service does not exist for many assets.

The units-of-output method may be used for certain types of machinery, equipment, and vehicles. For example, assume that a company finds from experience that it can obtain 70,000 miles of service from certain types of trucks before they become so worn out that the need for extensive repairs and replacements makes it advisable for the company to dispose of them. The company purchases a new truck of this type at a cost (apart from tires, which are separately depreciated) of $10,000. The company expects that the truck can be traded in for $3,000 after 70,000 miles of service. The estimated net cost to be charged to operations during the life of the truck, the depreciation per mile, and the first-year depreciation are therefore:

Net cost = $10,000 cost − $3,000 salvage = $7,000

$$\text{Depreciation per mile} = \frac{\$7{,}000 \text{ net cost}}{70{,}000 \text{ total miles}} = 10 \text{ cents}$$

First year depreciation = 28,000 miles @ 10 cents = $2,800.

Accelerated Cost Recovery System (ACRS) Depreciation. The Economic Recovery Tax Act of 1981 introduced **ACRS** (accelerated cost recovery system) **depreciation**. This method permits extremely rapid depreciation of long-term business assets for income tax purposes. A business can decrease its income tax expense by claiming large depreciation expense deductions in the early years of a long-term asset's life.

ACRS increases the rate of asset cost write-off by:

1. Designating four "recovery" periods of artificial length over which the costs of long-term assets can be written off. Most business property can be placed into one of three ACRS classifications—3-year, 5-year, and 18-year. These periods are noticeably shorter than the designated assets' useful lives:
   (a) Automobiles, light trucks, and special tools—3-year write off.
   (b) Heavy trucks, machinery, and equipment—5-year write-off.
   (c) Buildings and land improvements—18-year write-off if purchased after March 15, 1984.
2. Using a modified declining-balance depreciation rate, as the following table indicates:

ACRS Depreciation Rates

Year	3-Year Property	5-Year Property	18-Year Property
1	25	15	10
2	38	22	9
3	37	21	8
4		21	7
5		21	6
6			6
7			5
8			5
9			5
10			5
11			5
12			5
13			4
14			4
15			4
16			4
17			4
18			4
	100	100	100

For example, assume that a light delivery truck costing $15,000 is acquired. Even though its estimated useful life is four years, this truck qualifies as three-year ACRS property. The following schedule shows the calculation of the depreciation expense deduction for federal income tax purposes for each of the three years.

Delivery Truck Depreciation Deduction Schedule (ACRS for Income Tax)

Year	Calculation	Expense Deduction	Accumulated Depreciation	Undepreciated Cost
1	($15,000 × 25%)	$3,750	$ 3,750	$11,250
2	(15,000 × 38%)	5,700	9,450	5,550
3	(15,000 × 37%)	5,550	15,000	-0-

Observe that the undepreciated cost is zero at the end of Year 3. ACRS ignores salvage value. Another feature of the ACRS method is that for 3- and 5-year property there is no concern for fractional periods. Regardless of the time of year that an asset in these classes is acquired, depreciation is taken for a full year. Fractional periods are considered for 18-year property.

Comparison of Methods

The results of the different depreciation methods are experienced in two ways: (1) through the pattern of depreciation charges and the resultant periodic undepreciated cost amount on the balance sheet, and (2) through the periodic determination of net income on the income statement.

Depreciation Pattern and Undepreciated Costs. The following tabulation contrasts the results of using straight-line, declining-balance, and sum-of-the-years digits depreciation methods for an asset costing $1,000, with a 10 year estimated life and an estimated salvage value of $100:

	Straight-Line Method		Declining-Balance Method		Sum-of-the Years-Digits Method	
Year	Depreciation Charge	Undepreciated Cost End of Year	Depreciation Charge	Undepreciated Cost End of Year	Depreciation Charge	Undepreciated Cost End of Year
1	$90.00	$910.00	$200.00	$800.00	$163.64	$836.36
2	90.00	820.00	160.00	640.00	147.27	689.09
3	90.00	730.00	128.00	512.00	130.91	558.18
4	90.00	640.00	102.40	409.60	114.55	443.63
5	90.00	550.00	81.92	327.68	98.18	345.45
6	90.00	460.00	65.54	262.14	81.82	263.63
7	90.00	370.00	52.43	209.71	65.45	198.18
8	90.00	280.00	41.94	167.77	49.09	149.09
9	90.00	190.00	33.55	134.22	32.73	116.36
10	90.00	100.00	26.84	107.38	16.36	100.00

Under the straight-line method, the annual depreciation charge was determined by dividing the net cost of $900 ($1,000 cost − $100 salvage value) by 10 years.

Under the declining-balance method, salvage value was ignored since it is a built-in factor, and twice the straight-line rate was applied to the undepreciated cost at the start of each year. With a 10-year life, the straight-line rate is 10%, so twice this is 20%. The undepreciated cost at the end of 10 years ($107.38) is very close to the estimated salvage value of $100. If this were not the case, the declining-balance procedure could have been dropped at some point and in the years remaining, equal charges could have been made to write off all but the estimated salvage value.

Under the sum-of-the-years digits method, salvage value was taken into consideration. The sum of the digits, 1 through 10, is 55 $\left[10\left(\frac{10 + 1}{2}\right)\right]$. Therefore, the charge was 10/55 of the net cost in the first year, 9/55 in the second year, and so on.

Effect on Net Income Calculation. Over a number of years, the total of the amounts of the calculated annual net income will be about the same regardless of the method of depreciation used. For any one year, however, the method of depreciation used may make a significant difference in the amount of the calculated net income. For example, assume that a business acquired a number of new depreciable assets at a cost of $60,000, with an estimated life of 10 years and an estimated scrap value of $6,000. For the first year of operation, revenue was $150,000 and all costs and expenses except depreciation amounted to $120,000. Following is a comparison of three very condensed income statements of the new business showing the net income for the first year after applying the three depreciation methods:

	Straight-Line Depreciation Method Used		Declining-Balance Depreciation Method Used		Sum-of-the-Years-Digits Depreciation Method Used	
Revenue		$150,000		$150,000		$150,000
Costs and expenses other than depreciation	$120,000		$120,000		$120,000	
Depreciation	5,400	125,400	12,000	132,000	9,818	129,818
Net income		$ 24,600		$ 18,000		$ 20,182

To verify the depreciation calculation, refer to Year 1 of the example on page 400 and multiply by 60, since that example was based on a

$1,000 asset, and this illustration assumes that the depreciable assets cost $60,000.

Note that the calculated amount of net income in the first case is over one third greater than the amount in the second case. In contrast, the effect on net income will reverse itself in later years. During those years the reported net income will be larger for the accelerated methods than for the straight-line method. Clearly significant differences in net income may result from the choice of depreciation methods.

In the preceding chapter, the effects of the choice of inventory method on net income were noted It is apparent that periodic business income calculation is not an exact science, but rather an art involving careful judgment based on an understanding of acceptable alternatives and the consequences of their use.

BUILDING YOUR ACCOUNTING KNOWLEDGE

1. Describe five different ways of classifying long-term assets.
2. What may be included in the total amount at which a long-term asset is entered initially?
3. How should additions or improvements representing an increase in the value of long-term assets be entered?
4. How should the cost of such activities as landscaping grounds be entered?
5. What are the two major causes of depreciation?
6. What is meant by the "net cost" of a long-term asset?
7. What are the five most commonly used methods of calculating depreciation, and how do they differ in their application?
8. Why cannot the units-of-output method of depreciation be applied to all depreciable long-term assets?
9. What are the three types of business assets and respective recovery periods in ACRS depreciation?

APPLYING ACCOUNTING CONCEPTS

Exercise 13-1. A light truck is purchased on January 1 at a cost of $10,500. It is expected to serve for 5 years and to have a trade-in value of $1,500. Calculate the depreciation expense for the first and third years of use of the truck using the

1. Straight-line method.
2. Declining-balance method.
3. Sum-of-the-years-digits method.

Exercise 13-2. The truck purchased in Exercise 13-1 is expected to be used for 90,000 miles over its 5-year life. Calculate the depreciation expense for the first and third years of use if the truck is driven 25,000 miles in year 1 and 15,000 miles in year 3.

Exercise 13-3. The truck purchased in Exercise 13-1 is classified as 3-year property according to ACRS depreciation. Using the ACRS depreciation rates provided in the chapter, calculate the depreciation expense for tax purposes in the first and third years of use of the truck.

Report No. 13-1

Complete Report No. 13-1 in the study assignments and submit your working papers to the instructor for approval. Then continue with the textbook discussion until Report No. 13-2 is required.

ACCOUNTING PROCEDURE

The number of accounts for tangible long-term assets that will be kept in the general ledger will depend upon the number of depreciable assets, the type of information required by the management, and in the case of all but land, the sort of depreciation procedure that is to be followed. Land is not subject to depreciation in business accounting. If there are very few long-term assets, a separate account for each one with a related depreciation account can be kept in the general ledger. In such a case, the periodic depreciation for each asset should be calculated and entered separately.

Entering Depreciation

Depreciation usually is entered at the end of the period, along with other necessary adjusting entries. One or more depreciation expense accounts may be debited, and one or more accumulated depreciation accounts may be credited. The number of each of these accounts depends upon the degree of detail that is desired in the general ledger accounts and for the periodic statements. Often there is one depreciation expense account for each major type of asset, such as Depreciation Expense — Buildings, Depreciation Expense — Furniture and Fixtures, and Depreciation Expense — Delivery Equipment. A business that classifies expenses on a departmental basis may use a large number of depreciation expense accounts.

In the normal course of events, the only entries in the accumulated depreciation accounts are those made at the end of each period to enter the depreciation for the period then ended. When some disposition is made of a depreciable asset (such as its sale, exchange, retirement, or destruction by fire), depreciation should be entered for the interval between the date of the last regular adjustment of the accounts and the date of the disposition of the asset. Usually, the depreciation is calculated to the nearest full month.

To illustrate the depreciation accounting process, assume that a delivery truck was acquired on January 6, 1986 with a cost of $10,000, an estimated useful life of 4 years, and an estimated salvage value of $4,000. The annual depreciation using the straight-line method would be calculated as follows:

$$\frac{\$10{,}000 \text{ cost} - \$4{,}000 \text{ salvage}}{4 \text{ year life}} = \$1{,}500 \text{ annual depreciation}$$

The entry for the annual depreciation on the truck as of December 31, 1986 would appear in two-column form as follows:

Depreciation Expense—Delivery Truck	1,500	
Accumulated Depreciation—Delivery Truck		1,500
Annual depreciation on truck.		

The foregoing entry would be repeated each succeeding December 31 until the delivery truck was either fully depreciated or disposed of.

Assume that the truck was sold on May 1, 1989. The entry for the depreciation through the date of the sale of the asset would be as follows:

Depreciation Expense—Delivery Truck	500	
Accumulated Depreciation—Delivery Truck		500
Depreciation on truck for 1/3 year.		

Disposition of Long-Term Assets

A long-term asset may be disposed of in any one of the following ways:

1. It may be discarded or retired.
2. It may be sold.
3. It may be exchanged or traded in for property of like kind or for other property.

Discarding or Retiring Long-Term Assets. A long-term asset may be discarded or retired whether or not it has been fully depreciated. If it has been fully depreciated, no gain or loss will be realized. If it has not been fully depreciated, the undepreciated cost of the discarded asset will represent a loss. Such a loss may be the result of underestimating the depreciation of the asset for the period of time that it has been in use, or it may be the result of obsolescence. Often, it is better to scrap an obsolete machine and buy a new one even though a loss is realized on the old machine.

To illustrate, on July 15, postal scales that had no exchange or sale value were discarded. The property, plant, and equipment record indicated that the scales originally had cost $150 and that depreciation totaling $120 had been entered as a credit to the accumulated depreciation—store equipment account. This event involved a loss of $30 ($150 − $120) that was the undepreciated cost of the discarded asset. The transaction was entered as indicated by the following two-column journal entry:

Loss on Discarded Store Equipment	30	
Accumulated Depreciation—Store Equipment	120	
Store Equipment		150
Discarded postal scales.		

When this entry is posted, the debit of $120 to the accumulated depreciation account and the credit of $150 to the store equipment account will remove the amounts relating to the postal scales from the balances of these accounts. The debit of $30 to Loss on Discarded Store Equipment represents the realized loss that will be reflected on the income statement.

When a long-term asset is discarded after it has been fully depreciated, even though no gain or loss results from the transaction, the amounts relating to the discarded asset should be eliminated from the account balances by debiting the accumulated depreciation account and by crediting the asset account with the amount of the original cost of the asset.

Selling Long-Term Assets. If a long-term asset is sold, it is necessary to know its undepreciated cost before the proper amount of any gain or loss resulting from the transaction can be determined. The undepreciated cost of an asset is the difference between its cost and the total amount of accumulated depreciation entered to the date of sale. When a long-term asset is sold at its undepreciated cost, no gain or loss results from the transaction; when it is sold for more than its undepreciated cost, the difference represents a gain; when it is sold for less than its undepreciated cost, the difference represents a loss.

Assume that an electronic calculator costs $350, has no estimated salvage value, and depreciates at the rate of 10% a year. The annual depreciation is entered in two-column journal form as follows:

Depreciation Expense—Office Equipment	35	
Accumulated Depreciation—Office Equipment		35

$$\frac{\$350 \text{ cost} - 0 \text{ salvage}}{10\text{-year life}} = \$35 \text{ annual depreciation}$$

At the end of the 3 years, the undepreciated cost of the calculator will be $245, the difference between the cost price ($350) and the accumulated depreciation ($105).

$$\$350 \text{ cost} - (\$35 \text{ annual depreciation} \times 3) = \$350 - \$105 = \$245.$$

If the calculator was sold at the end of 3 years for $275 cash, the transaction should be entered in two-column journal form as follows:

Cash	275	
Accumulated Depreciation—Office Equipment	105	
Office Equipment		350
Gain on Sale of Office Equipment		30
Sold calculator.		

When this entry is posted, the debit of $105 to the accumulated depreciation account will offset the amounts entered previously as credits to the accumulated depreciation account over a period of 3 years. The amount credited to Office Equipment will offset the purchase price of $350 previously entered as a debit to Office Equipment. These entries have the effect of completely eliminating the amounts relating to the old calculator from the office equipment and accumulated depreciation accounts. The gain of $30 ($275 sales price – $245 undepreciated cost) realized from the sale of the calculator is reported as a Gain on Sale of Office Equipment. This gain should be listed under the heading of "Other revenue" in the income statement.

If the calculator was sold at the end of 3 years for $225 instead of $275, there would be a loss of $20 ($245 undepreciated cost – $225 sales price), instead of a gain of $30. The transaction should be entered in two-column journal form as follows:

Cash	225	
Accumulated Depreciation—Office Equipment	105	
Loss on Sale of Office Equipment	20	
Office Equipment		350
Sold calculator.		

When this entry is posted, the debit of $105 to the accumulated depreciation account and the credit of $350 to the office equipment account will eliminate the amounts relating to the old calculator from these accounts. The loss resulting from the sale of the old calculator for $20 less than its undepreciated cost will be reported as a Loss on Sale of Office Equipment. This loss should be listed under the heading of "Other expense" in the income statement.

Exchange or Trade-In of Long-Term Assets. A long-term asset may be exchanged or traded in for other property. Accepted financial accounting treatment, in most cases, is based on the fair market values of the asset exchanged. **Fair market value** is a value that is agreed upon in a current sales transaction by a willing buyer and a willing seller. On the other hand, tax regulations often allow the asset acquired to be assigned a cost equal to the undepreciated cost of the asset given up.

If one asset is traded in on the purchase of another, a **trade-in allowance** frequently is granted which may be equal to, greater than, or less than the undepreciated cost of the asset traded in. Trade-in allowances frequently do not reflect fair market values, so that any gain or loss calculated based on a trade-in allowance may not be an accurate measurement of the situation.

In financial accounting, long-term assets are classified into two categories for purposes of exchange or trade-in: similar (the tax laws refer to these as "of like kind") and dissimilar (the tax laws refer to these as "not of like kind"). In accounting for exchanges of similar assets, financial accounting recognizes all losses but no gains. For tax purposes, neither gains nor losses are recognized on such exchanges. In contrast, in accounting for exchanges of dissimilar assets, both financial accounting and the tax laws recognize gains and losses on the exchanges.

To illustrate the exchange or trade in of similar assets ("like kind"), assume that a delivery truck that cost $6,500 and has been owned for 3 years is traded in for another delivery truck which is to be used for a similar purpose. Depreciation in the amount of $1,800 has been taken each year—a total of $5,400. Thus, the undepreciated cost of the truck is $1,100 ($6,500 − $5,400). If the trade-in value of the old truck is $1,500 and the new truck has a fair market value of $8,000, $6,500 would be paid in cash ($8,000 − $1,500). This $6,500 balance paid to the supplier on the long-term asset trade-in is known as boot. The transaction should be entered in two-column journal form as follows:

Delivery Equipment (new truck)	7,600	
Accumulated Depreciation—Delivery Equipment	5,400	
Delivery Equipment (old truck)		6,500
Cash		6,500
Purchased a new truck.		

The new truck's cost ($7,600) is the sum of the undepreciated cost of the old truck ($1,100) and the boot paid ($6,500). This cost becomes the basis for future depreciation charges. Note that this journal entry does not recognize the $400 gain, which is the difference between the undepreciated cost of $1,100 and the trade-in value of the old truck of $1,500. When this entry is posted, the cost of the old truck will be eliminated from the delivery equipment account and that account will be charged with the cost of the new truck. The accumulated depreciation on the old truck will also be eliminated from the accumulated depreciation account, and no gain will be recognized in recording the transaction. This method of accounting also conforms to the tax laws.

If the fair market value of the new truck had been only $7,500, and the trade in value of the old truck only $1,000, boot of $6,500 would still be paid. Proper financial accounting would require the following two-column journal entry:

Delivery Equipment (new truck)	7,500	
Accumulated Depreciation—Delivery Equipment	5,400	
Loss on Exchange of Delivery Equipment	100	
Delivery Equipment (old truck)		6,500
Cash		6,500
Purchased a new truck.		

Note that in this situation the new truck is entered at its fair market value and that a $100 loss (the excess of the undepreciated cost over the trade-in allowance) on the exchange is charged to a special loss account. This method of accounting does not conform to the tax laws, because losses for tax purposes (like gains for tax purposes) are not recognized in connection with a "like kind" exchange. The proper entry for tax purposes would be the same as the entry previously illustrated on page 408 where a gain on the exchange was involved but not entered.

To illustrate the trade-in of dissimilar assets (not of like kind), assume that a typewriter that cost $300 and has been owned for 2 years is traded in for a new cash register. Depreciation in the amount of $60 has been taken each year for a total of $120. Thus the undepreciated cost of the typewriter is $180 ($300 − $120). The new cash register has a fair market value of $625. A trade-in allowance of $200 is granted, and the balance, $425, is paid in cash as boot. Since this transaction involves an exchange of dissimilar assets, any gain or loss should be recognized. Because $200 was allowed for an asset that had an undepreciated cost of $180 ($300 cost of asset − $120 accumulated depreciation), the transaction involved a gain of $20. The transaction should be entered in two-column journal form as follows:

Office Equipment	625	
Accumulated Depreciation—Office Equipment	120	
Office Equipment		300
Cash		425
Gain on Exchange of Office Equipment		20
Purchased a new cash register.		

When this entry is posted, the debit of $120 to the accumulated depreciation account will offset the amounts entered previously as credits to that account over a period of 2 years. The amount credited to Office Equipment will offset the purchase price of the typewriter previously entered as a debit to that account. These entries have the effect of completely eliminating the amounts relating to the old typewriter from the office equipment account and the accumulated depreciation account. The gain realized on the old typewriter is reported as a Gain on Exchange of Office Equipment. Had the trade-in allowance been less than the undepreciated cost of the typewriter, the difference would have represented a loss to be reported as a Loss on Exchange of Office Equipment.

The following chart summarizes the financial accounting and income tax accounting rules for recognition of gain or loss in "like kind" and "not of like kind" exchanges of long-term assets.

Asset

	Like Kind		Unlike Kind	
	Recognition of			
	Gain	*Loss*	*Gain*	*Loss*
Financial Accounting	No	Yes	Yes	Yes
Tax Accounting	No	No	Yes	Yes

Property, Plant, and Equipment Records

If the business has a large number of depreciable long-term assets, it is likely that a summary general ledger account will be kept for each major class of assets, such as one account for buildings, one for machinery and equipment, one for office furniture and equipment, and one for delivery trucks. Each of these summary accounts will have a related accumulated depreciation account. It is highly desirable that such summary accounts be supported by some sort of supplementary or subsidiary records. If depreciation is calculated on a unit basis (meaning a separate calculation and record of depreciation for each unit), it is common practice to maintain a subsidiary record of each unit. Such records commonly take the form of cards or computer disks. Space is provided on each card or disk record to show the details about the asset, including the cost of the unit (which supports the debit in the general ledger asset account), and the amount of depreciation taken each period (which supports the credits in the general ledger accumulated depreciation account). Space is also provided to enter the disposition of the asset. The following is a typical property, plant, and equipment record. Note that salvage value was considered in arriving at the amount of annual depreciation, $150 [($900 original cost − $150 estimated salvage value) ÷ 5 years]. Also note that the 20% rate

PROPERTY, PLANT, AND EQUIPMENT RECORD

Description	Typewriter	Account	Office Equipment
Age when acquired	New	Estimated salvage value	$150
Estimated life	5 years	Rate of annual depreciation based on cost less salvage value	20%

COST

Date Purchased		Description	Amount	
1984 Jan.	9	IBM Selectric II typewriter,	900	00
		Serial No. 8403637		
		Fletcher Typewriter Company, City		
		Less estimated salvage value	150	00
		Net cost	750	00

DEPRECIATION RECORD

Year	Rate	Amount		Total To Date	
19 84	20%	150	00	150	00
19 85	20%	150	00	300	00
19 86	20%	75	00	375	00
19					
19					
19					
19					
19					
19					
19					
19					
19					
19					
19					
19					

SOLD, EXCHANGED, OR DISCARDED

Date		Explanation	Amount Realized		More than ✓ Less than	Undepr. Cost		Accum. Depr.	
1986 July	1	Sold	550	00		25	00	375	00

Property, Plant, and Equipment Record

(100% ÷ 5 years) is applied to the original cost of $900, less the $150 estimated salvage value.

Following is a narrative of the transactions that were entered on the record:

January 9, 1984. Purchased IBM Selectric II typewriter, No. 8403637, from the Fletcher Typewriter Company, City, for $900.

December 31, 1984. Depreciation of typewriter at annual rate of $150 [($900 cost − $150 salvage value) × .20].

December 31, 1985. Depreciation of typewriter at annual rate of $150.

July 1, 1986. Depreciation of typewriter for one-half year, $75. Sold typewriter for $550 cash.

Note that before the sale of the typewriter on July 1, 1986, was entered, depreciation for the half year, amounting to $75, was entered on the card or disk record. The sale was also entered on the record, after which the record was transferred from a file of assets owned to a file of assets sold, exchanged, or discarded. (In a computer-based accounting system, the record would be transferred electronically from an "active asset" disk to an "inactive asset" disk.) Such an asset record, when properly kept, will provide all the information needed in claiming the proper amount of depreciation on each long-term asset as a deduction from gross income in the annual income tax returns.

Fully Depreciated Long-Term Assets

A long-term asset is said to be fully depreciated when the accumulated depreciation is equal to the cost of the asset. When an asset is fully depreciated, no further depreciation should be entered. Since the rate of depreciation is based on its estimated useful life, an asset may still be used after it is fully depreciated. In this case, the cost of the asset and an equal amount of accumulated depreciation are usually retained in the accounts. When a fully depreciated asset is scrapped, the cost of the asset and the total amount of depreciation should be removed from the accounts. Such an adjustment involves a debit to the proper accumulated depreciation account and a credit to the proper long-term asset account for the cost of the asset.

In some states a taxable value is placed on a fully depreciated long-term asset if the asset is in continued use. Under such circumstances, the taxable value of the fully depreciated asset should be stated in the property, plant, and equipment record as a guide in preparing the property tax schedule. The taxable values of fully depreciated long-term assets and the undepreciated costs of other long-term assets should be listed so that the total taxable value of the long-term assets may be determined.

Depreciation in the Financial Statements

Most accountants and business people consider depreciation to be an operating expense and so classify it in the income statement. There may be as much subclassification as the management desires. Depreciation of delivery equipment, for example, may be classed as a selling expense, while depreciation of office furniture and equipment may be classed as an office or general administrative expense.

In view of the close relationship between long-term asset accounts and their accumulated depreciation accounts, the accepted practice in the preparation of balance sheets is to show the amount of the accumulated depreciation as a deduction from the cost of the asset. The difference, representing undepreciated cost, is extended to be included in the asset total.

Accumulated depreciation accounts, like allowances for doubtful accounts, are sometimes called asset valuation accounts. An accumulated depreciation account, however, only values the asset in a very limited and remote sense. The difference between the cost of the asset and the balance of the accumulated depreciation account is not expected to have any relation to the market value of the asset. Such assets are not intended for sale. What they might bring, if sold, is usually of small consequence. The difference between the gross amount of the long-term assets and the related accumulated depreciation accounts simply represents costs not yet charged to operations. Some companies so describe this difference in their balance sheets.

Wasting Assets

A wasting asset is any real property which is acquired for the purpose of removing or extracting the valuable natural resource on or in the property. Stands of timber, mines, oil wells, gas wells, or land acquired in the belief that the property contains minerals, oil, or gas that can be extracted, are examples of wasting assets because, in most cases, it is expected that the valuable product eventually will be removed or exhausted so as to leave the property relatively valueless. In the case of many types of mines and wells, only the valuable materials below the surface are owned. The land, as such, may not be owned by the mining, oil, or gas company.

Depletion. The consumption or exhaustion of wasting assets is called depletion. Apart from income tax considerations, the accounting problem is to apportion the cost of such assets to the periods in which they are consumed. The procedure called cost depletion is very similar to that involved in computing depreciation on a units-of-output basis. The cost of the property is reduced by estimated salvage or residual value, if any, and the difference is divided by the estimated number of units that the property contains. The result is the depletion expense per unit. This amount times the number of units removed and sold during the period will give the depletion expense for the period.

To illustrate the computation of and proper accounting for depletion, consider the following example. A coal mine is acquired at a cost of $1,000,000. No salvage value is expected. The estimated number of units available for production is 1,000,000 tons. During the current year, 180,000 tons of coal are mined and sold. The computation of the amount of depletion expense is as follows:

$1,000,000 ÷ 1,000,000 tons = $1 per ton
180,000 tons × $1 per ton = $180,000 depletion expense

The depletion is entered in two-column journal form as follows:

Depletion Expense	180,000	
Accumulated Depletion—Coal Mine		180,000
Depletion based on 180,000 tons of coal @ $1 a ton.		

The difference between the cost of the mine and the amount of the accumulated depletion is the undepleted cost of the property:

Cost of coal mine	$1,000,000
Less accumulated depletion	180,000
Undepleted cost of mine	$ 820,000

It is customary to show the accumulated depletion as a deduction from the property account in the balance sheet in order to indicate the undepleted cost of the property. Depletion Expense is a temporary account that is closed into Expense and Revenue Summary at the end of the accounting period. It should be reported as an operating expense in the income statement. It is an expense that may be deducted in calculating taxable income.

From time to time the estimate of the quantity of the resource that remains in the property has to be changed. The usual practice is to make a new calculation of the depletion per unit, starting with the most recently determined undepleted cost of the property and dividing that amount (less estimated salvage value, if any) by the number of units extracted during the current year plus the current estimate of the number of units remaining. For example, the mine mentioned in the previous illustration had an undepleted cost of $820,000 at the start of the second year. Assume that during that year, 275,000 tons were extracted, and at the end of the year the engineers estimate that 925,000 tons remain. The calculation of the revised depletion expense per unit and depletion expense for the second year would be as follows:

$$\frac{\$820{,}000}{275{,}000 \text{ tons} + 925{,}000 \text{ tons}} = 68.33¢ \text{ per ton}$$

$$275{,}000 \text{ tons} \times 68.33¢ = \$187{,}907.50 \text{ depletion expense}$$

Depletion Expense for Federal Income Tax Purposes. Special rules govern the amount of the deduction for depletion expense that can be taken for federal income tax purposes. The taxpayer may compute the amount in the cost depletion manner explained in the preceding paragraphs. However, certain taxpayers who own and operate oil and gas wells (basically where the resource is regulated or sold under a fixed contract) and certain types of mines may use **percentage depletion**. Under this method, depletion is equal to certain specified percentages (which vary from 5% to 22%) of the amount of the sales of the period subject to stated maximum and minimum limits. The dollar amount deductible is limited to 50% of the taxable income exclusive of any depletion deduction.

BUILDING YOUR ACCOUNTING KNOWLEDGE

1. For what time interval should depreciation be entered when a depreciable asset is disposed of?
2. What are the three major ways in which a long-term asset may be disposed of?
3. From what two major causes may a loss result when a long-term asset is discarded or retired? Will a gain or loss result if a discarded or retired asset has been fully depreciated?
4. When a long-term asset is sold, what must be known about the asset in order to determine the proper amount of gain or loss on the sale?
5. Describe the major differences between accounting for a "similar" (or "like kind") exchange of long-term assets, and accounting for a "dissimilar" (or "not of like kind") exchange. Indicate the ways in which financial accounting and income tax procedures differ in dealing with long-term asset exchanges.
6. What details about a particular long-term asset are provided by a property, plant, and equipment record?
7. What does the difference between the gross amount of long-term assets and the related accumulated depreciation accounts represent to accountants?
8. What depreciation method is very similar to cost depletion? How does percentage depletion differ from cost depletion?

APPLYING ACCOUNTING CONCEPTS

Exercise 13-4. Shelving units which had cost $2,800 and had accumulated depreciation of $2,580 were discarded. Prepare the journal entry for this transaction.

Exercise 13-5. A delivery truck which had cost $11,000 and had accumulated depreciation of $8,900 was sold for $2,800.

(a) Prepare the journal entry for this transaction. **(b)** Assuming that the truck was sold for $1,900, prepare the journal entry for this transaction.

Exercise 13-6. A drill press which had cost $20,000 and had accumulated depreciation of $11,400 was traded in for a new drill press with a fair market value of $23,000. The old drill press and $13,000 in cash were given for the new drill press.

(a) Prepare the journal entry for this transaction. **(b)** Assuming that the old drill press and $15,000 in cash were given for the new drill press, prepare the journal entry for this transaction.

Exercise 13-7. Office partitions which had cost $2,400 and had accumulated depreciation of $1,900 were traded in on new typewriters with a fair market value of $2,100. The partitions and $1,150 were given for the typewriters. Prepare the journal entry for this transaction.

Exercise 13-8. A gravel pit was acquired at a cost of $900,000. It is estimated that the pit will produce 600,000 cubic yards of gravel. During Year 1, 180,000 cubic yards of gravel were mined and sold.

(a) The proper depletion expense for Year 1 is ______________.

(b) During Year 2, 200,000 cubic yards of gravel were mined and sold. At the end of the year, it is estimated that 300,000 cubic yards of gravel remain to be mined. The proper depletion expense for Year 2 is ______________.

Report No. 13-2

Complete Report No. 13-2 in the study assignments and submit your working papers for approval. Then continue with the textbook discussion in Chapter 14 until Report No. 14-1 is required.

EXPANDING YOUR BUSINESS VOCABULARY

What is the meaning of each of the following terms?

ACRS depreciation **(p. 399)**
amortization **(p. 388)**
book value **(p. 392)**
boot **(p. 408)**

capital assets **(p. 387)**
cost allocation **(p. 390)**
cost depletion **(p. 413)**
declining-balance method **(p. 394)**
depletion **(pp. 388, 413)**
depreciable assets **(p. 388)**
depreciation **(pp. 388, 390, 399)**
fair market value **(p. 407)**
fixed assets **(p. 387)**
functional depreciation **(p. 390)**
intangible **(p. 388)**
investments **(p. 388)**
long-term assets **(p. 387)**
marketable securities **(p. 388)**
net cost **(p. 391)**
percentage depletion **(p. 415)**
personal property **(p. 387)**
physical depreciation **(p. 390)**
property, plant, and equipment assets **(p. 387)**
real property **(p. 387)**
straight-line method **(p. 392)**
sum-of-the-years-digits method **(p. 396)**
tangible **(p. 388)**
trade-in allowance **(p. 407)**
undepreciated cost **(p. 392)**
unit basis **(p. 410)**
units-of-output (production) method **(p. 398)**
wasting assets **(pp. 388, 413)**

CHAPTER 14

Internal Accounting Control

CHAPTER OBJECTIVES

Careful study of this chapter should enable you to:

- Define internal accounting control and to explain its importance in operating a business.
- Identify the basic elements of good internal accounting control.
- Explain the application of internal accounting control concepts in the two major operating cycles of every business: **(1)** the expenditure cycle and **(2)** the revenue cycle.

There are enormous variations in size, type of operation, and product lines of companies. Each of these factors affects the type of control system appropriate for a particular company. For example, a very small business often uses only a limited number of formal control procedures and has little segregation of duties because there are few people to perform the duties in the first place. The key internal control element in this situation is the owner-manager who personally supervises the activities of the business. On the other hand, as the size and nature of a business become larger and more complex, it becomes impossible for the owner to maintain such close contact with all the activities of the business. Consequently, the owner must rely more on a formal internal accounting control system to ensure that the activities of the business are being conducted properly and errors or fraud are prevented or promptly detected. It is important to recognize that it is impossible to define the "correct" system of internal accounting control for all businesses.

In this chapter, certain basic internal accounting control concepts are explained and many aspects of the application of these concepts are illustrated. Some of the internal accounting controls, such as the use of prenumbered documents, are relevant for virtually every business. Other controls, such as an ideal segregation of duties, are not feasible for very small firms. Clearly, the exact system of internal accounting control for a given firm should be developed based on that firm's needs and business environment.

INTERNAL ACCOUNTING CONTROL CONCEPTS

In order to appreciate why many documents, records and procedures exist and are used in particular ways in accounting, an understanding of the concept of internal accounting control and the key elements of internal accounting control is needed.

Meaning and Importance of Internal Control

An **internal accounting control system** is defined as all the procedures, documents, and records used by a business to protect its assets and to ensure that the activities of the business are properly performed and documented. The system should provide assurance that (1) all transactions are properly authorized and accounted for, (2) access to assets is permitted only to authorized parties for authorized purposes, and (3) records of assets are verified periodically by examining the related physical properties.

Internal accounting control is essential to the functioning of a business. There is hardly an aspect of a business that is not affected by it. For example, the system must ensure that purchases are made only of goods to be used in the business and that bills are paid only for goods and services actually purchased and received by the business. Similarly, when shipments are made to customers, the system must ensure that the customers are billed and the related amounts collected. Then, the system must ensure that cash receipts from sales are received and entered by the business and not kept by an employee. In addition, management decisions often are based on accounting information; the control system must ensure that this information is accurate and up to date.

Internal accounting control systems can take many different forms in different businesses; they can be quite simple or very complex. Regardless of their form, however, internal accounting controls are critical to the efficient functioning of a business.

Key Elements of Internal Control

Before looking at specific applications of internal accounting control in individual areas of a business, it will help to examine the basic elements or principles underlying the entire concept. Four key elements of internal accounting control can be identified:

1. Segregation of duties.
2. Authorization procedures and related responsibilities.
3. Accounting procedures.
4. Independent checks on performance.

Segregation of Duties. Segregation of duties involves assigning duties in such a way that (1) different employees are responsible for different parts of a transaction, and (2) employees who maintain accounting records do not have custody of the firm's assets. Appropriate segregation of duties helps to detect errors promptly and reduces the possibility of employee fraud. For example, assume that one employee is responsible for ordering goods, a second employee for receiving goods, a third employee for paying for goods based on proper evidence of purchase, and a fourth employee for accounting for the purchase of and payment for the goods. Such a segregation of duties provides a built-in check of one employee on another in that the amounts ordered, received, paid for, and entered in the accounting records must agree; otherwise some error has occurred. Similarly, no one of these four employees can obtain goods for personal use or make improper payments for goods without being caught.

The duties of accounting and asset custody should be segregated in order to prevent employees from stealing business assets and concealing their theft by modifying the accounting records. For example, assume that one employee is responsible for receiving customer remittances on account, and a second employee is responsible for entering sales and customer remittances in the accounting records. This segregation of duties prevents the first employee from keeping the customers' remittances because the customer would complain if billed by the second employee for amounts that already had been remitted. Similarly, the second employee has no incentive to make improper entries in the accounting records because of lack of access to cash receipts.

Authorization Procedures and Related Responsibility. Sound authorization procedures involve assigning responsibilities so that only properly authorized activities take place in the business and the persons responsible for such activities and the related assets are identified at every step in the process. Basically, this element of internal accounting control should ensure that transactions do not occur without sufficient authorization. For some transactions this authorization can be general.

For example, a sales clerk in a department store has general authorization to make sales of particular goods using a particular cash register and perhaps keying in a specific clerk number. For other transactions, the authorization is likely to be specific. For example, major production equipment of a business normally is bought or sold only if specific written authorization is obtained from management at a relatively high level. Whether the authorization is general or specific, the control concept remains the same; someone should be responsible for every activity in which a business engages. Unless someone has authorized and assumed responsibility for an action, that action should not be taken by the business. Correspondingly, after some activity has occurred, it should be possible to determine who authorized it and therefore is held responsible.

Accounting Procedures. Proper **accounting procedures** include use of accounting records and documents in such a way that whenever business activities occur, the accounting system reacts. A major dimension of this internal accounting control element is the use of prenumbered documents that must be generated promptly when an activity occurs and then subsequently accounted for. Subsequent accounting for prenumbered documents can be simplified by entering the data and filing the documents in numerical order. This element of internal accounting control helps ensure that all valid activities of the business are included in the records and that only valid activities are included. For example, assume that prenumbered sales receipts are used, that one copy of the receipt is issued to a customer whenever a sale occurs and the other copy is retained in the firm's files. In this situation, if the numerical sequence of receipts is complete and there are no duplicate receipts entered, it is reasonable to assume that all sales transactions are accounted for and only valid sales transactions are entered.

Independent Checks on Performance. This last key element of internal accounting control includes the various methods used by a business to ensure that management's accounting rules and regulations are being followed. Perhaps the most easily recognized type of **independent check** on performance is that provided by the internal audit department of a business. The **internal audit department** has broad responsibility to see that the internal accounting control system is effective. This includes responsibilities for determining (1) that the system is properly designed and (2) that there is compliance with the segregation of duties, with authorization, and with accounting procedures dictated by the system. The first responsibility is fulfilled primarily by making sure that the system is characterized by the key elements of internal control that are described in this section. The second responsibility is fulfilled by testing and analyzing the business activities that occur during the year. For example, the numerical sequence of sales invoices or checks can be accounted for by maintaining numerical order. The sum of the balances in the accounts receivable ledger can be verified by comparing it with the general ledger accounts receivable balance. A bank reconciliation can be prepared. Canceled checks can be traced to appropriate supporting documents.

In addition to the specific performance checks provided by the internal audit department, a system of independent checks is built into many phases of the business. For example, if the accounts receivable records, sales journal, and general ledger are maintained by three different people in the accounting department, each of these employees provides an automatic independent check on a part of the work of the other two employees. If any one of these employees does not perform the prescribed procedures correctly, the accounting records will not agree. Another type of independent check built into the system literally involves some duplication of work. This happens whenever an employee is responsible for verifying the work of a fellow employee, such as when the price, quantity, and total dollar amount of a sales invoice must be verified by a second employee before it is mailed to a customer. Many of these built-in checks can exist throughout a company's accounting system and can help provide assurance that various procedures are being properly performed.

BUILDING YOUR ACCOUNTING KNOWLEDGE

1. Why is it impossible to define the "correct" system of internal accounting control for all businesses?
2. What assurance should be provided by an internal accounting control system?
3. How would appropriate segregation of duties prevent an employee responsible for receiving customer remittances on account from keeping the customers' remittances?
4. How do sound authorization procedures contribute to internal accounting control?
5. Why should documents be prenumbered and subsequently accounted for?
6. What are the responsibilities of an internal audit department?

APPLYING ACCOUNTING CONCEPTS

Exercise 14-1. Selected acquisition and payment transactions of Fraum Co. for the first month of operations are as follows:

1. Purchased equipment on account from Supay Co., $1,297.
2. Purchased merchandise for cash, $803.
3. Purchased merchandise on account from Selby Co., $915.
4. Paid $700 on account to Supay Co.
5. Purchased merchandise on account from Vency Co., $548.
6. Paid $600 on account to Selby Co.

(a) Prepare appropriate two-column journal entries for the above transactions. **(b)** Post appropriate entries to the accounts payable subsidiary ledger and to the accounts payable account. (Use T account forms.) **(c)** Prove the balance of the accounts payable account by preparing a schedule of accounts payable.

Exercise 14-2. Selected sales and collection transactions of Busher Co. for the first month of operations are as follows:

1. Sold merchandise on account to P. Cusae, $419.
2. Sold merchandise for cash, $610.
3. Sold merchandise on account to R. Clibee, $264.
4. Collected $300 on account from P. Cusae.
5. Sold merchandise on account to N. Percy, $317.
6. Collected $150 on account from R. Clibee.

(a) Prepare appropriate two-column journal entries for the above transactions. **(b)** Post appropriate entries to the accounts receivable subsidiary ledger and to the accounts receivable account. (Use T account forms.) **(c)** Prove the balance of the accounts receivable account by preparing a schedule of accounts receivable.

Report No. 14-1

Complete Report No. 14-1 in the study assignments and submit your working papers to the instructor for approval. Then continue with the textbook discussion until Report No. 14-2 is required.

APPLICATION IN THE EXPENDITURE CYCLE

The expenditure cycle includes all of the functions involved in acquiring and receiving goods from suppliers and in making payments for the goods purchased. Diagramming and briefly explaining the expenditure cycle will assist in understanding internal accounting control in the expenditure cycle. A flowchart of the basic elements of the expenditure cycle appears on the following page. Many variations of the expenditure cycle are possible for different businesses. For example, in a small business, all the purchasing and payment activities might be performed by a single owner/manager. Purchases might be

FLOWCHART OF EXPENDITURE CYCLE

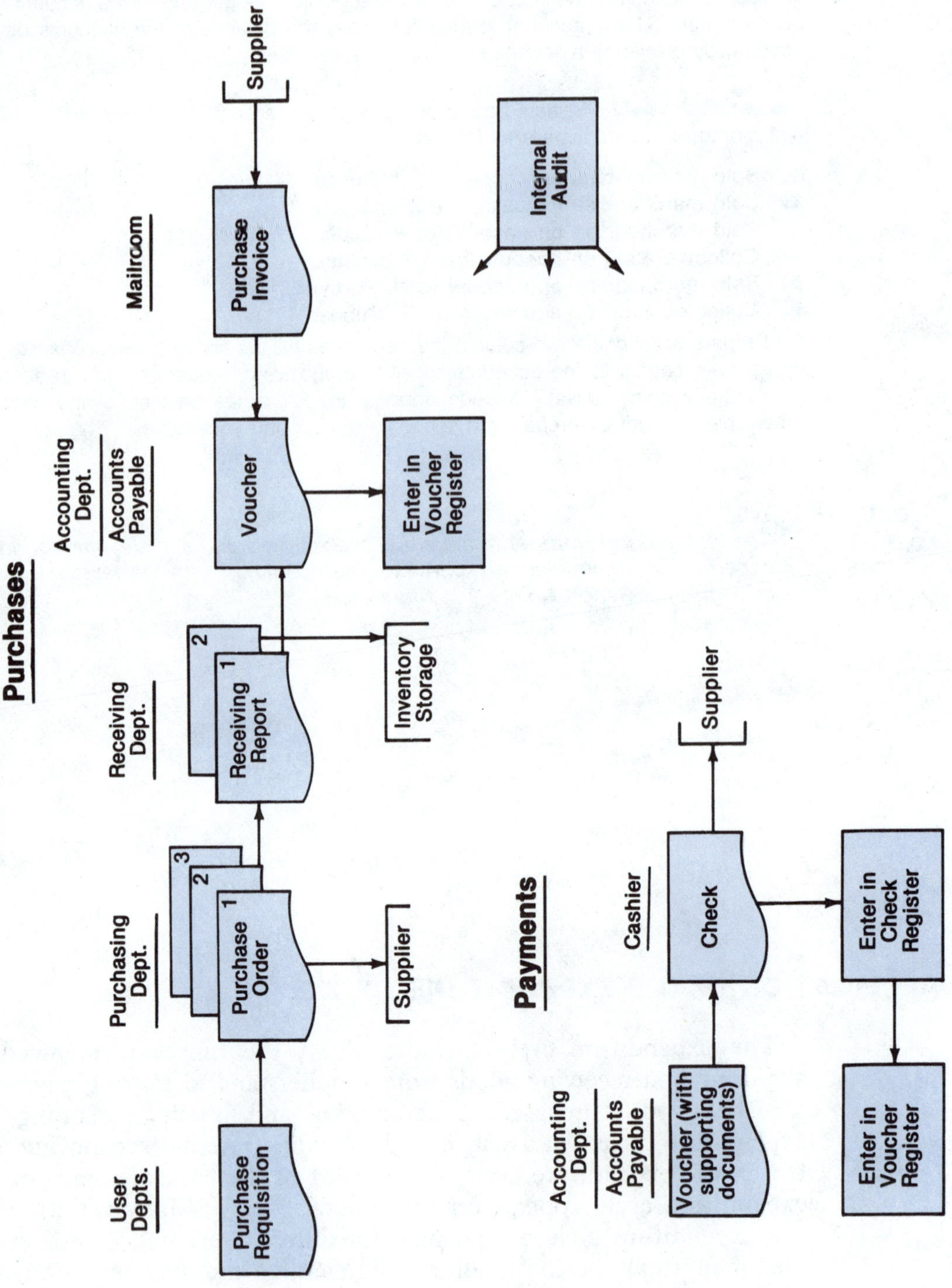

made directly from sales representatives who visit the store, perhaps with the goods ready for delivery. At the other extreme, in very large firms two or three different levels of authorization might be required in order to make expenditures above a specified dollar amount. The flowchart presented here assumes a medium-sized business that purchases tangible products.

The Purchases portion of the flowchart shows that any department or person in the firm wanting to purchase goods must prepare an authorized purchase requisition and forward it to the purchasing department. The purchasing department examines the purchase requisition and prepares a purchase order and sends it to the appropriate supplier. When the goods arrive from the supplier, a receiving report is prepared in the receiving department. This receiving report and a copy of the purchase order are sent to the accounting department where eventually they are matched with the purchase invoice received from the supplier. The purchase order, receiving report, and purchase invoice provide the basis for preparing a **voucher**, which is a document used to authorize payments for goods and services. The voucher is entered in the **voucher register**, an accounting record similar to a purchases journal.

The Payments portion of the flowchart indicates that the voucher and supporting documents are used by the cashier as a basis for preparing a check that is sent to the supplier in settlement for the goods received. The cashier also enters in the **check register** the date, amount, and payee of the check. The voucher and supporting documents are then returned to the accounts payable section where they are used to enter in the voucher register the fact that the voucher has been paid.

The Internal Audit Department has responsibility to oversee and monitor the entire system of internal accounting control shown in the flowchart. Its functions might include seeing that purchases are made only on the basis of authorized purchase orders or that all payments are properly entered.

Internal accounting control over the expenditure cycle will now be discussed in some detail. The partial records of Spinner & Thomas, a partnership engaged in the bakery business, are illustrated. The organization of this discussion follows the outline suggested by the expenditure flowchart.

Acquisition of Goods

A firm must have an internal accounting control system that ensures that it purchases only those goods and services that are necessary for the efficient and effective operation of the business. Documents and procedures that are relevant for controlling the purchasing process are illustrated and explained in the following sections.

Purchase Requisition. The **purchase requisition** is a document requesting that the purchasing department order specific goods. The following is a purchase requisition used by Spinner & Thomas. Purchase requisitions should be prenumbered and subsequently accounted for by number. This is to ensure that all requisitions are properly handled by the purchasing department and that the individual responsible for requesting that any merchandise be purchased can be subsequently identified if necessary.

Purchase Requisition No. 218

Spinner & Thomas Baking Co.
1604 N. Milburn
Indianapolis, IN 46202-9001

Date issued: May 1, 19--
Date required: May 6, 19--
Dept.: A
Deliver to: C. Thomas

Order From
Capital City Products
1021 E. 54 St.
Indianapolis, IN 46220-1693

Quantity	Description
20	Large bakery trays

Purchasing Dept. Memorandum
Date: May 1, 19--
Issued To: Capital City Products
1021 E. 54 St.
Indianapolis, IN 46220-1693

Placed by: C. Thomas
Approved by: H. Spinner
Purchase Order No. 302

Purchase Requisition

The purchase requisition itself does not authorize a purchase. The requisition must first be approved. For a minor purchase, the approval might come from a department supervisor, whereas a major purchase should be approved at a higher level of management. When approved, the purchase requisition authorizes the purchasing department to generate a purchase order.

Purchase Order. The **purchase order** is an explicit request by the firm to buy goods from a supplier. The following purchase order prepared by Spinner & Thomas was based on the purchase requisition illustrated on page 426. Purchase orders should be prenumbered and subsequently accounted for by number, in order to ensure either that all of the goods on an order are received or that the order is canceled, and that only goods that have been ordered are received and paid for subsequently. The number of copies of the purchase order that are prepared depends on the particular accounting information system. There are likely to be at least three copies. One copy is sent to the

Purchase Order No. **302**

Spinner & Thomas Baking Co.
1604 N. Milburn
Indianapolis, IN 46202-9001

Date May 1, 19--

Delivery by May 6, 19--

Terms Net

To Capital City Products
1021 E. 54 St.
Indianapolis, IN 46220-1693

Quantity	Description	Unit Price
20	Large bakery trays	$5.35

H. Spinner

Purchase Order

supplier, a second copy goes to the accounting department, and the third copy is retained by the purchasing department for its files. A fourth copy could be sent to the individual who requisitioned the goods, and a fifth copy could be sent to the receiving department for use as a receiving report.

Receiving Report. Whether or not a copy of the purchase order is used for this purpose, a document called a **receiving report** should be prepared promptly by the receiving department for all goods received by the firm. Receiving reports should be prenumbered and subsequently accounted for by number to ensure that all goods received are properly entered. There are normally two copies of the receiving report. One copy is sent to the accounting department, and the other remains with the goods for forwarding to the inventory storage area.

PAYMENT FOR GOODS USING THE VOUCHER SYSTEM

Much of the material covered thus far in this chapter was addressed previously in other sections of the text. For example, basic features of accounting for purchases and payments were explained in Chapter 6, and accounting for sales and collections was addressed in Chapter 7. For this reason, data entry procedures in these areas generally have not been explained and illustrated in detail in this chapter. However, the accounting system used to *control* payments for items purchased by the business warrants further attention. Therefore, the data entry aspects of internal accounting control over payments will be explained in greater detail in this section.

A system for controlling expenditures that is used by many businesses is known as a **voucher system**. Such a system is very useful for controlling cash payments, because written authorization is required for each payment. A voucher system usually involves the use of vouchers, a voucher register, a vouchers payable account in the general ledger, voucher checks, and a check register. There are several alternative accounting procedures applicable to the voucher system. For instance, ordinary checks may be used and entered in a simple cashbook or in a cash payments journal. Like most accounting processes, the voucher system is flexible and readily adaptable to various situations.

The use of the voucher system of accounting is not advisable under all conditions, but it usually may be used to advantage when one or more of the following circumstances exist:

1. When the volume of transactions is large enough to require a system of control over expenditures.
2. When the nature of the business is such that it is desirable to enter invoices at the time that they are received rather than when payment is made.
3. When it is the custom of the firm to pay all invoices in full at maturity instead of making partial or installment payments.

There are generally five key documents in a voucher system: a purchase order, a receiving report, a purchase invoice, a voucher, and a check. Purchase orders and receiving reports were described previously. The purchase invoice and voucher will now be explained.

Purchase Invoice. A **purchase invoice** is the supplier's bill for goods, materials, or other assets purchased or for services rendered. The following is a purchase invoice received by Spinner & Thomas for the purchase of bakery trays from Capital City Products. When the purchase invoice is received by the accounts (or vouchers) payable section of the accounting department, it should be compared with the purchase order and receiving report on file in that department to determine that the invoice is for the quantity ordered and received and for the proper price. In addition, mathematical accuracy of the invoice should be verified and the account to be charged for the purchase should be determined.

CAPITAL CITY PRODUCTS
1021 E. 54 ST.
INDIANAPOLIS, IN 46220-1693

Invoice No. 163

Sold to
Spinner & Thomas Baking Co.
1064 N. Milburn
Indianapolis, IN 46202-9001

Date May 6, 19--
Terms Net

Quantity	Description	Unit Price	Total
20	Large bakery trays	$5.35	$107.00

Received by S. Salstrom
Date 5/7

Purchase Invoice

An alternative approach to purchase invoice verification used by some firms is to have the different employees responsible for ordering and receiving goods participate in the verification process. The receiving clerk would verify receipt of the assets purchased and the purchasing agent would verify the quantities, prices, and terms of the order. The accounting department would then verify the mathematical accuracy of the invoice and determine the account distribution.

Voucher. Based on the verified purchase invoice, receiving report, and purchase order, a voucher is prepared by the vouchers payable section. The **voucher** is a key internal accounting control document which provides authorization for payment for goods or services. The voucher normally provides space to enter the invoice date, the goods or services purchased, accounts to be charged, authorization for payment, date of payment, and number of the check issued. There is no standard form of voucher; it varies depending on the nature of the business, the classification of accounts, and the distribution desired. Regardless of its form, however, for good internal accounting control the voucher should be prenumbered and subsequently accounted for by number in order to ensure that all payments are properly entered and that payments are made only for authorized purchases.

A voucher that was prepared by the voucher clerk for Spinner & Thomas is shown on page 431. The information entered on this voucher was obtained from the invoice shown on page 429. All of the information on the front and the account distribution on the back of this voucher would be entered when the voucher is prepared. The payment information would be entered when the voucher is paid.

Entering Vouchers. There are two accounting records involved in entering vouchers: the voucher register and the general ledger. All vouchers should be entered in the voucher register. The **voucher register** is basically an expanded purchases journal that is used to enter purchases of all types of assets and services. The voucher register represents the first point at which purchases activities are reflected in the accounting records. In addition, each entry in the voucher register is a key step leading to the payment of a specific amount. This makes the voucher register particularly important from a control standpoint. To the extent feasible, vouchers should be entered in the voucher register in numerical order to facilitate accounting for the numerical sequence of the vouchers.

The columnar headings of a voucher register depend upon the nature of the business and the desired classification of purchases and expenses. One form of voucher register is shown on page 432. That illustration shows that Voucher No. 164, which is reproduced on page 431, was entered by debiting Store Equipment, Account No. 181, and by crediting Vouchers Payable, Account No. 218, for $107.

Spinner & Thomas Baking Co.
1604 N. Milburn
Indianapolis, IN 46202-9001

VOUCHER No. 164

Date Issued May 7 19-- Terms Net Due May 7 19--

To Capital City Products

Address 1021 E. 54 St., Indianapolis, IN 46220-1693

Invoice Date	Description	Amount
May 6	20 Large bakery trays	$107.00

Authorized by H. Spinner

Prepared by S. Salstrom
Voucher Clerk

Voucher *(front)*

DISTRIBUTION

Purchases		Operating Expenses		Sundry Accounts	
Dept. A	Dept. B	Acct. No.	Amount	Acct. No.	Amount
				181	107.00

PAYMENT

Date of Payment May 7 19-- Check No. 519 Amount $ 107.00

CERTIFICATION

This voucher has been audited carefully and is correct in every respect.

J. Davis
Accountant

Voucher *(back)*

VOUCHER REGISTER FOR MONTH OF *May* 19 –

PAGE 13

	PURCHASES DR.		OPERATING EXPENSES DR.			SUNDRY ACCOUNTS DR.				VOU.		SUNDRY ACCOUNTS CR.			VOUCHERS	DISPOSITION		
	DEPT. A	DEPT. B	ACCT. NO.	AMOUNT	√	ACCT. NO.	AMOUNT	√	DAY	NO.	TO WHOM ISSUED	ACCT. NO.	AMOUNT	√	PAYABLE CR.	DATE	CK. NO.	
1											AMOUNTS FORWARDED							1
2			5443	1 500 00					1	158	Estate Leasing Co.				2 500 00	5/1	511	2
3			5406	1 000 00														3
4	2 928 00	1 291 00							5	159	Flowers Baking Co.				4 219 00	5/7	514	4
5	1 206 00	2 647 00							5	160	Heileman Baking Co.				3 853 00	5/7	515	5
6	2 033 00	2 034 00							5	161	International Bakers				4 067 00	5/7	516	6
7	4 114 00								5	162	Omar Bakeries				4 114 00	5/7	517	7
8	1 460 00	2 764 00							5	163	Tri-Baking Co.				4 224 00	5/7	518	8
9						181	107 00		7	164	Capital City Products				107 00	5/7	519	9
10			5433	186 00					8	165	Indianapolis Star				186 00	5/8	522	10
11			5431	899 00					16	166	Payroll	211	268 00		5 016 00	5/16	520	11
12			5432	994 00								214	576 00					12
13			5401	1 567 00														13
14			5402	1 200 00														14
15			5434	1 200 00														15
16																		16
28	52 940 00 52 940 00	39 143 00 39 143 00		14 824 00 14 824 00			4 917 00 4 917 00						1 728 00 1 728 00		110 096 00 110 096 00			28
29	(511)	(521)		(541)			(√)						(√)		(218)			29

Spinner & Thomas Voucher Register—*(Partial)*

Following is a description of the vouchers that have been entered in the voucher register:

May 1 No. 158, Estate Leasing Co.; store and office rent, Account No. 5443, $1,500, and Account No. 5406, $1,000.
5 No. 159, Flowers Baking Co.; merchandise, Account No. 511, $2,928, and Account No. 521, $1,291.
5 No. 160, Heileman Baking Co.; merchandise, Account No. 511, $1,206, and Account No. 521, $2,647.
5 No. 161, International Bakers; merchandise, Account No. 511, $2,033, and Account No. 521, $2,034.
5 No. 162, Omar Bakeries; merchandise, Account No. 511, $4,144.
5 No. 163, Tri-Baking Co.; merchandise, Account No. 511, $1,460, and Account No. 521, $2,764.
7 No. 164, Capital City Products; bakery trays, Account No. 181, $107.
8 No. 165, Indianapolis Star; advertising, Account No. 5433, $186.
16 No. 166, Payroll, May 1-16, $5,016. Distribution: Store Clerks Wage Expense, Account No. 5431, $899; Truck Drivers Wage Expense, Account No. 5432, $994; Office Salaries Expense, Account No. 5401, $1,567; Harlan Spinner, Salary Expense, Account No. 5402, $1,200; Carol Thomas, Salary Expense, Account No. 5434, $1,200. Taxes withheld: FICA Tax Payable, Account No. 211, $268; Employees Income Tax Payable, Account No. 214, $576.

Voucher No. 166 was based on a report of the payroll clerk. The amount payable is the net amount of the payroll after deducting the taxes withheld. The total wages and salaries earned during the pay period ended May 16 amounted to $5,860 represented by:

Store clerks wage expense	$ 899.00
Truck drivers wage expense	994.00
Office salaries expense	1,567.00
Harlan Spinner, salary expense	1,200.00
Carol Thomas, salary expense	1,200.00
Total	$5,860.00

Note that five lines were required to enter this transaction in the voucher register. This was because of the five entries in the Operating Expenses Dr. column.

To prove the voucher register, it is only necessary to determine that the sum of the debit footings is equal to the sum of the credit footings. The footings should be proved before the totals are forwarded and before the summary posting is completed.

Both individual posting and summary posting from the voucher register to the general ledger are required. In addition, individual posting from the voucher register to the operating expense ledger is required. (Use of the operating expense ledger is explained in Chapter 17.) The individual posting involves posting each item entered in the Sundry Accounts Dr. and Cr. Amount columns to the proper account in the general ledger, and posting each item in the Operating Expense Dr. Amount column to the proper account in the operating expense subsidiary ledger. As each item is posted, a check mark should be placed beside it in the check (√) column of the voucher register. The page number of the voucher register should also be entered in the Posting Reference column of the ledger account to which the amount is posted.

The summary posting of the voucher register required each month involves the following procedures:

1. The total of the column headed Purchases—Dept. A should be posted as a debit to the purchases—Dept. A account in the general ledger.
2. The total of the column headed Purchases—Dept. B should be posted as a debit to the purchases—Dept. B account in the general ledger.
3. The total of the column headed Operating Expenses Dr. should be posted as a debit to the operating expenses account in the general ledger, which is the control account for the operating expenses subsidiary ledger.
4. The total of the column headed Vouchers Payable Cr. should be posted as a credit to the vouchers payable account in the general ledger.

As the total of each column is posted from the voucher register, the account number should be entered in parentheses immediately below the total. The page number of the voucher register should also be entered in the Posting Reference column of the ledger account to which it is posted. Check marks in parentheses should be entered below the totals of the Sundry Accounts Dr. and Cr. amount columns in the voucher register to indicate that these totals should not be posted.

Paying Vouchers. After the vouchers are entered in the voucher register, they may be filed according to due date or alphabetically by supplier name in an unpaid vouchers file. Regardless of the way in which the vouchers are filed, they should be paid according to the terms stated in the invoice. Delay in payment may result in discounts being lost or in the loss of credit standing.

When they become due, the vouchers and supporting documents should be presented to the cashier or other proper disbursing officer for payment. The disbursing officer should review each voucher and supporting documents for propriety of the expenditure, prepare and sign the check, and mail it directly to the supplier. In no case should a check be written without a supporting voucher and documentation. Ordinary checks may be used. In some cases, however, a voucher check is used, which is a check with space for entering data from the invoice or other sources of information concerning the voucher to which the check relates. In the following illustration, a voucher check issued to Capital City Products in payment of its invoice of May 6 is reproduced. The statement attached to it provides space for details of the invoice, including its date, number, description, amount, deductions, if any, and net amount. The information given on the statement attached to the check is for identification purposes and serves as a remittance advice to the payee of the check. Whether an ordinary check or a voucher check is used, the checks should be prenumbered and subsequently accounted for by number to ensure that no unauthorized payments occur.

No. 519
Date May 7, 19--
To Capital City Products
Voucher No. 164
Amount of Voucher $107.00
Discount
Amount of Check $107.00
Remarks

Spinner & Thomas Baking Co.
1604 N. Milburn
Indianapolis, IN 46202-9001

3-4/740

May 7, 19 --   No. 519

Pay to the order of Capital City Products $ 107.00

One hundred seven 00/100 ---------------------------------- Dollars

FEDERAL NATIONAL BANK
Indianapolis, Indiana

Harlan Spinner
Treasurer

⑆074000009⑆ 92 646 8 ⑈

Detach this statement before depositing check.

Date May 7, 19--

Attached voucher check is full settlement of the following:

Invoice Date	Invoice Number	Description	Invoice Amount	Deductions For	Deductions Amount	Net Amount
May 6	163	20 Large bakery trays	107 00			107 00

Voucher Check

After the voucher has been paid, the disbursing officer should cancel the voucher and supporting documents to indicate payment. This ensures that a voucher will not be processed again to generate a duplicate payment. The canceled voucher and supporting documents are then returned to the vouchers payable section for filing either numerically or alphabetically in a paid vouchers file. In either case, the numerical sequence should be strictly controlled for possible missing or duplicate vouchers.

Entering Checks. Three accounting records are affected by the check entering process: the check register, voucher register, and general ledger. All checks issued in payment of vouchers may be entered in a **check register**. A check register is an accounting record of all checks written by a firm. When the charges pertaining to each voucher have been entered in the voucher register, it is not necessary to make provision for distribution of charges in the check register. It is not unusual, however, to find that columns are provided in the check register to enter deductions that may be made at the time of payment, such as purchases discounts. The form of check register shown below does not have such a column. After checks are entered in the check register, an entry should also be made in the Disposition columns of the voucher register to show that the voucher has been paid, as illustrated in the disposition columns of the voucher register on page 432. This entry, which would be made by the vouchers payable clerk based on a canceled voucher, serves the same purpose as a debit entry in a supplier's ledger account.

CHECK REGISTER FOR MONTH OF *May* **19 --** **PAGE** *13*

	VOUCHERS PAYABLE DR. NO.	VOUCHERS PAYABLE DR. AMOUNT	DAY	DRAWN TO THE ORDER OF	CASH CR. CHK. NO.	CASH CR. AMOUNT	
1				**AMOUNTS FORWARDED**			1
2	*158*	*2 500 00*	*1*	*Estate Leasing Co.*	*511*	*2 500 00*	2
3	*149*	*260 00*	*2*	*Walnut Paper*	*512*	*260 00*	3
4	*154*	*74 00*	*5*	*Stansifer's Garage*	*513*	*74 00*	4
5	*159*	*4 219 00*	*7*	*Flowers Baking Co.*	*514*	*4 219 00*	5
20							20
21		*99 186 00* *99 186 00*				*99 186 00* *99 186 00*	21
22		*(218)*				*(111)*	22

Spinner & Thomas' Check Register *(Partial)*

Following is a description of the checks that have been entered in the check register reproduced on page 436.

May 1 No. 511, Estate Leasing Co., $2,500, in payment of Voucher No. 158.
2 No. 512, Walnut Paper, $260, in payment of Voucher No. 149.
5 No. 513, Stansifer's Garage, $74, in payment of Voucher No. 154.
7 No. 514, Flowers Baking Co., $4,219, in payment of Voucher No. 159.

To prove the check register, it is only necessary to determine that the footing of the Cash Cr. column is equal to the footing of the Vouchers Payable Dr. column. The footings should be proved before the totals are forwarded and before the summary posting is completed.

No individual posting from the check register is required. It is only necessary to complete the summary posting at the end of each month.

The summary posting procedure is as follows:

1. The total of the column headed Vouchers Payable Dr. should be posted as a debit to the vouchers payable account in the general ledger.
2. The total of the column headed Cash Cr. Amount should be posted as a credit to the cash account in the general ledger.

As the total of each column is posted from the check register, the account number in parentheses should be entered immediately below the total. The page number of the check register should also be entered in the Posting Reference column of the ledger account to which the amount is posted.

Proving Vouchers Payable. When the voucher system is used, it is possible to dispense with a subsidiary accounts payable ledger. The file of unpaid vouchers serves as the detail to support the balance of the vouchers payable account after all posting has been completed. The voucher register itself partially performs this function. Every blank in the Disposition columns of the register shows that the indicated voucher is unpaid. The unpaid vouchers file can be consulted if more detail about any item is needed.

When a trial balance is prepared at the end of a period, the balance of the vouchers payable account should be verified by preparing a list of the vouchers contained in the unpaid vouchers file. The total amount of this list should be equal to the balance of the account.

If a subsidiary accounts payable ledger is not maintained and if unpaid vouchers are filed according to due date, there is no way of quickly finding out how much is owed to a particular supplier. This may not be considered important. Businesspeople using the voucher system tend to think in terms of unpaid invoices rather than being primarily concerned with the total amount owed to each of their suppliers. However, if the latter information is needed, copies of the vouchers may be filed according to the names of the suppliers. In addition, a subsidiary accounts payable ledger may be maintained if one is desired.

Purchases Returns and Allowances. When a voucher system of accounting is used, purchases returns and allowances must be entered in such a way that the accounts currently reflect such transactions, that the voucher register shows the proper amounts payable, and that the amount of the affected unpaid voucher is reduced. A commonly used procedure involves three steps:

1. A notation of the return or allowance is made on the affected voucher and the credit memo is attached to it.
2. A notation of the reduction is made in the voucher register beside the amount of the affected voucher.
3. The transaction is formally entered in the general journal.

A return or allowance relating to a merchandise purchase would require a debit to Vouchers Payable and a credit to Purchases Returns and Allowances. If the return or allowance is related to a purchase of a long-term asset or to some expense, the credit in the entry would be to the asset or expense account.

Partial Payments. When a business using the voucher system makes partial payments on invoices, special handling is required. If it is known at the outset that an invoice will be paid in installments, a separate voucher for each installment should be prepared in the first place. If it is decided to make a partial payment on an invoice already vouchered and entered, the original voucher should be canceled and two or more new ones issued. The total amount of the new vouchers should be equal to that of the old voucher. The vouchers would be entered in the voucher register by a debit to Vouchers Payable in the Sundry Accounts—Dr. column for the amount of the old voucher, and by a credit to Vouchers Payable in the Vouchers Payable Cr. column for the amounts of the new vouchers. A note should be entered in the Disposition columns of the voucher register indicating that the old voucher has been canceled and showing the numbers of the new vouchers issued. Payments of the vouchers should then be entered in the usual manner.

BUILDING YOUR ACCOUNTING KNOWLEDGE

1. What functions are included in the expenditure cycle?
2. Purchase orders are typically prepared in multiple-copy form. What is done with the different copies of the purchase order?
3. Why is a voucher system very useful for controlling cash payments?
4. Under what circumstances is there usually an advantage in using a voucher system?
5. What two accounting records are involved in entering vouchers?
6. What are the appropriate procedures for paying vouchers?
7. Why should the disbursing officer cancel a voucher and supporting documents to indicate payment after the voucher is paid?
8. When a voucher system is used, how is the vouchers payable account balance verified at the end of a period?

APPLYING ACCOUNTING CONCEPTS

Exercise 14-3. The following transactions occurred during the first month of operations of Lewell Co.

Sept. 2 Received an invoice for $800 from Klew Realty Co. for rent. (Rent Expense, Account No. 5443.)
5 Received an invoice for $1,520.85 from Cray Supply House for merchandise.
10 Received an invoice for $910.90 from Reese Equipment Co. for office furniture. (Office Equipment, Account No. 191.)
16 Received a bill for $110.07 for telephone service and installation from Inlet Telephone Co. (Telephone Expense, Account No. 5409.)
19 Received an invoice for $87.50 from the Daily Herald for advertising. (Advertising Expense, Account No. 5433.)
26 Received an invoice for $1,110.55 from Lema Co. for merchandise.

Enter the foregoing transactions in a voucher register similar to the one on page 432.

Exercise 14-4. The following payments were made during the first month of operations of Lewell Co. (See Exercise 14-3.)

Sept. 3 Issued Check No. 1 in payment of invoice from Klew Realty Co.
16 Issued Check No. 2 in payment of invoice from Cray Supply House.
17 Issued Check No. 3 in payment of invoice from Reese Equipment Co.
26 Issued Check No. 4 in payment of invoice from the Daily Herald.

Enter the foregoing transactions in a check register similar to the one on page 436.

Exercise 14-5. See Exercises 14-3 and 14-4.

(a) Foot the Vouchers Payable column in the voucher register and in the check register. Open a T-account for vouchers payable and post the footings to it. **(b)** Prove the balance of the vouchers payable account by preparing a schedule of unpaid vouchers from the voucher register.

Report No. 14-2

Complete Report No. 14-2 in the study assignments and submit your working papers to the instructor for approval. Then continue with the textbook discussion until Report No. 14-3 is required.

APPLICATION IN THE REVENUE CYCLE

The revenue cycle includes all the functions involved in receiving customer orders, providing goods and services, billing customers, and collecting payments—either on account or for cash sales. Diagramming and briefly explaining the revenue cycle will assist in understanding internal accounting control in the revenue cycle. A flowchart of the basic elements of the revenue cycle appears on the following page. Many variations of the revenue cycle are possible for different businesses. The flowchart shown here assumes a medium-sized business that deals in a tangible product.

The Credit Sales portion of the flowchart shows that a customer who purchases merchandise on account usually sends a purchase order to a particular business. In response to this order, a sales order would be generated by the business. This sales order is the basis for preparing a shipping order which causes goods to be shipped to the customer. One copy of the shipping order is sent to the customer with the goods and a second copy is sent to the Billing section so that a bill, the sales invoice, will be sent to the customer. A second copy of the sales invoice is sent to the General Accounting and Accounts Receivable sections for entry in the accounting system.

The Collections and Cash Sales portion of the flowchart depicts the processing of both collections on account and collections from cash sales. Collections on account are generally received by mail from customers. Normally included with the check is a remittance advice, which is a document indicating the purpose of the payment, that is, the bill that is being paid. Remittance advices are sent to the General Accounting and Accounts Receivable sections for entering in the accounting records and the checks are sent to the cashier, who prepares a deposit slip and sends it with the checks to the bank. The bank returns a validated deposit slip to the Accounting Department.

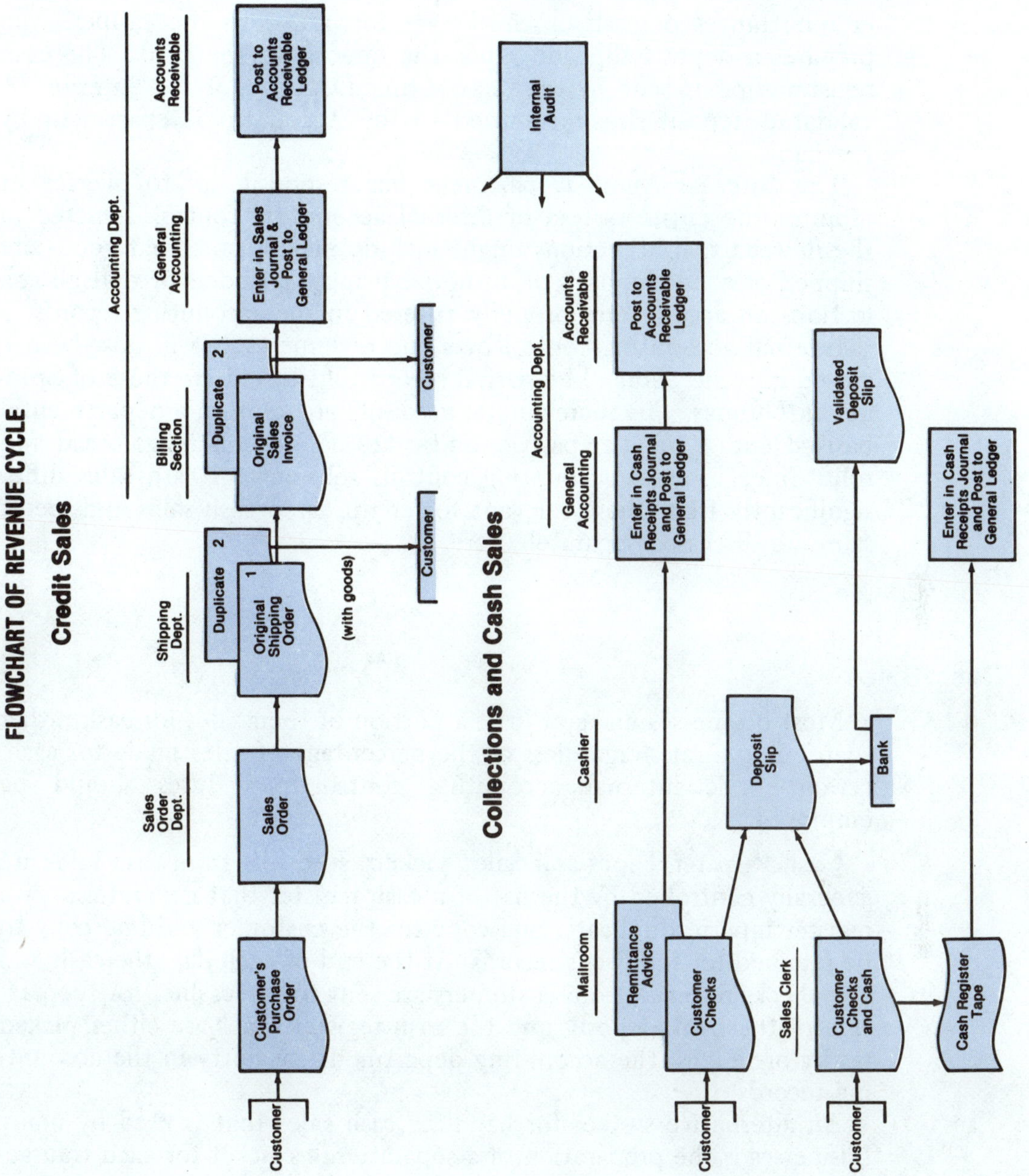

FLOWCHART OF REVENUE CYCLE
Credit Sales
Sales Order Dept.
Shipping Dept.
Billing Section
Accounting Dept.
General Accounting
Accounts Receivable
Customer
Customer's Purchase Order
Sales Order
Duplicate 2
Original Shipping Order 1
(with goods)
Customer
Duplicate 2
Original Sales Invoice
Customer
Enter in Sales Journal & Post to General Ledger
Post to Accounts Receivable Ledger
Collections and Cash Sales
Internal Audit
Mailroom
Cashier
Accounting Dept.
General Accounting
Accounts Receivable
Customer
Remittance Advice
Customer Checks
Deposit Slip
Bank
Validated Deposit Slip
Enter in Cash Receipts Journal and Post to General Ledger
Post to Accounts Receivable Ledger
Sales Clerk
Customer
Customer Checks and Cash
Cash Register Tape
Enter in Cash Receipts Journal and Post to General Ledger

Sales clerks normally use cash registers to handle cash sales. Customer remittances of cash or checks are forwarded to the cashier, who prepares a deposit slip and sends the deposit to the bank. The cash register tape is sent to the Accounting Department for entering. A validated deposit slip is returned to the Accounting Department by the bank.

The Internal Audit Department has responsibility to oversee or monitor the entire system of internal accounting control depicted in the flowchart. Its functions might include making sure that goods are shipped only on the basis of authorized shipping orders or that all collections on account are properly entered in the accounting records.

Internal accounting control over the revenue cycle will now be discussed in some detail. The partial records illustrated are those of Spinner & Thomas. The merchandise accounts are kept on a departmental basis—Dept. A handles pastries and cakes, Dept. B handles bread and rolls. Since internal accounting controls relevant for cash sales differ significantly from those relevant for credit sales, cash sales and credit sales are discussed separately here.

Cash Sales

Most businesses make at least a portion of their sales for cash rather than on account. Regardless of the percentage of sales made for cash, certain basic internal accounting control procedures should be employed.

Cash Register Tapes and Sales Tickets. Receipts from cash sales are generally controlled by the use of a cash register that generates a cash register tape in duplicate; one copy for the customer and one copy to be retained for the firm's records. At the end of each day, the cash and any checks received from customers are sent to the cashier for preparation of the bank deposit, and the cash register tapes are either picked up by or sent to the accounting department for entry in the accounting records.

An alternative system for handling cash sales that is used by many businesses is the preparation of a separate sales ticket for each transaction. A salesclerk prepares a sales ticket in duplicate for each sale, and these tickets and the related cash receipts are then handled in a manner similar to that used for cash register tapes and related cash receipts. The only additional control necessary when sales tickets are used is that the tickets should be prenumbered and subsequently accounted for by number.

Deposit Slip. The cashier prepares a deposit slip in duplicate for the cash and checks received from the salesclerks and sends both copies with the deposit to the bank. The validated deposit slip should be returned by the bank to the firm's accounting department.

Accounting Procedures for Cash Sales. The first accounting record affected by cash sales is the cash receipts journal. The cash register tapes, the sales tickets, or a listing of the tickets are the basis for the entries in the cash receipts journal. Examples of entries of cash sales can be seen in the portion of the cash receipts journal of Spinner & Thomas illustrated on page 452.

The second accounting record affected by cash sales is the general ledger. At the end of each month, a summary posting is made from the cash receipts journal to the general ledger cash and sales accounts for the appropriate amounts.

When each validated deposit slip is returned by the bank to the firm's accounting department, the amount deposited is compared with the amount entered in the cash receipts journal based on the cash register tapes or sales tickets. This procedure ensures that all cash sales collected by the salesclerks and forwarded to the cashier were in fact properly deposited.

This system appears to control adequately what happens to cash once a proper cash register or sales ticket record is made of each cash sale. A question might be raised, however, as to the control that exists over the salesclerks to see that a valid cash register entry or sales ticket is prepared in the first place. The answer essentially is the customer. Any customer purchasing merchandise expects to receive some kind of receipt for the amount remitted. In order to provide such a receipt, the salesclerk must generate either a cash register entry or a sales ticket. It would still be possible for the salesclerk to alter a sales ticket subsequently, but if these documents are reviewed by the accounting department or internal audit staff, frequent alterations in sales tickets would be questioned.

Credit Sales

Internal accounting control procedures for credit sales typically are more complicated than those for cash sales. By their nature, credit sales involve more documents, more people, and more accounting records.

Customer Purchase Order. The customer's purchase order initiates a sales transaction. Since the customer intends to purchase goods from another business, clearly one firm's purchase is another firm's sale. Customer orders can be received either by mail or by telephone. If an order is received by telephone, the customer order document usually is generated internally by the seller. Based on the customer order, a sales order is prepared.

Sales Order. The **sales order** is a document prepared by the sales order department which authorizes sales of merchandise to a customer. It would be possible to use the customer order as a sales order, but control and handling efficiency are improved if a separate sales order is generated. The following is a sales order prepared by Spinner & Thomas Baking Co. for a sale to Heritage House. Sales orders should be prenumbered and subsequently all numbers should be accounted for. If any numbers are missing, this would suggest that some orders have been lost and not properly processed. Sales orders are often prepared in duplicate so that the sales order department can retain one copy for its files. Many companies also have a separate credit department. If a credit department exists, the sales order is sent to the credit department to obtain approval of a sale to any charge customer. Note the credit approval that appears on the Spinner & Thomas sales order. After credit is approved, the sales order is sent to the shipping department.

SALES ORDER No. 303

Spinner & Thomas Baking Co.
1604 N. Milburn
Indianapolis, IN 46202-9001

Customer: Heritage House
4990 US Highway 31S
Indianapolis, IN 46227-5123

Date May 6, 19--

Quantity	Description	Amount	Total
50 dz.	Assorted danish	$260	
20	Assorted coffee cakes	54	
26	Assorted cakes	108	
225 dz.	Assorted buns and rolls	302	
115	Assorted breads	104	$828

Credit approval: CD

Sales Order

Shipping Order. The **shipping order** is the document that provides authorization to ship merchandise. It is an important control document in a firm's information system. An example of a shipping order for a shipment from Spinner & Thomas to Heritage House is shown below. This shipping order was prepared based on the preceding sales order. Shipping orders should be prenumbered and subsequently accounted for by number in order to ensure that all shipments are properly entered and that all goods shipped are billed to the purchasers. One copy of the shipping order is sent to the customer with the goods and the other copy is sent to the billing section so that a sales invoice can be prepared.

SHIPPING ORDER No. 295

Spinner & Thomas Baking Co.
1604 N. Milburn
Indianapolis, IN 46202-9001

Customer:

Heritage House
4990 US Highway 31S
Indianapolis, IN 46227-5123

Date May 6, 19--
Shipping instructions Our truck
To be delivered May 7, 19--

Quantity	Description	Amount	Total
50 dz.	Assorted danish	$260	
20	Assorted coffee cakes	54	
26	Assorted cakes	108	
225 dz.	Assorted buns and rolls	302	
115	Assorted breads	104	$828

Shipping Order

Sales Invoice. A multiple-copy **sales invoice**, which is the company's bill to the customer, is prepared in the billing section of the accounting department as soon as the copy of the shipping order has been received, indicating that the goods have been shipped. The following is a copy of a summary sales invoice that was generated based on the shipping order reproduced above. In Spinner & Thomas' system, this invoice showing sales summarized in terms of pastries and breads is supported by a detailed sales invoice (not shown) listing items

SUMMARY SALES INVOICE No. 291

Spinner & Thomas Baking Co.
1604 N. Milburn
Indianapolis, IN 46202-9001

Customer: Date May 7, 19--

Heritage House
4990 US Highway 31S
Indianapolis, IN 46227-5123

Description	Amount	Total
Pastries	$422	
Breads	406	$828

Summary Sales Invoice

purchased, unit prices, and extended amounts. This document is extremely important from a control standpoint. In conjunction with the shipping order, the sales invoice provides assurance that all goods shipped are also billed. Sales invoices should be prenumbered and subsequently accounted for by number in order to provide this assurance of proper billing. If any sales invoice number is missing from the sequence, it would suggest that some shipment was not billed or perhaps that the billing was not posted to the accounting records. In addition, each sales invoice should be supported by a shipping order to make certain that sales are entered only for goods actually shipped to customers. One copy of the sales invoice is sent to the customer and a second copy is sent to accounting. Other copies of the sales invoice might also be used in an accounting information system but the two copies described above are the minimum necessary. In many accounting information systems, the sales invoices must be verified as to price, quantity, and extended amounts before they are mailed to customers.

Accounting Procedures for Credit Sales. Accounting procedures for entering sales were explained to a great extent in Chapter 7. That discussion is extended here in order to emphasize the internal accounting control aspects of the data entry process.

The first accounting record affected by sales transactions is a firm's sales journal. The following is a portion of the sales journal for Spinner & Thomas. The individual sales invoices represent the basis for entries in the sales journal. In most accounting information systems, entries to such a journal represent the first point at which sales activities are reflected in the accounting records. Neither the customer order, nor the sales order, nor the shipping order, nor the preparation of the sales invoice directly affects any accounting record. This makes the sales journal particularly important from a control standpoint. Note that the sales invoices are entered in the sales journal not only in chronological order but also in numerical order. This feature of the data entry process makes the sales journal a convenient place to account for the numerical sequence of sales invoices.

SALES JOURNAL FOR MONTH OF *May* **19 --** **PAGE** *9*

	DEBIT								CREDIT					
	GENERAL LEDGER			ACCOUNTS RECEIVABLE	√	DAY	NAME	SALE NO.	SALES		GENERAL LEDGER			
	ACCT. NO.	AMOUNT	√						DEPT. A	DEPT. B	ACCT. NO.	AMOUNT	√	
1				1307 00	√	5	Ayres Department Stores	287	822 00	485 00				1
2				1075 00	√	5	Bakemeier's Bakery	288	672 00	403 00				2
3				798 00	√	5	Methodist Hospital	289	277 00	521 00				3
4				701 00	√	7	Brother Juniper's	290	508 00	193 00				4
5				828 00	√	7	Heritage House	291	422 00	406 00				5
6				645 00	√	7	Houlihan's Place	292	437 00	208 00				6
28				26827 00 26827 00					14884 00 14884 00	11943 00 11943 00				28
29				(131)					(411)	(421)				29

Spinner & Thomas' Sales Journal *(Partial)*

A second accounting record affected by sales transactions is the accounts receivable ledger. A portion of the accounts receivable ledger for Spinner & Thomas is reproduced on page 448. For good internal accounting control, the individual sales invoices should be the basis for posting to the individual customer accounts in the accounts receivable ledger. Note that the individual postings for sales invoices Nos. 287, 288, and 289 appear in these customer accounts, just as they appeared in the preceding sales journal. Posting to the individual customer accounts from the sales invoices rather than from the sales journal provides an independent check on the posting process. If the postings of

NAME *Ayres Department Stores* TERMS *Net*

ADDRESS *1 W. Washington St., Indianapolis, IN 46204-5174*

DATE		ITEM	POST. REF.	DEBIT	CREDIT	BALANCE
19-- May	1	Balance	✓			976 00
	5		S287	1 307 00		2 283 00

NAME *Bakemeier's Bakery* TERMS *Net*

ADDRESS *2039 N. Capitol Ave., Indianapolis, IN 46202-4240*

DATE		ITEM	POST. REF.	DEBIT	CREDIT	BALANCE
19-- May	1	Balance	✓			491 00
	5		S288	1 075 00		1 566 00

NAME *Methodist Hospital* TERMS *Net*

ADDRESS *1604 N. Capitol Ave., Indianapolis, IN 46202-5126*

DATE		ITEM	POST. REF.	DEBIT	CREDIT	BALANCE
19-- May	1	Balance	✓			650 00
	5		S289	798 00		1 448 00

Spinner & Thomas' Accounts Receivable Ledger *(Partial)*

customer accounts were made from the sales journal, any error in posting the sales journal would automatically be carried forward to the accounts receivable ledger. On the other hand, if both the sales journal and the customer accounts are posted from individual sales invoices by different accounting department employees, a posting error by either employee would cause the records to disagree, unless of course, both employees made exactly the same error. The posting error would be discovered at the end of the month because at that time, the individual customer account balances in the accounts receivable ledger would be scheduled, totaled, and compared with the general ledger accounts receivable control, which is posted from the total of the sales journal entries.

The third accounting record affected by sales transactions is the general ledger. As explained in Chapter 7, at the end of the month a summary posting would be made from the sales journal to the appropriate general ledger accounts. The accounts and amounts posted for May are indicated at the bottom of the columns in the sales journal on page 447. The posting that is of particular interest for purposes of the present discussion is the one to accounts receivable for $26,827. The following illustration shows the general ledger accounts receivable control account. After posting from the sales journal, the account has a balance of $33,653. This represents the total balances in all accounts receivable as of the end of May, after posting all charge sales made during May.

ACCOUNT *Accounts Receivable* ACCOUNT NO. *131*

DATE		ITEM	POST. REF.	DEBIT	CREDIT	BALANCE	
						DEBIT	CREDIT
19-- May	1	Balance	√			6 826 00	
	31		S9	26 827 00		33 653 00	

Accounts Receivable Control Account in General Ledger

Remittance Advice and Check. When a customer makes a remittance by mail, it is customary for the customer to include a remittance advice with the check. The **remittance advice** is a form showing the customer's name and address and the amount of the remittance. A good example of a remittance advice is shown on page 450. For good internal accounting control, the checks and remittance advices should be separated in the mailroom; the checks should be sent to the cashier and the remittance advices to the accounting department. If a customer remittance arrives without a remittance advice, a remittance advice should be prepared in the mailroom for forwarding to the accounting department.

The processing of the checks and remittance advices is designed to ensure that customer remittances on account are properly received, deposited, and entered in the firm's records. If employees in the mailroom attempt to retain any customer remittances for their own use, the fraud will be discovered because mailroom employees do not have access to the accounting records. Consequently, the customer will undoubtedly be billed again for the amount previously remitted but intercepted by the mailroom employees. When the customer complains about the billing, the theft will be discovered. The actions of the cashier who receives the remittances from the mailroom are simi-

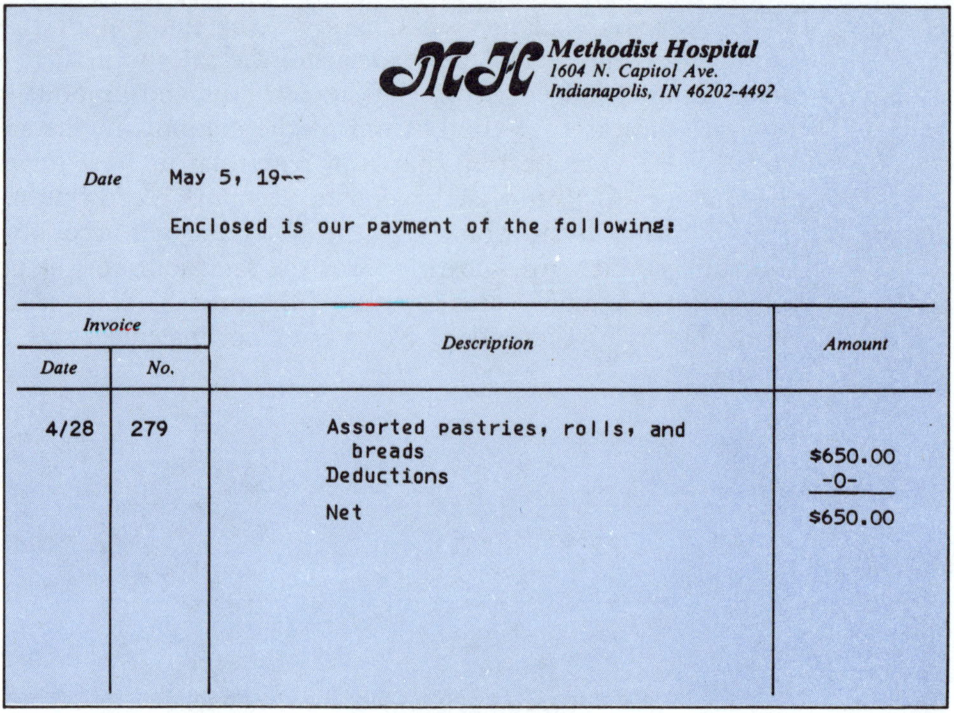

Methodist Hospital
1604 N. Capitol Ave.
Indianapolis, IN 46202-4492

Date May 5, 19--

Enclosed is our payment of the following:

Invoice Date	Invoice No.	Description	Amount
4/28	279	Assorted pastries, rolls, and breads	$650.00
		Deductions	-0-
		Net	$650.00

Remittance Advice

larly controlled. The accounting department employees have access to the accounting records and can fraudulently alter them, but these employees have no access to the remittances and therefore, no incentive to modify the accounting records.

Deposit Slip. The cashier prepares a deposit slip in duplicate for the checks and cash received from the mailroom, and sends both copies along with the checks and cash to the bank. The following is a common form of deposit slip. These deposit slips are often prenumbered. The bank validates the deposit slip and returns it to the depositing firm.

Spinner & Thomas Baking Co.
1604 N. Milburn
Indianapolis, IN 46202-9001

DEPOSIT SLIP 3-4/740

Date May 2 19 - -

FEDERAL NATIONAL BANK
Indianapolis, Indiana

Currency	2,452	20
Coin	139	80
Checks		
Total from other side		
Total	2,592	00

⑆074000009⑆ 92 641 8 ⑈

Deposit Slip

Accounting Procedures for Collections. The first accounting record affected by collections on account is the cash receipts journal, a special journal used to enter all but only cash receipts. The individual remittance advices are the basis for entries in this record. A portion of the cash receipts journal for Spinner & Thomas is shown on page 452.

A second accounting record affected by the collections is the accounts receivable ledger. The receipts are posted to the accounts receivable ledger in chronological order and the source of each receipt is indicated. For good internal accounting control, the individual remittance advices should be used to post to the individual customer accounts in the accounts receivable ledger. The portion of the accounts receivable ledger illustrated on page 448 is reproduced on page 453, with three additional items, the remittances on account by the three customers during May. Note that having different accounting department employees use the remittance advices to post separately to the accounts receivable ledger provides the same type of control over the cash receipts posting process that separate posting to the accounts receivable ledger from the individual sales invoices provided over the sales posting process. If an error was made in posting either to the general ledger or to the accounts receivable ledger, the error would be discovered at the end of the month when the total of the balances

CASH RECEIPTS JOURNAL FOR MONTH OF *May* **19 --** **PAGE** *12*

	DEBIT						CREDIT							
	GENERAL LEDGER								CASH SALES		GENERAL LEDGER			
	ACCT. NO.	AMOUNT	√	CASH NET AMOUNT	DAY	RECEIVED FROM DESCRIPTION	ACCOUNTS RECEIVABLE	√	DEPT. A	DEPT. B	ACCT. NO.	AMOUNT	√	
1						**AMOUNTS FORWARDED**								1
2				3368 00	1	*Cash Sales*			1896 00	1472 00				2
3				2592 00	2	*Cash Sales*			1434 00	1158 00				3
4				2941 00	5	*Cash Sales*			1571 00	1370 00				4
5				3260 00	6	*Cash Sales*			1798 00	1462 00				5
6				1232 00	6	*Ayres Department Stores*	1232 00	√						6
7				977 00	6	*Bakemeier's Bakery*	977 00	√						7
8				650 00	6	*Methodist Hospital*	650 00	√						8
27				110720 00 110720 00			30500 00 30500 00		42451 00 42451 00	37186 00 37186 00		583 00 583 00		27
28				(111)			(131)		(411)	(421)		(√)		28

Spinner & Thomas' Cash Receipts Journal (Partial)

in the accounts receivable ledger is compared with the general ledger accounts receivable control account balance. Even though the individual remittance advices are used to post the subsidiary accounts receivable ledger, the posting reference "CR12" is used to refer to the page of the cash receipts journal on which these collections were entered. This is because no other reference numbers are available for subsequent comparison or verification.

NAME *Ayres Department Stores* **TERMS** *Net*

ADDRESS *1 W. Washington St., Indianapolis, IN 46204-5174*

DATE		ITEM	POST. REF.	DEBIT	CREDIT	BALANCE
19-- May	1	Balance	√			976 00
	5		S287	1 307 00		2 283 00
	6		CR12		1 232 00	1 051 00

NAME *Bakemeier's Bakery* **TERMS** *Net*

ADDRESS *2039 N. Capitol Ave., Indianapolis, IN 46202-4240*

DATE		ITEM	POST. REF.	DEBIT	CREDIT	BALANCE
19-- May	1	Balance	√			491 00
	5		S288	1 075 00		1 566 00
	6		CR12		977 00	589 00

NAME *Methodist Hospital* **TERMS** *Net*

ADDRESS *1604 N. Capitol Ave., Indianapolis, IN 46202-5126*

DATE		ITEM	POST. REF.	DEBIT	CREDIT	BALANCE
19-- May	1	Balance	√			650 00
	5		S289	798 00		1 448 00
	6		CR12		650 00	798 00

Spinner & Thomas' Accounts Receivable Ledger (Partial)

Another accounting record affected by the collections is the general ledger. At the end of each month, a summary posting would be made from the cash receipts journal to the appropriate general ledger accounts. The accounts and amounts posted for May are indicated at the bottom of the columns in the cash receipts journal on page 452. The general ledger accounts receivable control account shown on page 449 is reproduced below, with one additional item, the credit total of $30,500 from the May cash receipts journal. After this posting, the account has a balance of $3,153. This represents the total of the balances in all individual customer accounts receivable as of the end of May, after crediting the customer accounts for all remittances received.

ACCOUNT *Accounts Receivable* ACCOUNT NO. *131*

DATE		ITEM	POST. REF.	DEBIT	CREDIT	BALANCE DEBIT	BALANCE CREDIT
19– May	1	Balance	√			6826 00	
	31		S9	26827 00		33653 00	
	31		CR12		30500 00	3153 00	

Accounts Receivable Control Account in General Ledger

In the previous discussion of deposit slips, it was noted that validated deposit slips are returned by the bank to the firm. Internal control is strengthened if these deposit slips are returned to the accounting department of the firm rather than to the cashier. An accounting department employee should compare the amount shown on the validated deposit slip with the amounts entered in the cash receipts journal as remittances on account. This procedure ensures that customer remittances on account as indicated on the remittance advices and entered in the cash receipts journal were in fact deposited by the cashier.

BUILDING YOUR ACCOUNTING KNOWLEDGE

1. What functions are included in the revenue cycle?
2. What purposes are served by the shipping order?
3. Why should postings to individual customer accounts receivable be made from the sales invoices rather than from the sales journal?
4. Why are checks and remittance advices separated in the mailroom, with the checks being sent to the cashier, and the remittance advices to the accounting department?
5. What control exists over salesclerks to see that a valid cash register entry is made or a sales ticket is prepared when a sale occurs?
6. What three accounting records are affected by collections on account?
7. Why should validated deposit slips be returned by the bank to the accounting department of the firm rather than to the cashier?

APPLYING ACCOUNTING CONCEPTS

Exercise 14-6. The following sales and collection transactions occurred during the first month of operations of the Robcar Co.

May 4 Made charge sale No. 1 to H. Inger, $310.50.
6 Made cash sales of $1,412.45.
11 Made charge sale No. 2 to P. Willems, $283.39.
12 Made charge sale No. 3 to F. Miller, $402.
18 Received $200 on account from H. Inger.
19 Made cash sales of $904.25.
24 Received $283.39 on account from P. Willems.
26 Made charge sale No. 4 to L. Fishel, $331.71.
29 Made charge sale No. 5 to H. Inger, $204.13.

Enter the foregoing transactions in a sales journal similar to the one on page 447 or in a cash receipts journal similar to the one on page 452.

Exercise 14-7. See Exercise 14-6.

(a) Foot the sales journal and cash receipts journal in Exercise 14-6. **(b)** Post the transactions from Exercise 14-6 to an accounts receivable subsidiary ledger, and the journal totals to an accounts receivable account. (Use T account forms.) **(c)** Prove the accounts receivable balance by preparing a schedule of accounts receivable.

Report No. 14-3

Complete Report No. 14-3 in the study assignments and submit your working papers for approval. Then continue with the textbook discussion in Chapter 15 until Report No. 15-1 is required.

EXPANDING YOUR BUSINESS VOCABULARY

What is the meaning of each of the following terms:

- accounting procedures **(p. 421)**
- authorization procedures **(p. 420)**
- cash receipts journal **(p. 451)**
- check register **(pp. 425, 436)**
- customer's purchase order **(p. 443)**
- independent check **(p. 421)**
- internal accounting control system **(p. 419)**
- internal audit department **(p. 421)**
- purchase invoice **(p. 429)**
- purchase order **(p. 427)**
- purchase requisition **(p. 426)**
- receiving report **(p. 427)**
- remittance advice **(p. 449)**
- sales invoice **(p. 445)**
- sales journal **(p. 447)**
- sales order **(p. 444)**
- segregation of duties **(p. 420)**
- shipping order **(p. 445)**
- voucher **(pp. 425, 430)**
- voucher check **(p. 435)**
- voucher register **(pp. 425, 430)**
- voucher system **(p. 428)**

CHAPTER 15

Accounting Concepts and Accepted Practices

CHAPTER OBJECTIVES

Careful study of this chapter should enable you to:

- Describe and explain the basic accounting concepts of:

  1. The Business Entity
  2. The Going Concern
  3. The Monetary Unit
  4. Transaction-Based Records and Historical Cost
  5. Periodicity, Realization, and Matching
  6. The Accrual Basis

- Describe and explain the widely accepted accounting practices of:

  1. Consistency and Comparability
  2. Adequate Disclosure
  3. Objectivity and Verifiability
  4. Materiality and Practicality
  5. Conservatism
  6. Legality

The framework that underlies modern business accounting is a blend of various assumptions, conventions, requirements, practical compromises, and constraints. Because these factors are so interrelated, it is not possible to list them in an unquestioned order of importance. The student should remember this in the discussion that follows. In the organization of this chapter, the various matters are grouped according to (1) those that can be regarded as concepts and (2) those that may be classed as accepted practices. However, it will soon become apparent that there is some overlap between the categories.

BASIC CONCEPTS IN FINANCIAL ACCOUNTING

The basic concepts in financial accounting include: (1) the business entity, (2) the going concern, (3) the monetary unit, (4) transaction-based records and the related concept of historical cost, (5) periodicity and the related concepts of realization and matching, and (6) the accrual basis.

The Business Entity

As applied to business accounting, the entity concept means that the business to which the records (or financial statements) relate is treated as a separately identifiable economic unit. This economic unit can be defined in various ways without regard to legal considerations of who actually owns the property and who is liable for the debts. In connection with the discussions and illustrations of the accounts of a single-owner business (a sole proprietorship), it was stressed that while the owner might possess various properties, only the property used in the business was taken into account. Likewise, the record of liabilities excluded any of the proprietor's debts of a nonbusiness or personal nature. Consequently, there was no accounting for any type of revenue and expense not connected with business operations. Of course, a business could be considered to include other, perhaps wholly unrelated, profit-seeking activities if the owner so desires. Or, the accounting entity could consist of the assets used by the business and the liabilities incurred on behalf of the business, even though, legally, the property belonged to the owner who was personally liable for the debts.

In the case of business partnerships, the separate entity is almost a legal reality. Property can be owned by a partnership. However, with limited exceptions, the debts of the firm may become personal liabilities of each of the partners. In the case of business corporations, the business entity is a legal reality, even though corporations are owned by their shareholders or stockholders. Corporations can own property, incur debt, sue, and be sued. The debts of a corporation are debts of the corporate entity, not personal debts of its owners (stockholders). This is one of the reasons for the wide popularity of the corporate form of business organization.

Probably the greatest extension of the entity concept occurs when one corporation owns most or all of another (or perhaps several others). While each corporation is a legal entity and each has a separate set of records, their individual financial statements are combined to present what is known as a consolidated income statement and a consolidated balance sheet. From the viewpoint of the stockholders of the parent corporation (the corporation that controls the other corporations in the consolidated group), there is, in effect, just one entity.

The Going-Concern

A well-established tradition in business accounting is that in the absence of strong reason to believe otherwise, a business should be assumed to have a continuing, indefinite life. This is called the going-concern concept, or concept of continuity. Several arguments are offered in support of this concept. Corporations can have virtually perpetual existence. In the other two forms of business organizations, proprietors and partners will die, but the businesses involved can be continued by others—perhaps by those who inherit the business, by remaining partners, or by those to whom the business may be sold. It is argued that, in most cases, the owners and managers of a business intend and hope that the business will continue indefinitely. They usually make decisions with a view to maintaining the existence of the business, often in the hope of expanding it.

The reality of the economic world does not give full support to the going-concern concept. Business failures are commonplace. The mortality rate among new businesses is especially high. However, the alternative to assuming that a business will continue indefinitely would be to make an estimate of its probable life. What is a reasonable estimate? Two years? Five years? Ten years? Whatever the estimated life, it would mean that the acquisition of a depreciable asset with a potential useful life greater than the expected life of the business might seem inadvisable. Whenever long-term assets were acquired, the nature of depreciation calculations could be affected. The estimated life of the business rather than the estimated useful life of the asset might become the controlling element. In addition, the longer a business were to survive, the greater would be the chance for its continued existence; thus some depreciation rates might have to be revised and rerevised. Since this alternative to a continuity concept is so unattractive (perhaps unworkable), the going-concern concept seems the more sensible alternative.

The Monetary Unit

The monetary unit concept means that business transactions are measured in terms of money and the purchasing power of money is assumed to be stable. The monetary unit used by American accountants (United States and Canada) to measure financial transactions is the dollar. In Great Britain, the unit is the pound, and in West Germany, the unit is the mark. Whatever form of monetary unit is used, it is not as reliable a measuring unit as is a physical measure, such as the meter or kilogram, because the value of money fluctuates. This can cause the monetary unit to have different values at different points in time.

For several decades, the question of whether changes in the value of the dollar should be recognized in the accounting process has been discussed and debated. It is well known that the purchasing power of the dollar is constantly changing—nearly always declining. The impact of this on the financial statements is greatest in the case of long-term assets. Quite apart from the question of whether the amounts reported on a balance sheet should approximate current market values of the assets as opposed to historical cost, is the problem that the amounts shown as the costs of long-term assets may be a mixture of some dollars spent perhaps 25 years ago, some 20 years ago, some 10 years ago, and some more recently. Almost certainly, the value of the dollar was not the same at those different times. The amount charged to depreciation expense would be, in consequence, a mixture of different-valued dollars. To a lesser extent, all this may apply to shorter-term assets whose costs become expenses within a shorter period of time; for example, inventories. Another point is that the dollars of revenue for a single period generally represent similar purchasing power, while the dollars of expense deducted may be a diverse mixture.

Awareness of the limitations of the monetary unit as a measuring device is not lacking. Accounting reports necessarily are limited in scope by the use of the monetary measure. Such matters as competitive advantage or disadvantage, employee attitudes, management talents, and working conditions often cannot be stated adequately in dollar terms. Accountants simply feel that the interpretation of the effects of any changes in the value of money should be made by the users of the accounting reports rather than by the accountants.

The effects of the instability of the dollar on accounting reports may be illustrated as follows. Assume that a business bought equipment for $50,000 ten years ago and it now costs $100,000 to replace the equipment because inflation has cut the value of the dollar in half during the ten-year period. If the old equipment is fully depreciated and the net income of the business over the ten-year period was equal to $50,000, this implies that the cost of the old equipment has been recovered and the firm has had a profit of $50,000. However, the firm has not really had a profit at all, because it will require both the recovered cost of the old equipment ($50,000) and the $50,000 of reported net income to purchase the new equipment for $100,000. Thus, the reported net income might be viewed as a mirage.

The monetary unit concept continues to be accepted, because money is still a common ingredient of all business transactions and does provide a practical measurement unit capable of lending objectivity and uniformity to financial data. Nevertheless, there is a growing interest in reporting accounting information either adjusted for general price level changes or in terms of replacement costs.

Transaction-Based Records and Historical Cost

Fundamental to business accounting is the idea that there is nothing to account for until a transaction occurs. Closely allied to this notion is the requirement that the amount to be entered when the transaction involves the acquisition of an asset is the acquisition cost, or historical cost, of that asset. The historical cost concept holds that, generally, no adjustment will be made to this amount in later periods, except to allocate the original cost of the asset to periodic expense as the asset is consumed.

Accountants do not deny that changes in the values of assets occur over time. Rather, accountants generally insist on objective, verifiable evidence before they are willing to enter information in the accounts. (Objective, verifiable evidence is discussed in a later section of this chapter.) Differences between the historical cost of a business's assets and the various market values of those assets that may exist at some later date may be difficult to measure and may never materialize. Consequently, accountants are reluctant to enter such value changes in the accounts. In contrast, when a transaction occurs, the objective, verifiable evidence that the accountant seeks becomes available. Add to this the application of the realization concept discussed in the next section and the case for transaction-based historical cost accounting gains strength.

Periodicity, Realization, and Matching

Central to business accounting is the concept that income determination may be made on a periodic basis, known as the periodicity concept. This means that income should always be determined annually, and in addition, sometimes for shorter periods, such as quarterly or monthly. Any period shorter than a year is described as an interim period. The requirement that income be determined on a periodic basis causes most of the problems associated with income measurement.

In order to determine income on a periodic basis, the accountant must decide when to recognize revenue and expenses. Revenue is recognized in accordance with the realization concept. Revenue generally is considered to be realized when there is a receipt of cash or a claim to cash in exchange for goods or services. For example, a car is taken to a service station for a tankful of gasoline (goods) and a car wash (services). The dealer may either receive cash or allow the use of a credit card (a claim to cash) in settlement. In either event, the dealer is considered to have realized revenue, even though the use of the credit card would create an account receivable on the dealer's books.

Once a decision is made regarding when to recognize revenue (using the realization concept), the expenses must next be recognized in accordance with the matching concept. The matching concept means that expenses incurred to generate particular revenues should be matched with those revenues that they helped to generate. For example, if the dealer in the previous example recorded the sale of gasoline, the cost of the gasoline sold should be matched against the revenue realized from the sale. Uncollectible accounts receivable represent a potential problem if revenue is considered realized when a claim to cash is created. The usual solution is the periodic estimation of uncollectible accounts expense, which then becomes part of the income calculation for the same period in which the receivables were recorded.

It is in attempting to perform the matching process that the periodic-income-determination requirement poses the largest problem. Two outstanding examples of expense-matching problems are: (1) the apportionment of merchandise cost between cost of goods sold and end-of-period inventory, where specific identification of the units sold is not possible, and (2) the allocation of the cost of most long-term assets by means of depreciation, depletion, or amortization. Considerable judgment and estimation are necessary in each of these cases. Nonetheless, the matching of revenues and expenses is a fundamental part of the accrual accounting process.

The Accrual Basis

According to the accrual basis concept, revenue is recognized in the accounting period in which it is earned, and expenses are recognized in the accounting period in which they are incurred, regardless of whether the receipt or disbursement of cash takes place in the same period. Revenue is recognized when money or a legal claim to money is obtained in exchange for something of value. Revenue accrues when an inflow of assets causes an increase in owner's equity other than from an investment of assets in the business by the owner. Expense accrues when an asset outflow or an additional liability causes owner's equity to decrease other than from a withdrawal of assets by the owner or owners.

The accrual basis of accounting involves the periodic matching of revenue with the expenses related to its realization. Revenue from sales must be matched with the cost of goods sold and the various other expenses incidental to conducting a business. The simple matching of cash receipts for a particular period with the cash paid for goods or services acquired in that period is meaningless for the most part. Collections may relate to sales of the current period and payments may relate to purchases during a previous period or vice versa. The expenses related to most long-term assets occur as the property loses its usefulness. The accrual basis recognizes changes in a variety of assets and liabilities in determining periodic net income—not just cash changes.

It is the combined effect of the realization and matching concepts coupled with the accrual basis concept, that provides some assurance that income is accurately measured and reported each period.

BUILDING YOUR ACCOUNTING KNOWLEDGE

1. Does the business entity concept identify only the legal property and legal debts of the business enterprise or may it be broader than this? Discuss.
2. What attribute of corporations supports the going-concern concept? What experiences of proprietors and partners support it?
3. Since the realities of the economic world do not fully support the going-concern concept, how is it justified by accountants? Discuss.
4. How do accountants justify the use of the monetary unit as a measuring device?
5. How is the historical cost concept related to transaction-based records?
6. How do the realization and matching concepts relate to the periodicity concept? Give two examples of this relationship.
7. When is revenue considered to be earned on the accrual basis? When is expense considered to be incurred on this basis?
8. What problems are created by a simple matching of cash received from customers during an accounting period with the cash paid for goods or services purchased in that same period?

APPLYING ACCOUNTING CONCEPTS

Exercise 15-1. J. Seary, who owns and operates J. S. Lock Service, engaged in the following transactions during the past month.

1. Received $85 for repairing lock on customer safe.
2. Paid $62 shop electric bill.
3. Paid $37 dental bill for daughter.
4. Received $140 for installing new bolt locks on customer doors.
5. Received $67 from sale of son's bicycle.
6. Paid $70 for cleaning service at shop.

Prepare two-column journal entries for each of the above transactions that should be considered part of J.S. Lock Service operations.

Exercise 15-2. K. Pearson purchased new office equipment for $3,000. The equipment is expected to last 10 years and have no salvage value. Pearson plans to sell the business in which the equipment is used in three years.

Compute the appropriate depreciation expense for the equipment for the first year of use, using the straight-line method.

Exercise 15-3. Prepare appropriate two-column journal entries for each of the following events and transactions that should be reflected in the accounting records.

1. Purchased manufacturing equipment for $3,400 on account.
2. Purchased merchandise for $1,550 cash.
3. Determined that the equipment in transaction (1) could now be purchased for $2,900.
4. Determined that the merchandise in transaction (2) could now be sold for $1,875.
5. Sold the merchandise in transaction (2) for $1,840 cash.

Exercise 15-4. U. Trust, who runs a car lot, engaged in the following transactions:

1. Acquired a used Mustang at auction for $3,100.
2. Acquired a used Omega at auction for $3,750.
3. Sold the Mustang for $4,050.
4. Acquired a used Dodge at auction for $2,940.
5. Sold the Omega for $4,800.
6. Paid lot rental and utilities of $360.

(a) Compute the amount of gross margin on the sale of the Mustang. **(b)** Compute the amount of the gross margin on the sale of the Omega. **(c)** Compute the net income from operating the lot during this time period.

Report No. 15-1

Complete Report No. 15-1 in the study assignments and submit your working papers to the instructor for approval. Then continue with the textbook discussion until Report No. 15-2 is required.

ACCEPTED ACCOUNTING PRACTICES

In an attempt to serve the interests of various groups of people concerned with business affairs as reported in periodic financial statements, several practices have become widely accepted in the accounting profession. Some of these practices have grown out of the concepts that have been discussed. Others are intended to help make accounting reports easier to understand. Many involve a compromise between partially-conflicting objectives. Six of the most important of these practices are discussed in the paragraphs that follow.

Consistency and Comparability

It has already been noted that the problems posed by the periodicity and matching concepts (which are fundamental to business accounting) preclude the attainment of absolute accuracy in the calculation of periodic income. Nevertheless, the users of financial statements invariably want to make comparisons between current and past results. This combination of circumstances makes it necessary to have a degree of consistency (e.g., the use of the same inventory or depreciation method from period to period) in accounting methods which makes comparability (the ability to identify similarities and differences in performance) between periods possible. One example of this need is found in the choice of an accounting method for merchandise inventory. Regardless of whether fifo or lifo is considered best, it is not difficult to imagine the possible consequence of switching from one to the other each year. This switching might make any comparison of the results of operations for several years almost meaningless. Frequent changes of the depreciation method could produce a similar undesirable result. Stated loosely, the rule is: "If you cannot be completely certain of your choice of method, at least use it consistently."

The consistency practice must not be carried to such an extreme that it is taken to mean that a method of accounting once adopted must never be changed. Changing circumstances may require a change in accounting method, but it is not expected that numerous and substantial changes will be needed each year. When important changes are made, it is essential that the financial statements clearly indicate (by footnote or otherwise) the changes made and the reasons therefor. Sometimes data are included in the explanation to show what the result might have been if the change had not been made. The act of providing an explanation of what was done, and why, is an example of compliance with the practice of adequate disclosure.

Adequate Disclosure

For at least the following three reasons, the practice of adequate disclosure must be followed in the preparation of accounting reports:

1. Financial statement users want to know which of the various generally accepted accounting principles and practices have been used.
2. There is a danger that significant facts about what has taken place during the period under review will somehow get "buried" among all the other information that the report contains or else remain undisclosed.
3. There has been an increasing demand from users of financial reports for more information about the business.

To meet the adequate disclosure requirement, a number of procedures have evolved. The use of explanatory notes, either in the body of financial statements or as footnotes, has become widespread. (Mention was made in the previous section of the importance of disclosing any important changes in the use of an accounting method.) What is termed the "all inclusive" type of income statement has become widely used. Such a statement not only shows the composition of the income (loss) from regular operations for the period, but, in addition, any unusual gains or losses that have occurred.

The annual reports of large corporations often include an assortment of tables and graphs intended to emphasize significant trends in their corporate business affairs. Often statistical data of a nonfinancial nature are included, such as the number of employees or the number of units produced. Annual reports of this type always include a message from the company president or board chairperson that draws attention to important things that happened during the year, including any major changes in management personnel and a general forecast for the year or years ahead.

In the interest of adequate disclosure, multiproduct-line companies are now required to provide information about major segments or product lines of the business by both the Securities and Exchange Commission and the Federal Trade Commission. It has also been proposed that annual reports should include a financial budget (forecast) so that interested parties can have an idea of "what's coming." Professional ethics rules prohibit auditors from vouching for the achievability of forecast data, although there is no rule against vouching for the basic assumptions and calculations involved. However, a published forecast might reveal information useful to competitors, and since the reported plans may not work out, many business managers and accountants fear that such a procedure might do more harm than good. Just how far adequate disclosure should go is an unsettled issue. Nevertheless, the inclusion of forecast data in published annual reports is increasing.

Objectivity and Verifiability

Data that are entered in the accounting records and later reported in the financial statements of a business generally should be supported by source documents or other records that are both objective and verifiable forms of evidence that certain transactions occurred. This is the practice of objectivity and verifiability. Sales tickets, purchase invoices, and employee paychecks are examples of source documents that provide objective evidential matter. When evidence is not completely objective, as in the case of doubtful accounts receivable or long-term asset depreciation, the most objective evidence available should be used. Records of past experience in collecting accounts receivable are an example of objective evidence for entering doubtful accounts expense.

The notion of objectivity is that such source documents or records of past experience provide unbiased, factual evidence of real transactions and events that have occurred. The notion of verifiability is that any two accountants looking independently at the same evidence probably would make the related entry in the same way.

Materiality and Practicality

In the field of law, there is a maxim of *de minimis non curat lex*, which means that the law is not concerned with trifles. The same can be said of accounting. In accounting, what is called the practice of materiality and practicality means that the concepts of accrual accounting need not be followed in the case of amounts that are too small to make any real difference. For example, even though a waste basket that cost $5 may be expected to be useful for many years, it is not necessary to account for it as an asset to be depreciated. Simply treat the expenditure as, perhaps, miscellaneous expense. It is an almost universal practice for each business to establish some "cut-off point" that the accountant should follow in entering such expenditures. In the case of a small business, the point might be $25 or $50; larger businesses may have a higher limit. Consistency of treatment is, of course, necessary.

In the handling of certain year-end adjustments, the amount involved may dictate whether an adjustment should be made. For example, it may be unnecessary to bother with accrued interest payable or receivable in the amount of $2.65 or to enter the fact that $15 of the supplies expense account balance (amounting to more than $400) actually relates to supplies that are still on hand.

Probably the most important application of the practice of materiality is in connection with the financial statements. Adequate disclosure does not require that a petty cash fund of $100 be shown by itself rather than being lumped together with cash in bank, or that the detail be shown for prepaid expenses whose total is equal to one percent of total assets. In fact, the interests of adequate disclosure are best served by preparing financial statements and schedules that are not so filled with detail that the significant matters may be obscured.

Another widespread practice that is followed in the interest of eliminating the immaterial aspects of financial statements is to eliminate cents; instead, each amount is rounded to the nearest dollar. In fact, the financial statements of very large companies frequently show amounts rounded to the nearest $1,000.

Conservatism

The customs, concepts, and conventions of modern business accounting involve a tendency (some say a bias) toward conservatism. Generally, this means that when two or more acceptable ways of allocating the cost of an asset between benefiting periods can be used, the one that causes reported assets and periodic income to be smaller usually is chosen. The widely-used "cost or market, whichever is lower" method for assigning a value to the end-of-period merchandise inventory will cause both the inventory and the income for the period just ended to be smaller than otherwise. As applied to depreciation, if equally good reasons exist to use either a ten-year or a twelve-year estimated life for a depreciable asset, most accountants would use the shorter life. For the years the asset is used, both the income of each of the periods and the undepreciated cost of the asset at the end of each period will be smaller than if the longer life were used. When the question arises whether to charge the total cost of an item to expense immediately or to treat it as an asset to be amortized, the "expense-it-now" option usually is followed.

Probably the most all-encompassing example of the practice of conservatism stems from the historical-cost and realization concepts, which do not permit "writing up" assets even if they are thought at a later date to be worth more than the accounts show. Some accountants contend that refusing to show current or present values for all assets causes many balance sheets to be almost worthless. However, if such write-ups were to become accepted practice, either accountants would have to be trained as appraisers or appraisers would have to be employed. It is questionable whether the values thus determined would qualify as objective, verifiable evidence. Historical costs, generally, do meet this test. Further, either the amount of the write-up would have to be considered as revenue even though there were no inflows of cash or receivables (or other assets), or provision would have to be made in the accounts for unrealized revenue. In the opinion of many accountants and business executives, so-called unrealized revenue is not revenue at all.

The conservatism practice is thought to have become deeply imbedded in accounting for two major reasons: (1) If unquestioned absolute accuracy in accounting is not possible, there is probably less danger of damaging the interests of existing and prospective owners and creditors by following conservative practices. (2) Conservative accounting practices lead to lower reported income for tax purposes and therefore lower taxes. Income tax laws do not require that most items be handled in the same way for tax purposes as they are in the accounts, but businesses typically find it easier to account for their activities in the same way for financial reporting purposes as for tax purposes. Further, a tax approach is easier to defend if it corresponds to what is done in the accounts.

Legality

Accounting records and reports must conform with certain legal requirements, such as tax regulations, contract provisions, and state incorporation laws, that relate to specific business transactions. This is the practice of legality. For example, it is illegal to evade taxes or reduce the required tax payments by ignoring or flaunting the law. It is also illegal to fail or refuse to enter payroll tax deductions when keeping employee payroll records. The structure of the equity section of a corporation balance sheet often is affected by the laws of the state in which the firm is incorporated. In addition, the ability of a corporation to pay dividends can be determined by state incorporation laws. The accounting system must be maintained in such a way that compliance with applicable laws can be determined.

BUILDING YOUR ACCOUNTING KNOWLEDGE

1. Why are consistency and comparability closely associated in business accounting?
2. If an important change in accounting method takes place, how should it be indicated to users of financial statements?
3. Give three reasons for observing the practice of adequate disclosure.

4. What attributes make source documents both objective and verifiable?
5. Explain why materiality is closely associated with practicality.
6. What is the relationship between materiality and adequate disclosure?
7. Give three examples of the application of the practice of conservatism.
8. Give two examples of legal requirements to which accounting records and reports must conform.

APPLYING ACCOUNTING CONCEPTS

Exercise 15-5. Massage Co. is considering making three accounting changes in the current year.

1. **From FIFO to LIFO inventory. FIFO inventory cost is $7,000, whereas LIFO inventory cost would be $5,200.**
2. **From straight-line to declining-balance depreciation. Straight-line depreciation is $6,600, whereas declining-balance depreciation would be $8,900.**
3. **From amortizing goodwill over 12 years to amortizing it over 5 years. Goodwill amortization on a 12-year basis is $2,000, whereas on a 5-year basis it would be $4,800.**

If Massage Co's net income for the year is $12,300 based on FIFO inventory, straight-line depreciation, and 12-year goodwill amortization, compute the net income if all three accounting changes are made.

Exercise 15-6. Matty Co. reported net income of $38,000 for the current year. In reviewing Matty's records, you discover the following items for which no adjustments were made at the end of the period.

1. **Supplies of $27 were on hand.**
2. **Interest revenue of $5 had accrued for four days on a note receivable.**
3. **Delivery charges of $13 on packages received in the current period were not entered until paid in the following period.**
4. **Petty cash expenditures of $7 were not entered because reimbursement of petty cash was not made at the end of the period.**
5. **Interest expense of $10 had accrued for six days on a note payable.**

(a) Compute the net income of Matty Co. for the year if adjustment were made for these items. **(b)** What accounting practice would support Matty's not making these adjustments?

Report No. 15-2

Complete Report No. 15-2 in the study assignments and submit your working papers for approval. Then continue with the textbook discussion in Chapter 16 until Report No. 16-1 is required.

EXPANDING YOUR BUSINESS VOCABULARY

What is the meaning of each of the following terms?

accrual basis concept **(p. 461)**
adequate disclosure **(p. 464)**
concept of continuity **(p. 458)**
conservatism **(p. 467)**
consistency and comparability **(p. 464)**
consolidated balance sheet **(p. 458)**
consolidated income statement **(p. 458)**
entity concept **(p. 457)**
going-concern concept **(p. 458)**
historical cost concept **(p. 460)**
interim period **(p. 461)**
legality **(p. 468)**
matching concept **(p. 461)**
materiality and practicality **(p. 466)**
monetary unit concept **(p. 459)**
objectivity **(p. 466)**
periodicity concept **(p. 460)**
realization concept **(p. 461)**
unrealized revenue **(p. 468)**
verifiability **(p. 466)**

CHAPTERS 11-15

Supplementary Practical Accounting Problems

PROBLEM 11-A Notes receivable register

Ann Allen is a dealer in paintings and framing materials. In accounting for notes received from customers in return for extensions of time in paying their obligations, Allen uses a notes receivable register similar to the one reproduced on pages 350 and 351. Following is a narrative of transactions involving notes received from customers during the current year.

Mar. 6 Received from Frank Soambee a 60-day, 12% note (No. 1) for $850 dated March 5, and payable at First National Bank, Willow Brook.

Apr. 27 Received from John Henry a 90-day, 10% note (No. 2) for $900 dated April 26, and payable at Second National Bank, Mayfield.

May 4 Received a check for $867.00 in payment for Frank Soambee's note due today plus interest.

20 Received from Knapp Logger a 60-day, 13% note (No. 3) for $1,200 dated May 19, and payable at Northern Trust Company, Park Ridge.

July 18 Received a check for $1,226.00 in payment for Knapp Logger's note due today plus interest.

25 Received a check for $922.50 in payment for John Henry's note due today plus interest.

Sept. 8 Received from Earl Fishhead a 90-day, 11% note (No. 4) for $800 dated September 7, and payable at Monroe State Bank, Monroe.

Dec. 6 Received a check from Monroe State Bank for $812.00 in payment of the note due yesterday plus interest less a $10 collection charge.

Required: (1) Prepare entries in two-column journal form for the transactions. Foot the amount columns as a means of proof. (2) Make the required entries in a notes receivable register similar to the one reproduced on pages 350 and 351, to provide a detailed auxiliary record of the notes received by Allen.

PROBLEM 11-B Notes payable

Denton Fenders operates a department store. Sometimes, Fenders finds it necessary to issue notes to suppliers to obtain extensions of time for payment of accounts. Unless otherwise stated, all notes are made payable to the Brown County Bank, Newburg. Following is a narrative of transactions involving notes issued by Fenders during the current year:

Feb. 3 Borrowed $1,500 from the bank on a 90-day, 11% note (No. 1).

Mar. 10 Issued a 60-day, 9% note (No. 2) for $660 to Budd & Decker Co.

Apr. 15 Issued a 60-day, 13% note (No. 3) for $1,000 to R. U. Irish & Co.

May 4 Issued a check for $1,541.25 to the bank in payment of note due today plus interest.

9 Gave Budd & Decker Co. a check for $9.90 in payment of the interest due today and a new note (No. 4), for $660, due in 60 days, with interest at 9%, in settlement of the note due today.

June 14 Issued a check for $1,021.67 to R.U. Irish & Co. in payment of note due today plus interest.

July 1 Borrowed $5,000 from the bank on a 90-day, 13% note (No. 5).

8 Issued a check for $669.90 to Budd & Decker Co. in payment of note due today plus interest.

Sept. 29 Gave Brown County Bank a check for $162.50 in payment of the interest due today and a new note (No.6) for $5,000.00, due in 60 days with interest at 13%, in settlement of the note due today.

Nov. 28 Issued a check for $5,108.33 to the bank in payment of note due today plus interest.

Required: (1) Prepare entries in two-column journal form for the transactions. Foot the amount columns as a means of proof. (2) Make the required entries in a notes payable register similar to the one reproduced on pages 356 and 357, to provide a detailed auxiliary record of the notes issued.

PROBLEM 12-A Application of fifo, weighted average, and lifo methods

The Earthbound Company is in the wholesale hardware business. Stock record cards are kept of all merchandise handled. The data with respect to Article X were assembled from the stock record cards and appeared as follows.

On hand at beginning of period	760 units
First purchase during period	850 units @ $42
Second purchase during period	800 units @ $50
Last purchase during period	900 units @ $48
In stock at end of period	750 units

Earthbound Company had sales of $173,000 during the period. Assume that the units in stock at the beginning of the period were assigned a cost of $41 each under the fifo method, $39 each under the weighted average method, and $37 each under the lifo method.

Required: Compute ending inventory, cost of goods sold, and gross margin under (1) the fifo method, (2) the weighted average method, and (3) the lifo method of cost assignment. (Carry the weighted average unit cost to four decimal places.)

PROBLEM 12-B Application of the lower of cost or market rule

Stanfield Distributors has four items in its ending inventory: Products W, X, Y, and Z. The quantities, costs, and market values of these items are given below:

Product	Quantity	Cost	Market
W	311	$12	$13
X	429	15	13
Y	223	18	19
Z	489	17	16

Assume that Stanfield uses the fifo lower of cost or market method of cost assignment.

Required: Calculate the dollar amount of ending inventory by applying the lower of cost or market rule to: (1) the total inventory, and (2) each item in the inventory.

PROBLEM 12-C Postage account

Watkins & Sinclair is a mail-order house. Metered postage is used on parcel post packages. Deposits are made for postage under the postal permit system. Postage stamps are purchased for other purposes. All prepaid postage is charged to Postage, Account No. 154, and periodically the postage used is charged to the following expense accounts:

557 Freight Out (Parcel Post)
558 Advertising Postage Expense
559 General Postage Expense

During the month of June, the postage used on parcel post packages amounted to $1,039, and on advertising matter, $516. On June 30, the unused stamps on hand amounted to $116, and the unused metered postage amounted to $437.

Required: **(1)** Open the necessary accounts and enter the debit balance of the postage account before adjustment, $2,432. **(2)** Make the required adjusting entry in general journal form for all postage expense for the month. **(3)** Post the entry to the appropriate accounts.

PROBLEM 13-A Depreciation of long-term assets; trade in

On February 1, 19A Simonis & Kosiba, a partnership, began the wholesale distribution of heating equipment. In accounting for their long-term assets, the following accounts are used:

171 Office Equipment
171.1 Accumulated Depreciation—Office Equipment
181 Store Equipment
181.1 Accumulated Depreciation—Store Equipment
183 Delivery Equipment
183.1 Accumulated Depreciation—Delivery Equipment
218 Accounts Payable
547 Depreciation Expense—Office Equipment
554 Depreciation Expense—Store Equipment
555 Depreciation Expense—Delivery Equipment

The following is a narrative of transactions involving the purchase of long-term assets during the year ended December 31, 19A:

Feb. 12 Invoice No. 218—Purchased cabinet file for office use on account from The Ironcase Co., $490; estimated useful life, 10 years; estimated trade-in value at end of 10 years, $70.

Mar. 7 Invoice No. 232—Purchased a small truck for delivery purposes on account from Mercurial Motors, Inc., $7,200; estimated useful life, 4 years; estimated trade-in value at end of 4 years, $900.

Apr. 18 Invoice No. 239—Purchased an office table on account from The City Furniture Co., $360; estimated useful life, 20 years; no salvage value.

July 2 Invoice No. 274—Purchased showcases on account from Campbell Co., $600; estimated useful life, 15 years; no salvage value.

Aug. 28 Invoice No. 291—Purchased used double-pedestal desk for use in storeroom on account from Harper Store Equipment Co., $280; estimated useful life, 20 years; no salvage value.

Sept. 9 Invoice No. 312—Purchased used Magic-write typewriter, No. 5837852-11 on account from Magic Corporation, $375; estimated useful life, 5 years; estimated trade-in value at end of 5 years, $75.

On February 7, 19C, after entering twenty-three months' depreciation, the delivery truck purchased on March 7, 19A, was traded in for a new truck with a market value of $7,900, and $4,000 in cash also was paid.

Required: **(1)** Enter the foregoing transactions in proper two-column journal form. **(2)** Foot the amount columns. **(3)** Determine the annual rate of depreciation (straight-line method) applicable to the net cost of each of the long-term assets purchased, compute the amount of depreciation accumulated during the current year ended December 31, 19A, and prepare an entry in two-column journal form for the depreciation. Depreciation is taken for a full month on assets purchased by the 15th of a month. **(4)** Prepare a two-column journal entry for the transaction on February 7, 19C. Recognize the gain or loss, if appropriate, for financial accounting purposes.

PROBLEM 13-B Wasting asset—depletion and sale

Graves Enterprises, Inc., owns a gravel pit that was purchased a few years before for $150,000. Depletion has been calculated on the basis of 20 cents for every cubic yard of gravel excavated. At the beginning of the current year, the balance of the accumulated depletion account was $9,350. During the first four months of this year, 19A, 60,000 cubic yards of gravel were excavated, and on May 2, 19A the pit was sold for $140,000 cash.

Required: Prepare entries in general journal form, for **(1)** the depletion accumulated for the first four months of the year, and **(2)** the sale of the gravel pit, recognizing any gain or loss on the sale.

PROBLEM 14-A Voucher register; check register; schedule of unpaid vouchers

Voltaic Electronics, a business just organized, uses a voucher register and a check register similar to those shown on pages 432 and 436.

Vouchers were entered using the gross-price basis. Checks were issued in payment of any invoices subject to discount on the day preceding the last day of the discount period.

The narrative of transactions of the month is as follows:

Oct. 3 Issued Voucher No. 1 for $200 to establish a petty cash fund and cashed Check No. 1 for that amount. (Petty Cash Fund, Account No. 112.)

3 Received an invoice for $695 from the Multnomah Real Estate Co. for rent. Issued Check No. 2 in payment of the invoice. (Rent Expense, Account No. 5443.)

4 Received an invoice for $2,193.75 from the Earblast Radio-Stereo Manufacturers, Inc., for merchandise. Date of invoice, September 29; terms, 1/10, n/30.

5 Received an invoice for $479 from Sturdee Equipment Co. for an office desk purchased. Date of invoice, October 3; terms, net 30 days. (Office Equipment, Account No. 191.)

6 Received a bill for telephone service from the Monopoly Telephone Co. and issued Check No. 3 for $27.80 in payment. (General Office Expense, Account No. 5418.)

Oct. 7 Received a bill for office supplies from Paper Chase Co. and issued Check No. 4 for $73.50 in payment. (Office Supplies, Account No. 152.)

8 Received an invoice for $894.50 from the Trendy Corporation for a shipment of merchandise. Date of invoice, October 6; terms, 2/15, n/60.

12 Received an invoice for $543.50 from the Radunn Advertising Agency for advertising service. Issued Check No. 6 in payment. (Advertising Expense, Account No. 5433.)

13 Received an invoice for $92.50 from the AllLand Insurance Co. for insurance. Issued Check No. 7 in payment. (Prepaid Insurance, Account No.155.)

14 Received an invoice for $2,197.25 from the Dundee Manufacturing Co. for a shipment of radio parts. Date of invoice, October 11; terms, 1/10, n/30.

15 Issued Payroll Voucher No. 11 covering wages earned for the half month as follows:

Warehouse salaries,$1,350.00
Delivery salaries, $170.00
Office salaries, $1,100.00
Sales salaries, $1,010.00

Taxes withheld:
FICA tax, $243.00
Employees' income tax, $768.50

Issued Check No. 8 in payment of Payroll Voucher No. 11. The following accounts will be affected in entering the payroll:

111	Cash
211	FICA Tax Payable
214	Employees' Income Tax Payable
218	Vouchers Payable
5401	Office Salaries Expense
5431	Sales Salaries Expense
5432	Delivery Salaries Expense
5439	Warehouse Salaries Expense

17 Issued a voucher for $100 to be used in purchasing stamps for the office. Cashed Check No. 9 for this amount and obtained the stamps. (Charge to Office Supplies, Account No.152.)

19 Received from the Last National Bank a notice of the maturity of a $1,500 non-interest-bearing note dated

September 30 due them. Issued Check No. 10 for that amount. (Notes Payable, Account No. 216.)

Oct. 20 Received an invoice from Toolers for $81.19, the cost of repairs on warehouse machinery. Issued Check No. 11 in payment. (Repairs, Account No. 5442.)

21 Received an invoice for $1,540.30 from Ultimate Radio & TV for a shipment of merchandise. Date of invoice, October 20; terms, 1/10, n/30.

24 Received an invoice for $219.00 for warehouse supplies purchased from the Central Container Co.; terms, on account. (Warehouse Supplies, Account No. 153.)

26 Received an invoice from Nuland Lifts for $10,279, the cost of a lift truck for use in the warehouse. Terms, net 30 days. (Warehouse Equipment, Account No. 182.)

28 Received an invoice for $1,160.00 from the Private Electric Co. for a shipment of merchandise. Date of invoice, October 27; terms, 2/10, n/30.

31 Issued Payroll Voucher No. 19 covering wages earned for the half month as follows:

Warehouse Salaries, $1,300.00
Delivery Salaries, $170.00
Office Salaries, $1,050.00
Sales Salaries, $1,070.00

Taxes withheld:
FICA Tax, $240.53
Employees' Income Tax, $770.15

Issued Check No. 15 in payment of Payroll Voucher No. 19.

Required: **(1)** Enter the foregoing transactions in the voucher register and check register. **(2)** Foot and prove the footings of both the voucher register and the check register. **(3)** Open an account for vouchers payable and post to it the footings of the Vouchers Payable columns in the voucher register and the check register. Use a T form of account. **(4)** Prove the balance of the vouchers payable account by preparing a schedule of the unpaid vouchers from the voucher register.

PROBLEM 14-B Cash sales and sales on account

Linda Fergy is the owner of a radio, television, and stereo equipment store. Following is a list of the general ledger accounts that are affected by this problem with the September 1 balances indicated:

111 Cash, $2,937.80
131 Accounts Receivable, $4,194.67
411 Sales, $30,657.18

As of September 1, the accounts receivable had debit balances as follows:

Hank Thun, 1512 Blackburn St., Wheaton; $583.22
Allen Gist, 1586 Briarcliffe Blvd., Lombard; $1,093.44
Ursula Flitner, 122 Main St., Wheaton; $1,215.67
Tim Gulstrom, 655 Roosevelt Rd., Glen Ellyn; $659.18
Pat Guhin, 542 Kenilworth, Batavia; $643.16

The narrative of September sales and collections transactions is as follows:

Sept. 1 (Wednesday) Charge sale No. 362, Tim Gulstrom, $408.
3 Cash sales of $512.
4 Collected $1,215.67 on account from Ursula Flitner.
6 Charge sale No. 363, Hank Thun, $167.
8 Collected $659.18 on account from Tim Gulstrom.
10 Charge sale No. 364, Allen Gist, $830.
11 Cash sales of $434.
14 Cash sales of $618.
16 Collected $583.22 on account from Hank Thun.
18 Charge sale No. 365, Pat Guhin, $188.
20 Collected $1,093.44 on account from Allen Gist.
22 Cash sales of $294.
24 Charge sale No. 366, Ursula Flitner, $167.
25 Cash sales of $609.
27 Collected $643.16 on account from Pat Guhin.
29 Charge sale No. 367, Tim Gulstrom, $544.

Required: **(1)** Open the necessary general ledger accounts and enter the September 1 balances, using four-column ledger paper. **(2)** Open the accounts receivable ledger and enter the September 1 balances, using three-column ledger paper. **(3)** Enter the charge sales for September and post directly to the proper customers' accounts, using a sales journal similar to the one reproduced on page 447. **(4)** Enter the cash sales and collections on account for September and post the collections directly to the proper customers' accounts, using a cash receipts journal similar to the one reproduced on page 452. **(5)** Foot, prove the footings, enter the totals, and rule the sales journal and the cash receipts journal. Complete the summary posting and update the account balances. **(6)** Prove the balance of the accounts receivable account by preparing a schedule of the accounts receivable as of September 30.

PROBLEM 15-A The business entity

Ward's Bakery, owned and operated by Lew D. Ward, is in the process of separating the assets and liabilities of the business enterprise from Ward's personal assets and liabilities as of December 31, 19--. Ward has solicited your help.

The list of assets, liabilities, income, and withdrawals is given below:

Cash in bank (Lyon National Bank) for business affairs	$13,950
Cash in bank (Washington Bank) for personal affairs	26,870
Accounts receivable owed to Ward's Bakery	18,470
Allowance for doubtful accounts on Ward's Bakery accounts receivable	795
Merchandise inventory of Ward's Bakery	68,440
Prepaid insurance:	
Lew D. Ward	400
Ward's Bakery	350
Supplies:	
Ward's Bakery	90
Lew D. Ward	115
Store equipment	9,900
Accumulated depreciation on store equipment	4,400
Delivery truck used by the business	9,500
Accumulated depreciation on delivery truck	3,500
Automobile for personal use	8,200
Store building owned as a personal asset (net)	12,600
Real estate investment owned by Ward	7,400
Notes payable to outsiders by Ward	2,000
Notes payable to outsiders by Ward's Bakery	4,000
Accrued interest payable on notes:	
Ward's Bakery	50
Lew D. Ward	40
Accounts payable to outsiders by:	
Lew D. Ward	3,000
Ward's Bakery	10,115
Sales tax owed by bakery	1,865
Taxes payable withheld—Ward's Bakery	880
Notes receivable owed to Ward	3,000
Mortgage due on Ward's home	28,800
Net income of Ward's Bakery for 19--	29,900
Lew D. Ward's withdrawals for 19--	21,000

Required: From the above list **(1)** separate those items that clearly relate to Ward's Bakery, and prepare a balance sheet as of December 31, 19--, in report form. **(2)** The separation of business assets and liabilities from personal assets and liabilities is an adaptation of what accounting concept?

CHAPTER 16

Accounting for Owner's Equity

CHAPTER OBJECTIVES

Careful study of this chapter should enable you to:

- Explain the characteristics, advantages, and disadvantages of the single proprietorship form of business operation, and to account for proprietary transactions.
- Explain the nature of a business partnership and its advantages and disadvantages.
- Explain the manner in which a partnership is formed, and to recognize a partnership agreement.
- Explain and prepare the accounting entries needed for:
  1. The formation of a partnership.
  2. The admission of a new partner, including the possible accounting for goodwill.
  3. The compensation of partners.
  4. The allocation of partnership profits and losses.
  5. The dissolution of a partnership.
- Prepare the owners' equity section of a partnership balance sheet.
- Explain the nature of business corporations and the accounting for corporate owners' (stockholders') equity, including:
  1. The advantages and major disadvantage of a private business corporation.
  2. The manner in which a corporation is organized.
  3. The nature of the ownership interest in a corporation and the nature of its operation.
  4. The preparation of the accounting entries peculiar to a business corporation.
  5. The preparation of the entries required for the incorporation of a single proprietorship and of a partnership.
  6. The preparation of the owners' equity section of a corporation balance sheet.

The accounting equation—ASSETS = LIABILITIES + OWNER'S EQUITY—reflects the fact that both outsiders and insiders have interests in the assets of a business. The claims of the outsiders are known as the liabilities of the business, while the interests of the insiders are known as the owners' or stockholders' equity in the assets of the business. Proper accounting for owners' equity in three types of business organizations will be discussed in this chapter: (1) the single proprietorship, (2) the partnership, and (3) the corporation. Whether an enterprise is operated by an individual as a single proprietorship, by two or more individuals as a partnership, or by stockholders through directors and officers as a corporation has little or no bearing on proper accounting procedure for entering routine transactions. However, there are significant differences in the owners' equity structures of these three types of businesses, and therefore differences in the accounting for and reporting of owners' or stockholders' equity transactions.

THE SINGLE PROPRIETORSHIP

A business that is owned and operated by one person is known as a single proprietorship. When there is only one owner, the amount of the owner's interest in the business is called owner's equity. Sometimes the designations net worth or capital are used.

In small merchandising enterprises and in personal service enterprises the single proprietorship form of organization predominates. The professions of medicine and dentistry, for example, are composed largely of individuals who are engaged in practice as sole owners. One reason for the popularity of the single proprietorship form of operation is that it is easily organized and does not involve formal legal agreement with others as to ownership or conduct. Anyone may engage in a lawful enterprise merely by complying with state and local laws.

Organization of a Single Proprietorship

When operating an enterprise as a sole owner, an individual decides the amount and the nature of the property that will be invested in the business. The original investment may consist of cash only, or of cash and any other property, such as merchandise, office equipment, store equipment, or delivery equipment. The property invested usually is segregated and accounted for separately from other property that may be owned by the proprietor, in accordance with the business entity concept. An individual may engage in more than one enterprise and may operate each enterprise separately as a single proprietorship. In such cases, it may be desirable to keep separate records of the activities of each enterprise.

In comparison with other forms of business organization, the single proprietorship offers certain advantages, such as:

1. Simplicity of organization.
2. Freedom of initiative and industry.
3. Minimizing of government reporting requirements.
4. Strengthening of incentive to individual effort.

The single proprietorship form of organization has some disadvantages, of which the following are the most significant:

1. The amount of available capital may be limited.
2. The amount of available credit may be restricted.
3. The proprietor has sole responsibility for all debts incurred.
4. The proprietor is legally obligated to assume all debts of the business as personal debts.

Accounting Procedure

The accounting procedure for handling the transactions uniquely related to a single proprietorship can be classified into six topics as follows:

1. Owner's equity accounts.
2. Opening entries.
3. Current period proprietary transactions.
4. Closing revenue, expense, and summary accounts.
5. Closing the owner's drawing account.
6. Owner's equity section of a single proprietorship balance sheet.

Owner's Equity Accounts. There are two types of owner's equity accounts: (1) permanent and (2) temporary.

In a single proprietorship, the owner's capital account is the only permanent owner's equity account. The account is usually given the name of the owner of the enterprise followed by "Capital" or "Proprietor."

The temporary owner's equity accounts are those in which increases and decreases in owner's equity arising from the transactions completed during an accounting period are entered, such as the owner's drawing or personal account and all of the revenue and expense accounts. At the end of each year, it is customary to close the temporary revenue and expense accounts by transferring their balances to one or more summary accounts. These summary accounts are then closed to the permanent owner's equity account. The owner's drawing account is also closed to the permanent owner's equity account.

Opening Entries. An individual may invest cash and other property in a single proprietorship enterprise. If the investment consists solely of cash, the opening entry will involve a debit to Cash and a credit to the owner's capital account for the amount invested.

If cash and other property, such as office equipment or store equipment are invested, the opening entry will involve a debit to Cash for the amount of the cash invested, debits to appropriate equipment accounts for the amounts of the other property invested, and a credit to the owner's capital account for the total amount of the investment.

If, at the time of organizing an enterprise, there are any liabilities applicable to the property invested, such as accounts payable, notes payable, or mortgages payable, the amounts of the liabilities should be credited to appropriate liability accounts and the owner's capital account should be credited only for the excess of the amount of the assets invested over the total amount of the liabilities.

For example, assume that Mary Roback starts a merchandising business by investing cash, $8,000, office equipment, $2,000, and store equipment, $1,500. Roback owes $600 on the office equipment. The opening entry in general journal form for the investment is:

Cash	8,000	
Office Equipment	2,000	
Store Equipment	1,500	
Accounts Payable		600
Mary Roback, Capital		10,900
Investment in business.		

Some small business enterprises start and operate with very few records. No journals or ledgers are used. Cash receipts and payments are kept on check stubs. The amounts of accounts receivable and payable can be found only by consulting files of uncollected charge-sales slips and unpaid bills. At the end of a period, various calculations relating to inventory, doubtful accounts, expired insurance, depreciation, and accruals are made in informal fashion and the several bits of information are pieced together to prepare an income statement and a balance sheet. These statements are often incorrect. Conditions and facts may have been overlooked. Business papers may have been lost. The absence of double-entry records means that one method of verifying the mathematical accuracy of the assembled figures is not available.

While such informal accounting practices may barely suffice when the enterprise is small and transactions are few, the time will come when a formal accounting information system is needed. To start such a system, it is necessary to prepare a balance sheet from the information at hand and to use this as a basis for an opening journal entry for the assets, liabilities, and owner's equity of the enterprise.

For example, assume that H. A. Erk has been operating a business without any formal, double-entry accounting records. After several months, Erk decides that proper records are necessary. With the help of an accountant, the following balance sheet for the business is constructed. The information supplied by the balance sheet is used in preparing the general journal entry shown at the top of page 486.

H. A. ERK
Balance Sheet
December 31, 1986

Assets			**Liabilities**		
Cash		$ 4,550	Notes payable	$ 4,000	
Accounts receivable	$ 7,200		Accounts payable	5,800	
Less allowance for doubtful accounts	800	6,400	Total liabilities		$ 9,800
Merchandise inventory		17,340			
Store equipment	$10,000		**Owner's Equity**		
Less accumulated depreciation	1,000	9,000	H.A. Erk, capital		27,490
Total assets		$37,290	Total liabilities and owner's equity		$37,290

Jan. 2	Cash	4,550	
	Accounts Receivable	7,200	
	Merchandise Inventory	17,340	
	Store Equipment	10,000	
	Notes Payable		4,000
	Accounts Payable		5,800
	Allowance for Doubtful Accounts		800
	Accumulated Depreciation—Store Equipment		1,000
	H.A. Erk, Capital		27,490

After the necessary accounts in the general ledger have been opened, the debits and the credits of the opening journal entry are posted in the usual manner. Each asset account is debited and each liability account, the allowance for doubtful accounts, and accumulated depreciation are credited for the respective amounts shown in the balance sheet. Erk's capital account is credited for the equity in the business. In opening the accounts receivable ledger, the balances of the accounts with customers are entered directly from a schedule of accounts receivable. In opening the accounts payable ledger, the balances of the accounts with suppliers are entered directly from a schedule of accounts payable.

Current Period Proprietary Transactions. Certain types of transactions may be referred to as proprietary transactions because they affect either the owner's drawing account or the capital account. The following are typical proprietary transactions:

1. Periodic withdrawals of cash for personal use of owner.
2. Payment of owner's personal or family bills with business cash.
3. Withdrawal of cash or other assets by the owner intended as a partial liquidation of the business.
4. Investment of cash or other assets by owner intended as a permanent increase in assets and owner's equity.

Cash withdrawn periodically by the owner for personal use is charged to the owner's drawing or personal account on the assumption that such amounts represent withdrawals in anticipation of income. These withdrawals are sometimes regarded as salary or compensation for personal services rendered; however, they actually represent decreases in the owner's equity in the business and cannot be treated as operating expenses of the enterprise.

The payment of personal or family bills with business funds should be entered as a withdrawal of cash by the owner. It is quite common for a sole owner of a business or professional enterprise to pay all personal, family or household bills by issuing checks against the same bank account that is used for business expenditures of the enterprise. However, care should be used in entering all checks issued. Those representing personal or family expenditures should be charged to the owner's drawing or personal account. Those representing business expenditures should be charged to the proper expense, asset, or liability accounts.

An owner may, at any time, permanently withdraw a portion of the cash or other assets invested in the business, or make additional investments in the business in the form of cash or other property. Withdrawals are considered to be decreases in the permanent invested capital and should be charged to the capital account. Additional investments are considered to be increases in capital and should be credited to the capital account.

Closing Revenue, Expense, and Summary Accounts. At the end of each year, it is customary to close the temporary owner's equity accounts. As the temporary accounts are closed, their balances usually are transferred to an account entitled Expense and Revenue Summary.

In a merchandising enterprise, however, there also may be a summary account called Cost of Goods Sold. In the closing process, the cost of goods sold account is debited for (1) the amount of the merchandise inventory at the beginning of the year, and (2) the amount of the purchases for the year; it is credited for (1) the amount of purchases returns and allowances for the year, and (2) the amount of the merchandise inventory at the end of the year. After transferring these amounts, the balance of the account represents the cost of goods sold during the year, and it is in turn transferred to Expense and Revenue Summary. Note that this is a more indirect closing procedure than the approach using only the Expense and Revenue Summary that was discussed in Chapter 10.

The difference between the amount of debits and the amount of credits to the Expense and Revenue Summary represents the amount of the net income or the net loss for the year. If the summary account has a credit balance, it represents net income; if the account has a debit balance, it represents net loss. The balance of the expense and revenue summary account at the end of the accounting period is then transferred to the owner's capital account by means of a journal entry. If the expense and revenue summary account has a credit balance, the journal entry will involve a debit to Expense and Revenue Summary and a credit to the owner's capital account for the amount of the net income. If the summary account has a debit balance, the journal entry will involve a debit to the owner's capital account and a credit to Expense and Revenue Summary for the amount of the net loss.

Closing the Owner's Drawing Account. The owner's drawing account usually is closed at the end of each year by transferring its balance directly to the owner's capital account. The drawing account usually has a debit balance, and it may be closed by means of a journal entry debiting the owner's capital account and crediting the drawing account for the amount of its balance.

After transferring the balances of the expense and revenue summary account and the owner's drawing account to the owner's capital account, the balance of the owner's capital account represents the owner's equity in the enterprise at the end of the year.

Owner's Equity Section of a Single Proprietorship Balance Sheet. The method of exhibiting the owner's equity of a single proprietorship in the balance sheet is shown on pages 11, 142, and 296. There may be some variation in the account titles used by different enterprises. However, the final results should be the same since the balance sheet is an exhibit of the accounting elements: (1) the assets, (2) the liabilities, and (3) the owner's equity. The owner's equity section of the balance sheet should be arranged to show the owner's equity in the business at the beginning of the accounting period, the net increase or the net decrease in the equity during the period, and the amount of equity at the end of the period.

BUILDING YOUR ACCOUNTING KNOWLEDGE

1. Identify four advantages of a single proprietorship in comparison with other forms of business organization.
2. Identify four disadvantages of a single proprietorship form of business organization.
3. What are the two types of owner's equity accounts? Give examples of each in a single proprietorship.

4. When a set of formal, double-entry accounting records is started by a single proprietor for the first time, what is the source of information for preparing the opening entry?
5. How should the payment of personal or family bills using business funds be entered by the single proprietorship?
6. Describe the use of a summary cost of goods sold account in the closing process of a merchandising type of enterprise.
7. How is the owner's drawing account usually closed at the end of each year?
8. How should the owner's equity section of a single proprietorship balance sheet be arranged?

APPLYING ACCOUNTING CONCEPTS

Exercise 16-1. Sherbette Drewry started her merchandising business on November 1 by investing cash, $9,500, office equipment, $6,000, and store furniture and fixtures, $4,500. Drewry owes $2,500 on the store furniture and fixtures.

Give the general journal entry for opening the business.

Exercise 16-2. Bob Petersen has been operating a small retail business without maintaining any formal, double-entry accounting records. On April 30 he decided that proper records are necessary and, with the help of his accountant, constructed a current balance sheet that consists of the following accounts:

Cash	$ 5,650
Accounts receivable	8,300
Allowance for doubtful accounts	1,900
Merchandise inventory	18,440
Store equipment	21,000
Accumulated depreciation on store equipment	12,000
Notes payable	5,100
Accounts payable	6,900
Bob Petersen, capital	27,490

Using this information from the balance sheet, prepare in general journal form the opening entry for Petersen's business.

Report No. 16-1

Complete Report No. 16-1 in the study assignments and submit your working papers to the instructor for approval. Then continue with the following textbook discussion until Report No. 16-2 is required.

THE PARTNERSHIP

When two or more individuals engage in an enterprise as co-owners, the organization is known as a partnership. This form of organization is common to practically all types of enterprises. However, it is more popular among personal service enterprises than among merchandise enterprises. For example, the partnership form of organization is quite common in the legal and public accounting professions.

Organization of a Partnership

The Uniform Partnership Act states that "a partnership is an association of two or more persons who carry on, as co-owners, a business for profit." The partners may, by agreement, unite their capital, labor, skill, or experience in the conduct of a business for their mutual benefit. While under certain circumstances a partnership may be formed by means of an oral or implied agreement, it is desirable that a partnership agreement be evidenced by a written contract. A written agreement containing the various provisions under which a partnership is to operate is known as a partnership agreement. There is no standard form of partnership agreement, but there are certain provisions that are essential, such as:

1. Date of agreement.
2. Names of the partners.
3. Kind of business to be conducted.
4. Length of time the partnership is to run.
5. Name and location of the business.
6. Investment of each partner.
7. Basis on which profits or losses are to be shared by the partners.
8. Limitation of partners' rights and activities.
9. Salary allowances to partners.
10. Division of assets upon dissolution of the partnership.
11. Signatures of the partners.

The conventional form of partnership agreement is reproduced on the following page.

In comparison with the single proprietorship form of organization, the partnership form offers certain advantages, such as the following:

PARTNERSHIP AGREEMENT

THIS CONTRACT, made and entered into on the first day of July 1, 19--, by and between Harlan Spinner of Indianapolis, Indiana, and Carol Thomas of the same city and state.

WITNESSETH: That the said parties have this day formed a partnership for the purpose of engaging in and conducting a wholesale and retail business in the city of Indianapolis under the following stipulations which are a part of this contract:

FIRST: The said partnership is to continue for a term of twenty-five years from July 1, 19--.

SECOND: The business is to be conducted under the firm name of Spinner & Thomas, at 1604 N. Milburn, Indianapolis, Indiana.

THIRD: The investments are as follows: Harlan Spinner, cash, $35,000; Carol Thomas, cash, $20,000. These invested assets are partnership property.

FOURTH: Each partner is to devote his/her entire time and attention to the business and to engage in no other business enterprise without the written consent of the other partner.

FIFTH: During the operation of this partnership, neither partner is to become surety or bonding agent for anyone without the written consent of the other partner.

SIXTH: Each partner is to receive a salary of $28,800 a year, payable $1,200 in cash on the fifteenth day and last business day of each month. At the end of each annual fiscal period, the net income or the net loss shown by the income statement, after the salaries of the two partners have been allowed, is to be shared as follows: Harlan Spinner, 60 percent; Carol Thomas, 40 percent.

SEVENTH: Neither partner is to withdraw assets in excess of his/her salary, any part of the assets invested, or assets in anticipation of net income to be earned, without the written consent of the other partner.

EIGHTH: In the case of the death or the legal disability of either partner, the other partner is to continue the operations of the business until the close of the annual fiscal period on the following June 30. At that time the continuing partner is to be given an option to buy the interest of the deceased or incapacitated partner at not more than 10 percent above the value of the deceased or incapacitated partner's proprietary interest as shown by the balance of his/her capital account after the books are closed on June 30. It is agreed that this purchase price is to be paid one half in cash and the balance in four equal installments payable quarterly.

NINTH: At the conclusion of this contract, unless it is mutually agreed to continue the operation of the business under a new contract, the assets of the partnership, after the liabilities are paid, are to be divided in proportion to the net credit of each partner's capital account on that date.

IN WITNESS WHEREOF, the parties aforesaid have hereunto set their hands and affixed their seals on the day and year above written.

Harlan Spinner (Seal)

Carol Thomas (Seal)

Partnership Agreement

1. The ability and the experience of the partners are combined in one enterprise.
2. More capital may be raised because the resources of the partners are combined.
3. Credit may be improved because each general partner is personally liable for partnership debts.

There are some disadvantages that are peculiar to the partnership form of organization, such as the following:

1. Each partner is individually liable for all of the debts of the partnership. The liability of each partner is not limited to a pro rata share of the partnership debts. Each partner is personally liable for all of the debts of the business to the same extent as if the business were a sole proprietorship. Under the laws of some states, certain partners may limit their liability. At least one partner, however, must be a general partner who is responsible for all of the debts of the partnership.
2. The interest of a partner in the partnership cannot be transferred without the consent of the other partners.
3. Termination of the partnership agreement, bankruptcy of the firm, or death of one of the partners dissolves the partnership.

Accounting Procedure

In accounting for the operations of a partnership, it is necessary to keep a separate capital account for each partner. It is also customary to keep a separate drawing or personal account for each partner. While no new principles are involved in keeping these accounts, care should be used in preparing the opening entry and in entering any transactions thereafter that affect the respective interests of the partners.

Opening Entries. Partners may invest cash and other property in the partnership. Certain liabilities may be assumed by the partnership, such as accounts payable, notes payable, and mortgages payable. In opening the books for a partnership, it is customary to prepare a separate journal entry for the investment of each partner. The proper asset accounts should be debited for the amounts invested, the proper liability accounts should be credited for the amounts of obligations assumed, and each partner's capital account should be credited for the residual equity in the assets. The opening entries for Spinner & Thomas based on the partnership agreement reproduced on page 491 may be made in general journal form, as follows:

Cash	35,000	
Harlan Spinner, Capital		35,000
H. Spinner invested $35,000 in cash.		

Cash	20,000	
Carol Thomas, Capital		20,000
C. Thomas invested $20,000 in cash.		

If, instead of investing $35,000 in cash, Spinner invested office equipment valued at $4,000 on which is owed $1,050, delivery equipment valued at $4,600 on which is owed $950 represented by a note, and $28,400 in cash, the proper opening entry in general journal form for the investment should be as follows:

Cash	28,400	
Office Equipment	4,000	
Delivery Equipment	4,600	
Vouchers Payable		1,050
Note Payable		950
Harlan Spinner, Capital		35,000
H. Spinner's investment in partnership.		

Two or more individuals who have been engaged in business as sole owners may form a partnership for the purpose of combining their businesses. Their respective balance sheets may be the basis for the opening entries for the investments of such partners. For example, assume that on April 1, S. H. Schoen and L. A. Starks form a partnership under the firm name of Schoen & Starks to continue the conduct of the businesses which they have been operating as sole owners. The balance sheets reproduced on page 494 are made a part of the partnership agreement. They agree to invest their assets and also that the partnership shall assume the liabilities shown in their respective balance sheets. Each partner is to receive credit for the equity in the assets invested, and the profits and losses are to be shared on a 50-50 basis. In case of dissolution, the assets are to be distributed between the partners in the ratio of their capital interests at the time of dissolution.

S. H. SCHOEN
Balance Sheet
March 31, 1986

Assets			Liabilities		
Cash		$ 3,172	Notes payable	$ 1,800	
Accounts receivable	$ 2,762		Accounts payable	5,041	
Less allowance for doubtful accounts	215	2,547	Total liabilities		$ 6,841
Merchandise inventory		12,287			
Store equipment	$ 1,920		**Owner's Equity**		
Less accumulated depreciation	500	1,420	S. H. Schoen, capital		12,585
Total assets		$19,426	Total liabilities and owner's equity		$19,426

L. A. STARKS
Balance Sheet
March 31, 1986

Assets			Liabilities		
Cash		$ 1,772	Notes payable	$ 3,000	
Accounts receivable	$ 2,640		Accounts payable	6,619	
Less allowance for doubtful accounts	360	2,280	Total liabilities		$ 9,619
Merchandise inventory		14,846			
Supplies		143			
Office equipment	$ 2,160		**Owner's Equity**		
Less accumulated depreciation	550	1,610	L.A. Starks, capital		12,832
Store equipment	$ 2,400				
Less accumulated depreciation	600	1,800			
Total assets		$22,451	Total liabilities and owner's equity		$22,451

When two single proprietors decide to combine their businesses, generally accepted accounting principles usually require that non-cash assets (primarily inventories and long-term assets) be taken over at their fair market values as of the date of formation of the partnership. Since it probably cannot be determined as of March 31, 1986, which of the accounts receivable may later prove to be uncollectible in whole or in part, the amount of each accounts receivable balance cannot be adjusted for the currently accumulated allowance for doubtful accounts. It is, therefore, usual practice to enter the full amount of the accounts receivable as a debit and the amount of the allowance for doubtful accounts as a credit in placing each partner's investment in the books of the partnership. In this way, the accounts receivable are entered at their approximate fair market value. Subsequent end-of-period adjustments of the allowance for doubtful accounts on the books of the partnership will reflect future collection experience with respect to the combined accounts receivable of Schoen & Starks. Any accounts receivable on either set of books considered to be uncollectible as of March 31, 1986, should be written off by a debit to the Allowance for Doubtful Accounts and a credit to Accounts Receivable. None was so considered in this case.

Because both Schoen & Starks had been using the fifo method of inventory costing, the values shown for merchandise inventories on their respective balance sheets are mutually acceptable as approximations of fair market value as of March 31, 1986. This is because under the fifo method, the most recently purchased inventory is considered to be still on hand. If Schoen or Starks had been using some other inventory costing method, the merchandise inventory amounts might require restatement to reflect the appropriate fair market value, with effects on the partner's capital accounts similar to those for long-term assets discussed below.

It is determined that the fair market value of Schoen's store equipment as of March 31, 1986, is $1,800, so this amount should be entered on the books of the new partnership, rather than the undepreciated cost of $1,420 ($1,920 − $500) shown on Schoen's balance sheet as of that date. In like manner, it is determined that the fair market values of Starks' office equipment and store equipment as of March 31, 1986, are $1,925 and $2,100 respectively, so these amounts should be entered on the books of the new partnership, rather than the respective undepreciated costs of $1,610 ($2,160 − $550) and $1,800 ($2,400 − $600) shown on Starks' balance sheet as of that date. The differences between the fair market values and the undepreciated costs of the long-term assets contributed by each partner are reflected in the respective credits to the partners' capital accounts of $12,965 and $13,447 shown in the opening entries at the top of the following page.

For tax purposes, S. H. Schoen must use the undepreciated cost of $1,420 to value the store equipment investment, and L. A. Starks must use the undepreciated costs of $1,610 and $1,800 to value the office equipment and store equipment respectively. Their net capital investments for tax purposes would thus be $12,585 and $12,832 respectively, which are the amounts shown as owner's equity on their March 31, 1986, balance sheets.

April 1	Cash	3,172		
	Accounts Receivable	2,762		
	Merchandise Inventory	12,287		
	Store Equipment	1,800		
	Notes Payable		1,800	
	Accounts Payable		5,041	
	Allowance for Doubtful Accounts		215	
	S. H. Schoen, Capital		12,965*	
	S. H. Schoen's investment in partnership.			

*S. H. Schoen, Capital (before partnership)		$12,585	
Add: Fair market value of store equipment	$1,800		
Undepreciated cost	1,420	380	
		$12,965	

April 1	Cash	1,772		
	Accounts Receivable	2,640		
	Merchandise Inventory	14,846		
	Supplies	143		
	Office Equipment	1,925		
	Store Equipment	2,100		
	Notes Payable		3,000	
	Accounts Payable		6,619	
	Allowance for Doubtful Accounts		360	
	L. A. Starks, Capital		13,447*	
	L. A. Starks' investment in partnership.			

*L. A. Starks, Capital (before partnership)			$12,832
Add: Fair market value of office equipment	$1,925		
Undepreciated cost	1,610	$315	
Fair market value of store equipment	$2,100		
Undepreciated cost	1,800	300	615
			$13,447

Observe that the ratio of the partners' investments in the partnership ($12,965 to $13,447) is not exactly the same as their profit-and-loss sharing ratio (50% each). The basis on which profits and losses are to be shared is a matter of agreement between the partners, and not necessarily the same as their investment ratio. There are factors other than the assets invested that may enter into a profit-and-loss sharing agreement. For example, one partner may contribute most of the assets but render no services, while the other partner may contribute less in assets but devote full time to the activities of the partnership.

Admitting a New Partner. A new partner may be admitted to a partnership by agreement among the existing partners. The admission of a new partner calls for the dissolution of the old partnership and the creation of a new partnership. A new partnership agreement that includes all of the necessary provisions should be prepared. For example, assume that Schoen and Starks admit G. E. Monahan as a new partner as of July 1, and agree to share profits and losses on the basis of their capital interests. If Monahan's investment consisted of cash only, the proper entry to admit Monahan to the partnership would involve a debit to the cash account and a credit to Monahan's capital account for the amount invested. If Monahan has been operating a business as a sole owner and the business is taken over by the partnership, Monahan's balance sheet reproduced below will serve as a basis for preparing the opening entry. Assume that, as of July 1, Monahan

G. E. MONAHAN
Balance Sheet
June 30, 1986

Assets			Liabilities		
Cash		$ 2,992	Notes payable	$ 4,524	
Accounts receivable	$ 7,145		Accounts payable	3,775	
Less allowance for doubtful accounts	539	6,606	Total liabilities		$ 8,299
Merchandise inventory		13,645			
			Owner's Equity		
			G.E. Monahan, capital		14,944
Total assets		$23,243	Total liabilities and owner's equity		$23,243

was admitted to the partnership. The assets listed in the balance sheet are taken over, the liabilities are assumed, and Monahan is given credit for the equity in the assets of the business.

The proper entry in general journal form to admit Monahan as a partner is as follows:

July 1	Cash	2,992	
	Accounts Receivable	7,145	
	Merchandise Inventory	13,645	
	Notes Payable		4,524
	Accounts Payable		3,775
	Allowance for Doubtful Accounts		539
	G.E. Monahan, Capital		14,944
	G.E. Monahan admitted to partnership.		

Because Monahan has no knowledge of any uncollectible accounts receivable as of June 30, 1986, and has been using the fifo method of inventory costing, no fair market value adjustments of the noncash asset account balances were made for purposes of this entry.

Goodwill. Some business organizations earn profits that are very large in relation to the stated amounts of the assets. The unique earning power of a business, which may be due to exceptional management, good location, or other factors, is called **goodwill**. Since goodwill is difficult to measure and may not prove to be permanent, accountants do not permit its formal recognition as an asset unless it has been purchased.

For example, assume that Schoen & Starks purchased the business of G. E. Monahan for $20,000 cash, acquiring all of the business assets except cash and assuming the business liabilities. If the book values of Monahan's net accounts receivable and merchandise inventory were considered to be reasonable approximations of their fair market values ($6,606 + $13,645 = $20,251), and Monahan's total liabilities of $8,299 were assumed, Schoen & Starks paid $20,000 for assets with net values of $11,952 ($20,251 − $8,299). The $8,048 difference between the $20,000 paid and the $11,952 of specific assets acquired may be considered to be the price paid for the goodwill of Monahan's business. The transaction may be entered as follows:

July 1	Accounts Receivable	7,145	
	Merchandise Inventory	13,645	
	Goodwill	8,048	
	Notes Payable		4,524
	Accounts Payable		3,775
	Allowance for Doubtful Accounts		539
	Cash		20,000
	Purchased G.E. Monahan's business.		

It is also permissible to recognize goodwill if a new partner is taken into a firm and is allowed a capital interest in excess of the net assets that were invested. For example, suppose that instead of purchasing Monahan's business, Schoen and Starks had agreed to give Monahan a capital interest of $22,992 in exchange for Monahan's business assets and liabilities (including the business cash). Also assume that, as in the previous case, the book values of Monahan's noncash assets were considered to be reasonable approximations of their fair market values. Monahan's investment may be entered as follows:

July 1	Cash	2,992	
	Accounts Receivable	7,145	
	Merchandise Inventory	13,645	
	Goodwill	8,048	
	Notes Payable		4,524
	Accounts Payable		3,775
	Allowance for Doubtful Accounts		539
	G.E. Monahan, Capital		22,992
	G.E. Monahan admitted to partnership.		

Goodwill is considered to be an intangible long-term asset. It is usually reported in the balance sheet as the last item in the asset section. Under present accounting rules, it may be amortized over a future period not to exceed 40 years.

Compensation of Partners. The compensation of partners (other than their share of profits) may be in the nature of salaries, royalties, commissions, bonuses, or other compensation. The amount of each partner's compensation and the method of accounting for it should be stated in the partnership agreement. For example, the partnership agreement between Spinner & Thomas shown on page 491 states that each partner is to receive a salary of $2,400 a month. When all partners receive the same salaries and when profits and losses are shared equally, it is immaterial whether the salaries are treated as an expense of the partnership or as withdrawals of anticipated profits. Under the federal income tax law, salaries or other compensation paid to partners for services rendered may not be claimed as a deduction from gross income in the income tax information return of the partnership unless such salaries are guaranteed. In such event, the amounts may be treated as deductions. (The partners, of course, must report compensation income in their individual returns.) However, apart from income tax considerations, the partnership agreement may provide that partners' salaries are to be treated as operating expenses in computing the net income or the net loss to be shared by the partners.

If partners' salaries are treated as operating expenses, it is usually advisable to keep a separate salary account for each partner. For example, the salaries specified in the partnership agreement between Harlan Spinner and Carol Thomas are to be treated as operating expenses. If the salaries are paid regularly, such as monthly or semi-monthly, it will be necessary only to debit each partner's salary account and to credit the cash account. Instead of paying partners' salaries regularly in cash, they may be credited to the partners' drawing accounts. The partners may then draw against such salaries at will. Under this plan, the proper entry for each partner's salary on each payday is to debit the salary account and to credit the drawing account for the proper amount. If partners' salaries are not treated as an expense of the partnership, it is not necessary to keep a salary account for each partner. Thus, amounts withdrawn by the partners as compensation for services may simply be charged to their respective drawing accounts.

Allocation of Partnership Profits and Losses. The partnership agreement should specify the basis on which profits and losses are to be shared by the partners. In the absence of any agreement between the partners, profits and losses must be shared equally regardless of the ratio of the partners' investments. If the partnership agreement specifies how profits are to be shared but does not specify how losses are to be shared, the losses must be shared on the same basis as that indicated for the profits.

After closing the temporary accounts into Expense and Revenue Summary at the end of the accounting period, the balance of the summary account represents either net income or net loss. If the account has a credit balance, it represents net income; if the account has a debit balance, it represents net loss.

The balance of the expense and revenue summary account should be allocated in accordance with the partnership agreement. If the account has a credit balance, the entry to close the account requires a debit to Expense and Revenue Summary and credits to the partners' drawing or capital accounts for the proper share of the net income in each case. Because the partners may formally or informally agree that they will not withdraw any of their permanent investments without mutual consent, it may be preferable to credit their drawing accounts with their respective shares of net income. Any credit balances in partners' drawing or personal accounts can then be reduced by withdrawals without restriction.

Dissolution of a Partnership. Dissolution of a partnership may be brought about through bankruptcy or the death of one of the partners. No partner can retire from the partnership without the consent of the remaining partners. To do so would constitute a violation of the partnership agreement and would make the retiring partner liable to the remaining partners for any loss resulting from the retirement.

By agreement, a partner may retire and be permitted to withdraw assets equal to, less than, or greater than the amount of the retiring partner's interest in the partnership. The book value of a partner's interest is shown by the credit balance of the partner's capital account after all profits or losses have been allocated in accordance with the agreement and the books are closed. If upon retirement cash or other assets equal to the credit balance of the retiring partner's capital account are withdrawn, the transaction will have no effect upon the capital of the remaining partners.

Suppose, for example, that sometime after G. E. Monahan had been taken into the partnership of Schoen & Starks, Monahan expressed a desire to retire and the partners agreed to the withdrawal of cash equal to the amount of Monahan's equity in the assets of the partnership. After closing the temporary owner's equity accounts into Expense and Revenue Summary, and after allocating the net income and closing the partners' drawing accounts, assume that the partners' capital accounts had credit balances as follows:

S. H. Schoen	$11,000
L. A. Starks.....................	14,000
G. E. Monahan	19,000

This indicates that the book value of Monahan's interest in the partnership amounts to $19,000. If this amount is withdrawn in cash, the entry in general journal form for the transaction on the books of the partnership is as follows:

G. E. Monahan, Capital................................	19,000	
Cash		19,000
G. E. Monahan retired, withdrawing $19,000 in equity settlement.		

While the transaction involves a decrease in cash with a corresponding decrease in the total capital of the partnership, it does not affect the equity of the remaining partners. Schoen still has an equity of $11,000 and Starks an equity of $14,000 in the partnership assets.

If a retiring partner agrees to withdraw less than the book value of the interest, the effect of the transaction will increase the capital accounts of the remaining partners. To enter such a transaction it is necessary to debit the retiring partner's account for the amount of its credit balance, to credit the assets withdrawn, and to credit the difference to the capital accounts of the remaining partners. Thus, if Monahan agreed to withdraw only $15,000 in settlement of the interest, the transaction should be entered in the books of the partership as follows:

G. E. Monahan, Capital	19,000	
Cash		15,000
S. H. Schoen, Capital		1,760
L. A. Starks, Capital		2,240
G. E. Monahan retired, withdrawing $15,000 in equity settlement.		

The difference between Monahan's equity in the assets of the partnership and the amount of cash withdrawn is $4,000 ($19,000 − $15,000). This difference is divided between the remaining partners on the basis stipulated in the partnership agreement; i.e., the ratio of their capital interests after allocating net income and closing their drawing accounts. On this basis, Schoen is credited for 11/25 [$11,000 ÷ ($11,000 + $14,000)] of $4,000, or $1,760, while Starks is credited for 14/25 [$14,000 ÷ ($11,000 + $14,000)] of $4,000, or $2,240.

If a partner is permitted to withdraw more than the book value of the interest, the effect of the transaction will decrease the capital accounts of the remaining partners. Thus, if Schoen and Starks agreed to the withdrawal of $25,000 in settlement of Monahan's interest, the transaction should be entered in the books of the partnership as follows:

G.E. Monahan, Capital	19,000	
S.H. Schoen, Capital	2,640	
L.A. Starks, Capital	3,360	
Cash		25,000
G.E. Monahan retired, withdrawing $25,000 in equity settlement.		

The excess of the amount of cash withdrawn over Monahan's equity in the partnership ($6,000) is divided between the remaining partners on the basis stipulated in the partnership agreement. Thus, Schoen is debited for 11/25 of $6,000 or $2,640, while Starks is debited for 14/25 of $6,000 or $3,360.

When a partner retires from the business, the partner's interest may be purchased by one or more of the remaining partners or by an outside party. If the retiring partner's interest is sold to one of the remaining partners, the retiring partner's equity is merely transferred to the other partner. Thus, if instead of withdrawing cash in settlement of the equity in the partnership, Monahan's equity is sold to Schoen, the entry for the transaction on the books of the partnership is as follows:

G.E. Monahan, Capital	19,000	
S.H. Schoen, Capital		19,000
S.H. Schoen purchased G.E. Monahan's interest in the partnership.		

The amount paid to Monahan by Schoen is a personal transaction not entered on the books of the partnership. Any gain or loss resulting from the transaction is a personal gain or loss of the withdrawing partner and not of the firm. Thus, whatever amount is involved, the credit in Monahan's account is to be transferred to Schoen's account.

Owners' Equity Section of a Partnership Balance Sheet. The method of showing the equity of the partners in the balance sheet of a partnership is similar to that of a single proprietorship, except that the equity of each partner should be shown separately. An illustration of the owners' equity section of a balance sheet for the partnership of Schoen and Starks is shown below, assuming the following:

Net income for the year	$25,000
Profit and loss ratio	50-50
Withdrawals during the year:	
Schoen	$5,000
Starks	6,000

Owners' Equity

S.H. Schoen:			
Capital, April 1, 1986		$12,965	
Net income (50% of $25,000)	$12,500		
Less withdrawals	5,000	7,500	
Capital, March 31, 1987			$20,465
L.A. Starks			
Capital, April 1, 1986		$13,447	
Net income (50% of $25,000)	$12,500		
Less withdrawals	6,000	6,500	
Capital, March 31, 1987			19,947
Total owners' equity			$40,412

BUILDING YOUR ACCOUNTING KNOWLEDGE

1. Identify eleven essential provisions of a partnership agreement.
2. Identify three advantages of a partnership in comparison with a single proprietorship.
3. Identify three disadvantages of a partnership form of business organization.
4. When two single proprietors decide to combine their businesses, at what values do generally accepted accounting principles usually require that noncash assets be taken over by the partnership?
5. When a new partner who has been the sole owner of a business is admitted to a partnership by having the partnership take over the old business, what usually serves as the basis for preparing the opening entry?
6. Why do accountants not permit the formal recognition of goodwill as an asset unless it has been purchased? Over what maximum future period may goodwill be amortized?
7. In the absence of any agreement between the partners, how must profits and losses be shared? If the partnership agreement specifies how profits are to be shared, in the absence of any agreement between the partners as to how losses are to be shared, what must be true with respect to losses?
8. Identify two ways in which a partnership may be dissolved without the consent of the remaining partners. What form of partnership dissolution requires the consent of the remaining partners?

APPLYING ACCOUNTING CONCEPTS

Exercise 16-3. J.R. Scronce and S.L. Machol agreed on September 1 to go into business as partners. According to the agreement, Scronce is to contribute $45,000 in cash. Machol is to contribute office equipment valued at $3,000 on which $1,000 is owed, delivery equipment valued at $3,500 on which $850 is owed in the form of a note, and enough cash to make his capital investment equal to that of Scronce.

Provide the opening entry in general journal form for the investment.

Exercise 16-4. Designer Carpets, owned by Larry Smythe, and Rudy's Carpets, owned by Rudy Reaves, have decided to combine their business on January 1.

Designer Carpets has the following assets and liabilities:

Cash	$ 25,145
Accounts receivable	32,000
Allowance for doubtful accounts	1,600
Store equipment	27,000
Accumulated depreciation on store equipment	9,000
Merchandise inventory	115,000
Notes payable	65,000
Accounts payable	38,000

Rudy's Carpets has the following assets and liabilities:

Cash	$ 36,362
Accounts receivable	25,500
Allowance for doubtful accounts	1,300
Merchandise inventory	69,000
Office equipment	33,000
Accumulated depreciation on office equipment	11,000
Notes payable	30,000
Accounts payable	57,500

Smythe and Reaves agree that since both have been using the fifo method of valuing the inventory, these amounts are stated at fair market value. The fair market value of the store equipment is $16,000 and the fair market value of the office equipment is $20,000.

Prepare the opening entries in general journal form to enter the investments of Smythe and Reaves.

Exercise 16-5. Smythe and Reaves decided to admit Ralph Anderson, the sole owner of another carpet store, as a new partner on January 1. Anderson's business has the following assets and liabilities:

Cash	$ 30,993
Accounts receivable	18,200
Allowance for doubtful accounts	1,600
Merchandise inventory	85,600
Notes payable	30,000
Accounts payable	10,100

Anderson has no knowledge of any uncollectible accounts receivable as of January 1 and has been using the fifo method of inventory costing, so that no fair market value adjustments of the noncash asset account balances are necessary.

Give the entry in general journal form to admit Ralph Anderson as a partner.

Exercise 16-6. Refer to Exercise 5. Assume that Smythe and Reaves purchased the Anderson business for $77,100 cash, acquiring all of the noncash business assets and assuming the business liabilities. Determine the price paid for the goodwill of Anderson's business and give the entry in general journal form to enter the transaction in the accounting records of the Smythe and Reaves partnership.

Exercise 16-7. Refer to Exercise 16-4. Assume the following end-of-the-year information related to the Smythe and Reaves partnership. Net income for the year was $88,000; Smythe received 60% of the profits and Reaves received 40%; Smythe withdrew $16,000 during the year and Reaves withdrew $12,000.

Prepare the owners' equity section of the balance sheet for the partnership as of December 31, 19--.

Report No. 16-2

Complete Report No. 16-2 in the study assignments and submit your working papers to the instructor for approval. Then continue with the textbook discussion until Report No. 16-3 is required.

THE CORPORATION

A private corporation is an artificial person created by law for a specific purpose. A corporation differs from a single proprietorship or a partnership with respect to organization, ownership, and distribution of net income or net loss.

In comparison with a partnership, the corporate form of organization has several advantages. The most important of these are:

1. Except in very unusual cases, the owners (stockholders) have no personal liability for the debts of the corporation.
2. The shares of ownership are easily transferred from one person to another.
3. The corporation has a perpetual life that is independent of the lives of its owners.
4. More capital may be raised because the resources of numerous stockholders are combined.

A major disadvantage of the corporate form of organization is that the net income of a corporation is taxed and any cash dividends resulting from that income are also taxable to the stockholders, resulting in so-called double taxation.

Organization of a Corporation

In order to incorporate an enterprise, a charter must be obtained from the state in which the corporation is to be formed. The persons who file articles of incorporation are known as the incorporators. Such persons must be competent to contract, some or all of them must be citizens of the state in which the articles are to be filed, and usually each incorporator is required to be a subscriber for one or more shares of the capital stock. All of the incorporators must sign the articles of incorporation.

The procedure in incorporating an enterprise must conform to the laws of the state in which it is desired to incorporate. The laws of the different states vary considerably in their provisions relating to the organization of corporations. Persons desiring to incorporate a business should acquaint themselves with the laws of the particular state in which they wish to incorporate, as it will be necessary to comply with the laws of that state.

Ownership of a Corporation. The owners' equity in a corporation is called capital stock. To make it possible to have many owners—often with different ownership interests—the capital stock is divided into units called shares. The persons forming a corporation (the incorporators) and those who wish to become owners subscribe for shares. Each subscriber agrees to buy a certain number of shares for a certain amount per share. Typically, payment is made in cash, although assets other than cash are used sometimes. All parties owning shares of stock in a corporation are known as stockholders (sometimes called shareholders).

Capital Stock. The charter obtained by a business corporation specifies the amount of capital stock that it is authorized to issue. Capital stock may or may not have par value. Par value is a technical legal matter. In general, par value represents the smallest amount that the corporation can accept in exchange for a share of stock at the time it is originally issued without the buyer of the stock incurring some liability to the corporation. In many states, par-value stock cannot be sold originally by the corporation for less than par value, but can be sold either above or below par value after the original sale. In most states, it is possible for corporations to issue stock that has no par value.

If the corporation issues only one type of capital stock, it is called common stock. The stockholders own the corporation "in common." Among other things, the stockholders have the right to vote for directors and upon certain other matters, and the right to share in dividends. Dividends are distributions to stockholders resulting either from profitable operations or from the fact that the corporation is being dissolved. In all cases, these rights are in direct proportion to the number of shares of stock owned.

Some corporations have more than one class or type of stock. The classes differ with respect to the rights which go with the ownership of the stock. In addition to common stock, a corporation may have one or more types of preferred stock, which may entitle the owner to receive a limited share of the earnings before the common stockholders receive any dividends or may involve a prior claim upon assets in the event that the corporation is dissolved. Sometimes preferred stock has a preference as to both dividends and assets. Frequently, preferred stockholders do not have voting rights.

Transactions and Accounts Unique to a Corporation

The day-to-day operating transactions of a corporation are similar to those of a single proprietorship or of a partnership of a like nature. Certain transactions involving the owners' equity of a business are unique if the enterprise is incorporated. Examples of such transactions include:

1. Capital stock subscriptions.
2. Amounts received to apply on capital stock subscriptions.
3. Issuance of capital stock to subscribers.
4. Transfer of capital stock from one stockholder to another stockholder.
5. Declaration and payment of dividends.

In order to account for these types of transactions, certain accounts are required by a corporation. The following is a list of the major accounts and related classifications that are unique to the corporate form of organization:

Account	Classification
Capital Stock	Owners' equity
Subscriptions Receivable	Asset
Capital Stock Subscribed	Owners' equity
Retained Earnings (sometimes called Earnings Retained in the Business)	Owners' equity
Dividends Payable	Liability

Accounting Procedure

In accounting for the operations of a corporation, two major stockholders' equity or owners' equity accounts are kept—Capital Stock and Retained Earnings. In addition, an asset account—Subscriptions Receivable—and an owners' equity account—Capital Stock Subscribed—are kept to enter unpaid subscriptions to capital stock. A liability account—Dividends Payable—is kept to enter the corporation's liability for any dividends declared but not yet paid. The use of these accounts will be discussed fully in the remainder of this chapter.

Owners' Equity Accounts. One of the features of accounting for corporate owners' equity is the distinction that is maintained in the records between owners' equity that results from investments by stockholders—referred to as **paid-in capital**; and owners' equity that results from profitable operations—referred to as **retained earnings**. In the case of certain types of corporate transactions, this distinction as to the source of the owners' equity is not evident, but in most cases the difference is reflected in the accounts. For example, when the corporation exchanges its stock for cash or other property equal in amount to the par value of the shares issued, the transaction is entered by debiting the proper asset account and by crediting Capital Stock. If there is more than one type of capital stock, there should be an account for each type.

Starting a Business Corporation. A business corporation may be started in a variety of ways. A corporation may sell its stock directly to new stockholders for cash or may obtain subscriptions to its stock. A **subscription** is an agreement to buy a certain number of shares at an agreed price and to pay for them at or within a specified time, either in full at one time or in installments over a period of time. For example, assume that a subscription is received for 1000 shares at a price of $10 each (assumed to be the par value of each share in this case). The transaction is entered by debiting Subscriptions Receivable and by crediting Capital Stock Subscribed for $10,000. Collections on the subscription are debited to Cash (or whatever is accepted in lieu of cash) and credited to Subscriptions Receivable. When the subscription is paid in full, the stock is issued and an entry is made debiting Capital Stock Subscribed and crediting Capital Stock for $10,000. As long as the subscriptions receivable account has a balance representing an amount that is expected to be collected, the account is treated as an asset and is shown on the balance sheet. Capital Stock Subscribed is a stockholders' equity account, the balance of which indicates the amount that eventually will be added to Capital Stock.

Following is a narrative of selected corporate common stock transactions with illustrative general journal entries:

(1) The Hilgert Company, Inc., was incorporated with an authorized issue of 10,000 shares of common stock, par value $10 per share. (This would be indicated by the following memorandum in the Description column of the general journal: "Aug. 1. The Hilgert Company, Inc., is authorized to issue 10,000 shares of common stock, par value of $10 per share.") At the time of incorporation, subscriptions had been received as follows:

R. L. Hilgert	5000 shares
Sue Cohen	2500 shares
Sharon Tucker	2500 shares

The stock was subscribed for at par value and one half of the subscription price was paid in cash, the balance to be paid on demand.

To enter this transaction completely, it is necessary (a) to enter the stock subscriptions received, and (b) to enter the cash received to apply on the subscription price. These entries may be made in general journal form as follows:

(a)

Subscriptions Receivable	100,000	
Capital Stock Subscribed		100,000
Received subscriptions to capital stock at par, as follows:		
R.L. Hilgert, 5000 shares		
Sue Cohen, 2500 shares		
Sharon Tucker, 2500 shares		

(b)

Cash	50,000	
Subscriptions Receivable		50,000
Received cash on account for subscriptions to capital stock, as follows:		
R.L. Hilgert, $25,000		
Sue Cohen, $12,500		
Sharon Tucker, $12,500		

(2) Received cash from subscribers to capital stock in settlement of balances due, as follows:

R.L. Hilgert	$25,000
Sue Cohen	12,500
Sharon Tucker	12,500

This transaction involves an increase in the asset Cash and a decrease in the asset Subscriptions Receivable. The transaction may be entered in general journal form, as follows:

Cash	50,000	
Subscriptions Receivable		50,000
Received cash in settlement of the balance due from subscribers to capital stock, as follows:		
R.L. Hilgert, $25,000		
Sue Cohen, $12,500		
Sharon Tucker, $12,500		

(3) Issued certificates of stock to the following subscribers who had remitted their subscriptions in full:

R.L. Hilgert	5000 shares
Sue Cohen	2500 shares
Sharon Tucker	2500 shares

Usually, certificates of stock are not issued until subscriptions are remitted in full. In this case, the subscribers remitted their subscriptions in full and the stock certificates are issued. The transactions are entered in general journal form, as follows:

Capital Stock Subscribed	100,000	
Capital Stock[1]		100,000
Capital stock issued to subscribers as follows:		
R.L. Hilgert, 5000 shares		
Sue Cohen, 2500 shares		
Sharon Tucker, 2500 shares		

After posting the above entry, the capital stock account will have a credit balance of $100,000, which is the par value of the capital stock outstanding.

(4) R. L. Hilgert's stock certificate for 5000 shares was returned and Hilgert requested that 2000 shares be transferred to G. B. Waymire. A new certificate for 3000 shares is to be issued to Hilgert.

This transaction indicates that out of 5000 shares owned by Hilgert, 2000 shares were sold to Waymire. Transferring capital stock from one stockholder to another involves the cancellation of the old certificate and the issuance of new certificates for the proper numbers of shares. In this case, it is necessary to cancel the original certificate for 5000 shares issued to Hilgert and to issue two new certificates, one to Waymire for 2000 shares and the other to Hilgert for 3000 shares. This transaction has no effect upon the assets, liabilities, or capital of the corporation. It is merely a transfer of stock between stockholders and the only entry required is a transfer entry in the capital stock records kept by the corporation.

Corporation Profits, Losses, and Dividends. At the end of each accounting period, the balance of the expense and revenue summary account is transferred to the retained earnings account. If a corporation is operated at a loss, the amount of the net loss which is transferred from the expense and revenue summary account to the retained earnings account might result in the retained earnings account having a debit balance. This balance is termed a deficit and will appear as a deduction in the stockholders' equity section of the corporation's balance sheet.

A decision on the part of the directors of a corporation to pay a dividend is commonly referred to as a declaration of dividends. The directors usually specify that the dividends shall be paid to the stockholders of record as of a certain date, which means that only stock-

[1]When both common stock and preferred stock are authorized in the charter of a corporation, separate accounts should be kept for each class of stock. A memorandum entry of the number of shares authorized should be entered in the item column of each capital stock account.

holders whose stock is entered in their names on that date are entitled to receive dividends. Any stockholder who acquires stock after that date is not entitled to share in the dividend previously declared.

Dividends may be paid immediately upon being declared or at some later date. Large corporations usually do not pay dividends until some time after the date of declaration. When dividends are declared and such dividends are payable in cash at a later date, the dividends declared represent a liability of the corporation. It is customary to enter the declaration by debiting Retained Earnings and by crediting Dividends Payable.

To illustrate, assume that the board of directors at its annual meeting held on July 15 voted to pay a cash dividend of 90¢ per share to be paid on Aug. 1 to stockholders of record July 15. As of the date of declaration, there are 10,000 shares issued and outstanding. The transaction may be entered in general journal form, as follows:

July 15	Retained Earnings	9,000	
	Dividends Payable		9,000
	Dividend declared by board of directors.		

The dividends payable account will have a credit balance until all dividends declared are paid in full. When dividends are paid immediately upon being declared, there is no need for setting up a dividends payable account.

To enter the payment of the dividend declared in the foregoing transaction, it is necessary to debit Dividends Payable and to credit the cash account, as follows:

Aug. 1	Dividends Payable	9,000	
	Cash		9,000
	Paid dividend declared July 15.		

This transaction has the effect of decreasing the liability, Dividends Payable, by $9,000 with a similar decrease in the asset Cash. After the transaction is posted, the dividends payable account will have no balance.

Incorporating a Single Proprietorship. The legal steps involved in incorporating a single proprietorship are the same as in organizing a new corporation. Usually, the sole proprietor becomes the principal stockholder in the corporation and transfers the assets of the proprietorship business to the corporation in exchange for capital stock. The business liabilities may also be assumed by the corporation. The same books of account may be continued or an entirely new set of books may be installed.

Assume that The Binder Company, Inc., was organized to take over the business formerly conducted by J. J. Binder as sole owner. Binder subscribes for 5000 shares of the capital stock of The Binder Company, Inc., at $10 per share and transfers the equity in the proprietorship (on a fair market value basis, as usually required by generally accepted accounting principles) to apply on the subscription. Just before the transfer at the end of the year, the balance sheet of the business appeared as reproduced below.

J. J. BINDER
Balance Sheet
December 31, 1986

Assets			**Liabilities**		
Cash		$ 7,400	Notes payable	$ 1,800	
Accounts receivable	$ 5,930		Accounts payable	4,990	
Less allowance for doubtful accounts	620	5,310	Total liabilities		$ 6,790
Merchandise inventory		12,410			
Office equipment	$ 2,400				
Less accumulated depreciation	600	1,800			
Store equipment	$ 1,900				
Less accumulated depreciation	500	1,400	**Owner's Equity**		
Delivery equipment	$ 4,600		J.J. Binder, capital		23,730
Less accumulated depreciation	2,400	2,200			
Total assets		$30,520	Total liabilities and owner's equity		$30,520

Binder's net accounts receivable are believed to be collectible and the merchandise inventory is costed on a fifo basis. However, the fair market values of the long-term assets as of December 31, 1986, are considered to be: office equipment, $2,100; store equipment, $1,700; and delivery equipment, $2,400. A comparison of these values with the undepreciated cost amounts shown in the balance sheet reveals that the fair market values are larger by a total of $800 ($6,200 fair market value − $5,400 undepreciated costs). Thus, Binder's equity in the business is considered to be $24,530, or $800 more than the amount of $23,730 that is shown on the balance sheet dated December 31, 1986.

The following entry is made on Binder's books to recognize the fair market values of the long-term assets:

Office Equipment	300	
Store Equipment....................................	300	
Delivery Equipment	200	
J.J. Binder, Capital..............................		800
Adjustment of long-term assets to fair market values.		

If Binder intends to continue to use the same set of books with only those modifications needed because of the change to the corporate form of enterprise, the entries for the subscription and its partial payment by the transfer of the business assets and liabilities to the corporation should be as follows:

Subscriptions Receivable	50,000	
Capital Stock Subscribed		50,000
J.J. Binder subscribed for 5000 shares of stock at par.		
J.J. Binder, Capital..................................	24,530	
Subscriptions Receivable		24,530
Assets and liabilities of J.J. Binder transferred to corporation at fair market value.		

After the foregoing entries are posted, Binder's capital account will have no balance. The corporate accounts listed below will take the place of Binder's capital account in the general ledger:

Capital Stock	Capital Stock Subscribed
Subscriptions Receivable	

As in the case of the Schoen & Starks partnership, for tax purposes, Binder must use the undepreciated costs of the three long-term assets as shown by the December 31, 1986, balance sheet on page 513, and the net capital investment for tax purposes would be considered to be $23,730, as shown also by the balance sheet.

If, instead of using the same books of account that were used by Binder, a new set of books is installed by the corporation, a general journal entry should be made for the transfer of the accounts of the single proprietorship to the corporation. Since the long-term assets are being taken over at their fair market values, they should be entered on the books of the corporation at these values, which represent the costs of the assets to the corporation. The accounts of Binder are then transferred to The Binder Company, Inc., by means of a general journal entry on the books of the corporation, as follows:

Cash	7,400	
Accounts Receivable	5,930	
Merchandise Inventory	12,410	
Office Equipment	2,100	
Store Equipment	1,700	
Delivery Equipment	2,400	
Notes Payable		1,800
Accounts Payable		4,990
Allowance for Doubtful Accounts		620
Subscriptions Receivable		24,530
Assets and liabilities of J.J. Binder transferred to corporation at fair market value.		

Assuming that the balance due on the subscription was paid, a stock certificate for 5000 shares is issued to Binder and the transactions are entered on the books of the corporation, as follows:

Cash	25,470*	
Subscriptions Receivable		25,470
Cash received from J.J. Binder in settlement of balance due on subscription to capital stock.		

*$50,000 Subscriptions Receivable Dr.
less $24,530 Subscriptions Receivable Cr.

Capital Stock Subscribed	50,000	
Capital Stock		50,000
Issued 5000 shares of capital stock to J.J. Binder.		

Incorporating a Partnership. When a partnership is incorporated, the partners may become stockholders of the corporation. The same books of account may be continued or a new set of books may be installed by the corporation. Assume that The Madeo Company, Inc., is organized with an authorized capital of $200,000 to take over the business formerly conducted by Madeo & Madeo, a partnership. The partners subscribe for capital stock of the corporation, as follows:

Larry Madeo, 6000 shares @ $10.......	$60,000
Silvia Madeo, 4000 shares @ $10.......	$40,000

Madeo & Madeo, as individuals, are to receive credit toward their subscription for their respective equities in the assets of the partnership.

The subscriptions to the capital stock should be entered as indicated in the following general journal entry:

Subscriptions Receivable..........................	100,000	
Capital Stock Subscribed		100,000
Received subscriptions to capital stock as follows:		
Larry Madeo, 6000 shares		
Silvia Madeo, 4000 shares		

The following balance sheet for the partnership was prepared just prior to the time of incorporating the business on April 1, 1986. It has already been adjusted to recognize the fair market values of the inventory and long-term assets as of that date, and the Madeos had no

MADEO & MADEO
Balance Sheet
March 31, 1986

Assets			Liabilities		
Cash		$17,000	Notes payable..........	$ 6,000	
Notes receivable	$ 2,000		Accounts payable	9,720	
Accounts receivable	9,900		Total liabilities		$15,720
	$11,900				
Less allowance for doubtful accounts	800	11,100			
Merchandise inventory..		25,500			
Office equipment	$ 4,000		**Owners' Equity**		
Less accumulated depreciation	1,200	2,800	Larry Madeo, capital....	$25,368	
Delivery equipment	$ 3,200		Silvia Madeo, capital ...	16,912	
Less accumulated depreciation	1,600	1,600	Total owners' equity..		42,280
Total assets...........		$58,000	Total liabilities and owners' equity		$58,000

knowledge of any specific uncollectible accounts receivable at the date of incorporation.

If the books of the partnership are to be continued in use by the corporation, the transfer of the partners' equities to the corporation may be made by means of the following general journal entry:

Larry Madeo, Capital	25,368	
Silvia Madeo, Capital	16,912	
Subscriptions Receivable		42,280
Assets and liabilities of Madeo & Madeo transferred to corporation at fair market value.		

After this entry is posted, the partners' accounts will have no balances.

As in the previous cases, for tax purposes, Madeo & Madeo must use the undepreciated costs of their long-term assets and the book value of their inventory as of March 31, 1986, prior to any fair market value adjustments, and value their net capital investments accordingly.

If instead of using the same books of account that were used by Madeo & Madeo, a new set of books is installed by the corporation, a general journal entry on the books of the corporation is required to transfer the accounts of the partnership to the corporation. This journal entry is:

Cash	17,000	
Notes Receivable	2,000	
Accounts Receivable	9,900	
Merchandise Inventory	25,500	
Office Equipment	2,800	
Delivery Equipment	1,600	
Notes Payable		6,000
Accounts Payable		9,720
Allowance for Doubtful Accounts		800
Subscriptions Receivable		42,280
Assets and liabilities of Madeo & Madeo transferred to corporation at fair market value.		

Assuming that Madeo & Madeo paid the balance due on their subscriptions and that stock certificates were issued to them, the transactions should be entered on the books of the corporation, as follows:

Cash	57,720	
Subscriptions Receivable		57,720
Received cash from subscribers as follows:		
Larry Madeo, $34,632		
Silvia Madeo, $23,088		
Capital Stock Subscribed	100,000	
Capital Stock		100,000
Issued capital stock to subscribers.		

Owners' Equity Section of a Corporation Balance Sheet. The difference between the amounts of the assets and of the liabilities of a corporation is called either "Capital" or "**Stockholders' Equity**" and is so described in the balance sheet of the corporation. Generally, the amount resulting from the issuance of capital stock and the amount resulting from undistributed earnings are shown. At the end of the first year of operations, the owners' equity section of the balance sheet of The Madeo Company, Inc., appeared as follows:

Stockholders' Equity

Capital stock (20,000 shares authorized; 10,000 shares issued and outstanding)	$100,000
Retained earnings	32,000
Total stockholders' equity	$132,000

Because of differences in capital structure, there may be considerable variation in the capital sections of balance sheets prepared for different corporations. If more than one kind of capital stock is issued, each kind should be listed separately. There may be retained earnings (accumulated income) or a deficit (accumulated losses) at the end of the year. A deficit should be shown as a deduction from the amount resulting from the issuance of the capital stock in arriving at the total stockholders' equity of a corporation.

BUILDING YOUR ACCOUNTING KNOWLEDGE

1. Identify four advantages of the corporate form of business organization in contrast to a partnership. Identify a major disadvantage of the corporate form.
2. What qualifications are necessary to be one of the incorporators of a corporation?
3. What are the usual rights of common stockholders?

4. Identify the five major accounts unique to the corporate form of business organization and give their balance sheet classifications.
5. Describe the accounting effect and the necessary entry or entries for the transfer of shares from one corporate stockholder to another.
6. When do dividends become a liability of the corporation?
7. When an existing single proprietorship or partnership is incorporated, at what values do generally accepted accounting principles usually require that noncash assets be taken over by the corporation?
8. Identify the two major divisions of the stockholders' equity section of a corporate balance sheet.

APPLYING ACCOUNTING CONCEPTS

Exercise 16-8. Space Center Industries was incorporated on April 1, 19--, with an authorized issue of 10,000 shares of common stock, par value of $10 per share. At the time of incorporation, subscriptions had been received from Amelia Eckart for 5,000 shares and from Tina Wyckott for 2,500 shares. The stock was subscribed for at par value, and one half of the subscription price was paid in cash with the balance to be paid on the first day of the following month.

In general journal form, enter the following transactions: **(a)** memorandum entry to be made on April 1; **(b)** stock subscriptions received; **(c)** cash received to apply on the subscription price; **(d)** receipt of final cash payment on the stock subscriptions; and **(e)** issue of the capital stock.

Exercise 16-9. The board of directors of Space Center Industries, Inc., at its annual meeting held on June 15, voted to pay a cash dividend of $3 per share on July 15 to stockholders of record on June 30. As of the date of declaration, there were 7,500 shares issued and outstanding.

Enter the following transaction in general journal form: **(a)** declaration of the dividend, and **(b)** payment of the dividend.

Exercise 16-10. Sunshine Health Foods, owned by Josefa Remalius, has been operating as a sole proprietorship. On December 31, Remalius decided to incorporate and subscribed for 1,000 shares of the capital stock of Sunshine Health Foods, Inc., at $100 par value per share and transferred the equity in the proprietorship (on a fair market value basis) to apply on the subscription.

Prior to the incorporation at the end of the year, the balance sheet of the proprietorship showed the following assets and liabilities:

Cash	$ 8,500
Accounts receivable	6,059
Allowance for doubtful accounts	950
Merchandise inventory	33,040
Office equipment	3,600
Accumulated depreciation on office equipment	900
Delivery equipment	5,700
Accumulated depreciation on delivery equipment	2,000
Notes payable	2,900
Accounts payable	5,690
Josefa Remalius, capital	44,459

The net accounts receivable are believed to be collectible and the merchandise inventory is costed on a fifo basis. The fair market value of the office equipment is $2,500 and the fair market value of the delivery equipment is $4,200.

(a) Assuming that Remalius intends to continue with the same set of books with only those modifications needed to change to the corporate form of organization, give the entries in general journal form to enter the following transactions:

1. Adjustment of long-term assets to fair market value.
2. Subscription for the 1,000 shares of stock at par value.
3. Transfer of assets and liabilities to the corporation at fair market value.

(b) Assuming that Remalius intends to open a new set of books for the corporation, give the general journal entry for the transfer of the accounts of the single proprietorship to the corporation.

Report No. 16-3

Complete Report No. 16-3 in the study assignments and submit your working papers to the instructor for approval. Then continue with the textbook discussion in Chapter 17 until Report No. 17-1 is required.

EXPANDING YOUR BUSINESS VOCABULARY

What is the meaning of each of the following terms?

capital (p. 482)
capital stock (p. 506)
common stock (p. 507)
corporation (p. 506)
declaration of dividends (p. 511)
deficit (p. 511)
dividends (p. 507)
double taxation (p. 506)
goodwill (p. 498)
incorporators (p. 506)
net worth (p. 482)
owner's equity (p. 482)
paid-in capital (p. 508)
par value (p. 507)
partnership (p. 490)
partnership agreement (p. 490)
preferred stock (p. 507)
retained earnings (p. 508)
shares (p. 507)
single proprietorship (p. 482)
stockholders (or shareholders) (p. 507)
stockholders' equity (p. 518)
stockholders of record (p. 512)
subscription (p. 509)

CHAPTER 17

Accrual Accounting Applied to a Medium-Scale Wholesale-Retail Business

CHAPTER OBJECTIVES

Careful study of this chapter should enable you to:

- Describe how accrual accounting is applied to a medium-size wholesale-retail business with two departments operated as a partnership.
- Explain for such a business the information processing phases of the accounting cycle (source documents, books of original entry, ledgers, and auxiliary records).
- Prepare the following new books of original entry:

  1. Departmental sales journal
  2. Departmental cash receipts journal
  3. General journal with special columns

- Describe the accounting for temporary investments, using the account for government notes as an example.
- Describe the use of departmental cost of goods sold accounts.
- Prepare a subsidiary operating expense ledger with its own chart of accounts.

In the wholesale portion of a wholesale-retail merchandising enterprise, the merchandise handled is usually purchased directly from manufacturers, importers, or producers. The merchandise is sold to retailers and distributors, who in turn sell to consumers at retail prices. The wholesaler usually buys in sizable quantities and has storage facilities that make it possible to carry a large stock of merchandise. Goods may be purchased for cash or on account and, likewise, the goods may be sold for cash or on account. A large percentage of the wholesale business involves the use of credit. The retail portion of such a business is handled in a manner similar to that explained and illustrated in Chapters 8, 9, and 10.

This chapter introduces departmental accounting and applies it to a partnership operated both as a wholesaler and as a retailer. It also illustrates the use of a departmental sales journal, a departmental cash receipts journal, and a general journal with special columns. The voucher register and check register introduced in Chapter 14 are also utilized here. Temporary investment accounts and departmental cost of goods sold accounts are introduced. Finally, a subsidiary operating expense ledger with a separate chart of accounts is utilized for the first time.

Factors Affecting Accounting Records Used

The books of account and the auxiliary records of a wholesale-retail business will vary depending upon a number of factors, such as the following:

1. Type of business organization.
2. Volume of business.
3. Office equipment used.
4. Information desired by the management and others concerned with the operation of the business.

Type of Business Organization. A wholesale-retail merchandising enterprise may be conducted as a single proprietorship, a partnership, or a corporation. The type of organization will affect the accounts that are kept. In a single proprietorship, it may be necessary to keep two accounts for the proprietor—one for capital and the other for personal transactions. In a partnership, it is necessary to keep separate accounts for each partner. In the case of a corporation, it is necessary to keep separate accounts for capital stock, retained earnings, and dividends payable.

Volume of Business. The volume of business is an important factor in determining the types of records and the number of accounts to be maintained. Obviously, the records and the accounts of a firm with annual sales of a million dollars or more will differ considerably from one with annual sales of only $50,000 a year. In a business with numerous departments, management may demand more financial statistical information and have a greater need for adequate control.

When manual methods are used, there is a fairly direct relationship between the size of a business and the number of persons engaged in keeping its records. When several persons are required, the work must be divided in some logical fashion. This means that a separate record or book of original entry will be kept for each major type of business transaction. For example, one journal may be provided to enter purchases, another to enter sales, another to enter cash receipts, another to enter checks written, and a general journal to enter transactions that cannot be entered in the special journals. The books of final entry (the ledgers) also will be subdivided. It is likely that there will be one or more subsidiary ledgers to enter the details about some of the elements that are shown in summary in some of the general ledger accounts. For example, one subsidiary ledger may be for individual customers' accounts (accounts receivable) and another may be for individual operating expense accounts. (A subsidiary ledger for individual accounts payable would not be used if a voucher system is maintained.) Each employee engaged in an accounting activity may specialize in keeping one of these records.

A functional division of the accounting activity may have many advantages. Some of the more important ones are that the functional division:

1. Becomes an integral part of the internal control system, as discussed in Chapter 14.
2. Makes possible a more equitable distribution of the work load among several employees.
3. Provides for a more detailed classification of transactions in the books of original entry.
4. Makes possible periodic summary posting to the general ledger.

Office Equipment. The accounting system is certain to be affected by the use of various types of office equipment. In recent years there has been a great expansion in the use of computer-based accounting systems. In the modern office of a big business enterprise, a large share of the data entry work is done with the aid of electronic data processing equipment. Many companies utilize personal computers and other associated equipment.

Regardless of the extent to which equipment is used in performing the accounting function, the fundamental principles involved in keeping the accounts continue to apply. A knowledge of accounting theory and practice on the part of those employed in accounting positions is just as essential as if no machines were used.

Information Desired. The accounting information system must be designed to provide the desired information for management and others concerned with the operation of a business. Management would like to know where the business stands financially from time to time, as well as the results of operations for given periods of time. Accounting may be required to supply such information of a statistical nature as well as the usual accounting reports. For example, the accounts must be kept so as to provide all the information needed for the various tax reports required by the federal, state, and local governments. In recent years there has been a tremendous increase in the number of tax reports and in the amount of tax information that must be furnished. Many large firms have found it necessary to organize a tax accounting department separate from the general accounting department.

Accounting Procedure

Harlan Spinner and Carol Thomas are partners who conduct a wholesale-retail bakery business. Pastries and cakes are handled in Department A, breads and rolls in Department B. Such merchandise is purchased on account from various bakery suppliers. The bakery products are sold primarily for cash to retail customers. A small number of sales on account also are made to restaurants and wholesale customers. In the following sections, the books of account and accounting procedures for Spinner & Thomas are explained and illustrated.

Books of Account

The records maintained by Spinner & Thomas consist of the following:

1. Books of original entry
   - (a) Voucher register
   - (b) Sales journal
   - (c) Cash receipts journal
   - (d) Check register
   - (e) General journal
2. Books of final entry
   - (a) General ledger
   - (b) Subsidiary ledgers:
     - Accounts receivable ledger
     - Operating expense ledger
3. Auxiliary records
   - (a) Petty cash payments record
   - (b) Long-term asset record

Voucher Register. A comparison of the format of Spinner & Thomas' voucher register shown on pages 542-543 with that of the voucher register reproduced on page 432 reveals that they are identical. This form of voucher register was described in detail in Chapter 14.

Sales Journal. Spinner & Thomas keeps a multi-column sales journal as illustrated on page 544. Since there is no sales tax on food sales in the state in which Spinner & Thomas operates, no sales tax collections are necessary. Note that General Ledger Debit amount, Credit amount, and Account No. columns are provided. In addition, a special debit amount column is provided for Accounts Receivable, and special credit columns are provided for (1) Sales, Department A, and (2) Sales, Department B. A Sale No. column is provided to tie in the entry for each sale with the related source document.

Proving the Sales Journal. The sales journal may be footed and the footings proved daily or periodically by comparing the sum of the debit footings with the sum of the credit footings. When a page is filled and the amount columns footed, the footings should be proved, and the totals carried forward to the top of the next page. It is customary to start a month at the top of a new page.

Posting from the Sales Journal. Completing the posting from the sales journal involves both individual and summary posting. Individual posting is required from the General Ledger Debit and Credit columns, and may be required from the Accounts Receivable Debit column in some accounting information systems. In Spinner & Thomas' system, however, individual posting to the accounts receivable ledger is done directly from the sales invoices. This posting usually is done daily. As each item is posted, a check mark is entered in the Check (√) column following the General Ledger Debit, Accounts Receivable Debit, or General Ledger Credit Amount column of the sales journal.

The summary posting usually is completed at the end of each month and involves the following procedure (Account Nos. relate to the chart of accounts shown on page 530).

1. The total of the column headed Accounts Receivable should be posted as a debit to Accounts Receivable, Account No. 131, in the general ledger.
2. The total of the column headed Sales, Dept. A, should be posted as a credit to Sales—Department A, Account No. 411, in the general ledger.
3. The total of the column headed Sales, Dept. B, should be posted as a credit to Sales—Department B, Account No. 421, in the general ledger.

As the total of each column is posted, the account number should be written in parentheses immediately below the total in the sales journal. The final step in both individual and summary posting to the general ledger is to enter the initials "SJ" and the page number of the sales journal in the Posting Reference column of the proper general ledger account to the left of the amount posted. The final step in individual posting to the accounts receivable ledger is to enter the letter "S" and the sale number in the Posting Reference column of the proper customer's account to the left of the amount posted. A check mark should be placed in parentheses below the totals of the General Ledger Debit and Credit columns to indicate that these totals are not posted.

Cash Receipts Journal. Spinner & Thomas keeps a multi-column cash receipts journal. In the cash receipts journal reproduced on page 545, General Ledger Debit amount, Credit amount, and Account No. columns are provided. In addition, a special debit amount column is provided for Cash. All cash and cash items are entered by debiting the cash account immediately. This practice usually is followed when a business deposits all its cash receipts in a bank on the day they are received and makes all its payments (other than petty cash) by check. On the credit side, special amount columns are provided for Accounts Receivable, Cash Sales—Department A, and Cash Sales—Department B.

Proving the Cash Receipts Journal. The cash receipts journal may be footed and the footings proved daily or periodically by comparing the sum of the debit footings with the sum of the credit footings.

When a page is filled, the amount columns should be footed, the footings proved, and the totals carried forward to the top of the next page. It is customary to start a month at the top of a new page.

Posting from the Cash Receipts Journal. Completing the posting from the cash receipts journal involves both individual posting and summary posting. Individual posting is required from the General Ledger Debit and Credit columns. Individual posting to the accounts receivable ledger is done directly from the remittance advices. This posting usually is done daily. As each item is posted, a check mark is entered in the Check (√) column following the General Ledger Debit, Accounts Receivable Credit, or General Ledger Credit Amount column of the cash receipts journal.

The summary posting usually is completed at the end of each month and involves the following procedure:

1. The total of the column headed Cash should be posted as a debit to Cash, Account No. 111, in the general ledger.
2. The total of the column headed Accounts Receivable should be posted as a credit to Accounts Receivable, Account No. 131, in the general ledger.
3. The total of the column headed Cash Sales, Dept. A, should be posted as a credit to Sales—Department A, Account No. 411, in the general ledger.
4. The total of the column headed Cash Sales, Dept. B, should be posted as a credit to Sales—Department B, Account No. 421, in the general ledger.

As the total of each column is posted, the account number should be written in parentheses immediately below the total in the cash receipts journal. The final step in both individual and summary posting to the general ledger is to enter the initials "CRJ" and the page number of the cash receipts journal in the Posting Reference column of the proper general ledger account to the left of the amount posted. The final step in individual posting to the accounts receivable ledger is to enter the letter "C" (for collection) in the Posting Reference column of the proper customer's account to the left of the amount posted. A check mark should be placed in parentheses below the totals of the General Ledger Debit and Credit columns to indicate that these totals are not posted.

Check Register. A comparison of the format of Spinner & Thomas's check register reproduced on page 546 with that of the check register reproduced on page 436 will reveal that the formats are identical. This form of check register was described in detail in Chapter 14.

General Journal. The general journal is used for entering all transactions that cannot be entered in the special journals. Spinner &

Thomas uses a general journal (reproduced on page 547) with three amount columns—Detail, Debit, and Credit—as well as an Account No. column. The Detail column is used to enter debits to specific operating expense ledger accounts to support each of the debits to the control account, Operating Expenses, Account No. 541 in the general ledger. Adjusting, closing, and reversing entries also are entered in the general journal.

Proving the General Journal. The general journal may be footed and the footings proved daily or periodically by comparing the Debit footing with the Credit footing. When a page is filled, the three amount columns should be footed, the Debit and Credit footings proved, and the totals carried forward to the top of the next page. It is customary to start a month at the top of a new page.

Posting from the General Journal. Completing the posting from the general journal involves only individual posting from the Detail, Debit and Credit columns. This posting usually is done daily. Since the account numbers normally are entered in the Acct. No. column when the entries are made, posting is indicated by entering a check mark in the Check (√) column following each of the amount columns as each item is posted. The initials "GJ" and the page number of the general journal then should be entered in the Posting Reference column of the proper general ledger (or operating expense ledger) account to the left of the amount posted.

Although no summary posting is required, a check mark should be placed in parentheses below the Detail, Debit, and Credit column totals at the end of each month to indicate that these totals are not posted. Check marks should also be placed in parentheses below the proving totals of the adjusting and closing entries in the general journal after each of these sets of entries has been posted.

General Ledger. Spinner & Thomas uses a general ledger with four-column ledger account format. The accounts are arranged in this ledger in numerical order according to the chart of accounts reproduced on page 530. Note that the chart includes some accounts not used in previous presentations. A brief discussion of these new accounts follows.

Government Notes, Account No. 121. This account is used to enter the cost of United States government notes owned by Spinner & Thomas. From time to time, the partners find that the firm's bank balance is larger than necessary. To supplement earnings from regular operations, the excess cash is temporarily invested in certain types of government notes which earn a relatively high rate of return. The

SPINNER & THOMAS

CHART OF GENERAL LEDGER ACCOUNTS

Current Assets*

Cash

111 Cash
112 Petty Cash Fund

Temporary Investments

121 Government Notes

Receivables

122 Accrued Interest Receivable
131 Accounts Receivable
131.1 Allowance for Doubtful Accounts

Inventories

141 Merchandise Inventory—Department A
142 Merchandise Inventory—Department B

Supplies and Prepayments

151 Store Supplies
152 Office Supplies
155 Prepaid Insurance

Long-Term Assets

181 Store Equipment
181.1 Accumulated Depreciation—Store Equipment
185 Delivery Equipment
185.1 Accumulated Depreciation—Delivery Equipment
191 Office Equipment
191.1 Accumulated Depreciation—Office Equipment

Current Liabilities

211 FICA Tax Payable
212 FUTA Tax Payable
213 State Unemployment Tax Payable
214 Employees Income Tax Payable
216 Notes Payable
217 Accrued Interest Payable
218 Vouchers Payable

Owners' Equity

311 Harlan Spinner, Capital
311.1 Harlan Spinner, Drawing
321 Carol Thomas, Capital
321.1 Carol Thomas, Drawing
331 Expense and Revenue Summary

Revenue from Sales

411 Sales—Department A
411.1 Sales Returns and Allowances—Department A
421 Sales—Department B
421.1 Sales Returns and Allowances—Department B

Other Revenue

431 Interest Earned

Cost of Goods Sold

511 Purchases—Department A
511.1 Purchases Returns and Allowances—Department A
521 Purchases—Department B
521.1 Purchases Returns and Allowances—Department B
531 Cost of Goods Sold—Department A
532 Cost of Goods Sold—Department B

Operating Expenses

541 Operating Expenses

Other Expenses

571 Interest Expense

*Words in bold type represent headings and not account titles.

notes can be sold or redeemed with little risk of loss. Because there is no intention to hold the notes for a long period of time, they are regarded as temporary investments and classified as a current asset of the firm. In the end-of-period adjustment process, any interest accrued on the notes is entered as a debit to Accrued Interest Receivable, Account No. 122 and a credit to Interest Earned, Account No. 431.

Cost of Goods Sold—Department A and Cost of Goods Sold—Department B, Account Nos. 531 and 532. These two accounts are similar to Expense and Revenue Summary in that they are used only at the end of the accounting period in the closing process. Each of these accounts is used to summarize the elements that enter into the calculation of the cost of goods sold by each department. The debit balances of the merchandise inventory account (representing the beginning inventory) and the purchases account, together with the credit balance of the purchases returns and allowances account, are closed to the cost of goods sold account. When the amount of the ending inventory is entered by a debit to the merchandise inventory account, the cost of goods sold account is credited. The balance of this account then represents the cost of goods sold for the indicated department. These balances then are closed to the expense and revenue summary account.

Accounts Receivable Ledger. Spinner & Thomas uses an accounts receivable ledger with balance-column account format. The accounts are arranged in this ledger in alphabetical order. A control account, Accounts Receivable (Account No. 131), is kept in the general ledger. At the end of each month, it is customary to prepare a schedule of the accounts receivable, the total of which should be the same as the balance of the accounts receivable control account.

Posting to the customers' accounts in the accounts receivable ledger may be done either from the books of original entry or directly from the documents that represent the transactions. The accountant for Spinner & Thomas follows the latter practice, using copies of sales invoices, remittance advices, and credit memorandums. A check mark is placed in the Check (√) column next to the Accounts Receivable amount column either in the sales journal or cash receipts journal, or next to the credit column in the general journal, each time an entry is made. This reminds the accountant that posting is done directly from source documents.

Operating Expense Ledger. Spinner & Thomas uses an operating expense ledger with balance-column account format. The accounts are arranged in numerical order. A chart of the accounts for Spinner &

Thomas appears below. A control account, Operating Expenses (Account No. 541), is kept in the general ledger. At the end of each month, it is customary to prepare a schedule of the operating expenses, the totals of which should be the same as the balance of the operating expenses control account.

SPINNER & THOMAS

CHART OF OPERATING EXPENSE LEDGER ACCOUNTS

Administrative Expenses

5401 Office Salaries Expense
5402 Harlan Spinner, Salary Expense
5403 Office Supplies Expense
5404 Depreciation of Office Equipment
5405 Office Equipment Insurance Expense
5406 Office Rent Expense
5407 Payroll Taxes Expense
5408 Heat, Light, and Water Expense
5409 Telephone Expense
5416 Postage Expense
5417 Uncollectible Accounts Expense
5422 Miscellaneous General Expense

Selling Expenses

5431 Store Clerks Salary Expense
5432 Truck Drivers Wage Expense
5433 Advertising Expense
5434 Carol Thomas, Salary Expense
5435 Depreciation of Delivery Equipment
5436 Delivery Equipment Insurance Expense
5437 Depreciation of Store Equipment
5438 Store Equipment Insurance Expense
5441 Truck Gas and Oil Expense
5442 Truck Repairs & Maintenance Expense
5443 Store Rent
5444 Store Supplies Expense
5452 Miscellaneous Selling Expense

All posting to the operating expense accounts is done from the books of original entry. As each item is posted, the initials and the page of the journal from which it is posted are entered in the Posting Reference column of the account.

As each entry involving an operating expense account is made in either the voucher register or general journal, the appropriate subsidiary ledger account number is written in the Acct. No. column to the left of the proper amount column. Then, when each of these amounts is posted to the operating expense ledger, a check mark is placed in the Check (√) column just to the right of the proper amount column.

Auxiliary Records. Spinner & Thomas keeps certain auxiliary records such as a petty cash payments record, a long-term asset record, voucher check stubs, and vouchers.

The format of the petty cash payments record is similar to that of the petty cash payments record illustrated on pages 262 and 263 of Chapter 8. The format of the long-term asset record is similar to the format of the long-term asset record illustrated on page 411 of Chapter 13. The voucher check and voucher formats were illustrated on pages 435 and 431 of Chapter 14. To conserve space, Spinner & Thomas' auxiliary records are not illustrated in this chapter.

Accounting Procedure Illustrated

The accounts of Spinner & Thomas are kept on the basis of a fiscal year ending June 30. The books of original entry (voucher register, sales journal, cash receipts journal, check register, and general journal) are shown on pages 542-543, 544, 545, 546, and 547. The general ledger and subsidiary ledgers are not reproduced in this illustration. Following is a narrative of the June transactions that are shown entered in the illustrations.

SPINNER & THOMAS

Narrative of Transactions

Monday, June 2

Issued Voucher No. 196 to Estate Leasing Co., Indianapolis, for $2,500, of which $1,500 represents store rent expense and $1,000 represents office rent expense.

Since the type of voucher used by Spinner & Thomas was illustrated in Chapter 14, it will not be illustrated in this chapter. Instead, sufficient detail will be given to explain each entry in the voucher register illustrated on pages 542-543. The voucher register illustration also begins with three unpaid vouchers from the previous month, May.

Issued Check No. 601 in payment of Voucher No. 171, and Check No. 602 in payment of Voucher No. 196.

The voucher register illustration on page 542 shows the payees and amounts of these two checks. Note that, in addition to the check register entries, the date and number of each check are written in the Disposition columns of the voucher register.

Cash sales for the day were $1,882 for Dept. A and $1,718 for Dept. B.

Cash sales are entered in the cash receipts journal illustrated on page 545. Note that the cash sales of Dept. A bakery goods are carefully separated from the cash sales of Dept. B bakery goods.

Tuesday, June 3

Received checks from customers on account as follows:
Brother Juniper's, $808, for merchandise sold on May 29.
Houlihan's Place, $514, for merchandise sold on May 29.
The Tin Star, $782, for merchandise sold on May 29.

Checks sent in by customers are accompanied by remittance advices, which are used to enter the transactions in the cash receipts journal illustrated on page 545 and to post to the individual customer accounts receivable ledger (not shown).

Cash sales for the day were $1,782 for Dept. A and $1,675 for Dept. B.

Wednesday, June 4

Issued Checks Nos. 603 and 604 in payment of Vouchers Nos. 194 and 195.

Issued Voucher No. 197 to Walnut Paper, Indianapolis, for store paper supplies, $201. (Charged to Account No. 151.)

Made charge sales as follows:

Bakemeier's Bakery, Indianapolis, pastries, $734; breads, $269; Sale No. 297.

Heritage House, Indianapolis, pastries, $392; breads, $354; Sale No. 298.

Sam's Deli, Indianapolis, pastries, $234; breads, $504; Sale No. 299.

Entries in the sales journal and postings to individual customer accounts receivable (not shown) are made from copies of the sales invoices. The sales

journal is illustrated on page 544. Note that pastries are Dept. A sales and breads are Dept. B sales. All sales are numbered consecutively.

Cash sales for the day were $1,681 for Dept. A and $1,524 for Dept. B.

Thursday, June 5

Issued Voucher No. 198 to Indiana Bell, Indianapolis, for June telephone service, $101.

Received checks from customers on account as follows:

Ayres Department Stores, $1,180, for merchandise sold to them on May 31.

Bakemeier's Bakery, $983, for merchandise sold to them on May 31.

Methodist Hospital, $605, for merchandise sold to them on May 31.

Cash sales for the day were $1,808 for Dept. A and $1,402 for Dept. B.

Friday, June 6

Issued vouchers as follows:

Voucher No. 199 to Flowers Baking Co., Indianapolis, $4,566; pastries, $2,960; breads, $1,606.

Voucher No. 200 to International Bakers, Anderson, $4,373; pastries, $2,136; breads, $2,237.

Voucher No. 201 to Omar Bakeries, Indianapolis, pastries, $4,460.

Invoices for the previous week's purchases are received from suppliers on Friday and on the last day of the month for any other purchases through that date.

Made charge sales as follows:

Ayres Department Stores, Indianapolis, pastries, $767; breads, $421; Sale No. 300.

Brother Juniper's, Indianapolis, pastries, $450; breads, $152; Sale No. 301.

Houlihan's Place, Indianapolis, pastries, $332; breads, $148; Sale No. 302.

Cash sales for the day were $1,582 for Dept. A and $1,336 for Dept. B.

Saturday, June 7

Cash sales for the day were $1,566 for Dept. A and $1,361 for Dept. B.

End-of-the-Week Work

(1) Footed the amount columns in the books of original entry, entered the footings in small figures immediately below the line on which the last entry appeared, and proved the footings. (2) Proved the cash balance in the following manner:

Cash balance, June 1	$26,122*
Add receipts June 1-7 per cash receipts journal	24,189
Total	$50,311
Subtract checks issued June 1-7 per check register	12,186
Cash balance, June 7	$38,125

*From General Ledger Account No. 111 not shown in this illustration.

(3) Completed the individual posting from the books of original entry to the general ledger and operating expenses ledger accounts. (Accounts receivable ledger accounts were posted directly from the sales invoices and remittance advices.)

Monday, June 9

Issued Credit Memorandum No. 7 to Brother Juniper's, $7, as an allowance for having delivered the wrong pastry order.

The pastry had been billed as a part of Sale No. 301. The allowance transaction was entered in the general journal illustrated on page 547, after which the credit memorandum was posted immediately as a credit to the account of Brother Juniper's in the accounts receivable ledger. ("CM" stands for credit memorandum in the journal entry explanation.)

Cash sales for the day were $1,715 for Dept. A and $1,433 for Dept. B.

Tuesday, June 10

Received checks from customers on account as follows:

Bakemeier's Bakery, $1,003, for merchandise sold on June 4.

Heritage House, $746, for merchandise sold on June 4.

Sam's Deli, $738, for merchandise sold on June 4.

Cash sales for the day were $1,777 for Dept. A and $1,484 for Dept. B.

Wednesday, June 11

Issued Checks Nos. 605, 606, 607, and 608 in payment of Vouchers Nos. 197, 199, 200, and 201.

Made charge sales as follows:

Bakemeier's Bakery, Indianapolis, pastries, $631; breads, $308; Sale No. 303.

Methodist Hospital, Indianapolis, pastries, $236; breads, $506; Sale No. 304.

The Tin Star, Indianapolis, pastries, $312; breads, $215; Sale No. 305.

Cash sales for the day were $1,738 for Dept. A and $1,446 for Dept. B.

Thursday, June 12

Issued Voucher No. 202 to Indianapolis Power & Light, Indianapolis, for May electricity bill, $239.

Received checks from customers on account as follows:

Ayres Department Store, $1,188, for merchandise sold on June 6.

Brother Juniper's, $595, for merchandise sold on June 6, less the $7 allowance for having delivered the wrong pastry order.

Houlihan's Place, $480, for merchandise sold on June 6.

Cash sales for the day were $1,812 for Dept. A and $1,532 for Dept. B.

Friday, June 13

Issued Vouchers as follows:

Voucher No. 203 to Heileman Baking Co., Fort Wayne, $3,860; pastries, $1,256; breads, $2,604.

Voucher No. 204 to Omar Bakeries, Indianapolis, pastries, $4,410.

Voucher No. 205 to Tri-Baking Co., Indianapolis, $4,236; pastries, $1,459; breads, $2,777.

Made charge sales as follows:

Ayres Department Stores, Indianapolis, pastries, $763; breads, $482; Sale No. 306.

Brother Juniper's, Indianapolis, pastries, $436; breads, $145; Sale No. 307.

Houlihan's Place, Indianapolis, pastries, $342; breads, $227; Sale No. 308.

Cash sales for the day were $1,524 for Dept. A and $1,201 for Dept. B.

Saturday, June 14

Issued Voucher No. 206 to Indianapolis Water Co., Indianapolis, for May water bill, $172.

Cash sales for the day were $1,423 for Dept. A and $1,120 for Dept. B.

End-of-the-Week Work

(1) Footed the amount columns in the books of original entry, entered the footings in small figures immediately below the line on which the last entry appeared, and proved the footings. (2) Proved the cash balance in the following manner.

Cash balance, June 1	$26,122
Add receipts, June 1-14 per cash receipts journal	47,144
Total	$73,266
Subtract checks issued June 1-14 per check register	25,786
Cash balance, June 14	$47,480

(3) Completed the individual posting from the books of original entry to the general ledger and operating expenses ledger accounts.

Monday, June 16

Issued Voucher No. 207 to the Federal National Bank for the payment of the following taxes:

Employees' income tax (withheld during May)		$1,120
FICA tax imposed —		
on employees (withheld during May)	$569	
on the employer	569	1,138
Total		$2,258

Issued Voucher No. 208 to Payroll for the semimonthly wages, $5,452.

Spinner & Thomas follows the policy of paying employees on the 15th (or the next business day) and the last day of each month. The business is subject to the taxes imposed under the Federal Insurance Contributions Act (for old-age benefits and hospital insurance), and the Federal Unemployment Tax Act (for unemployment insurance purposes), and is required to make contributions to the state unemployment compensation fund. The company is also required to withhold a percentage of employees' wages both for FICA and for income tax purposes. In addition to the wages paid to employees, the Spinner & Thomas partnership agreement provides that each partner is to receive a salary of $2,400 a month, payable semimonthly. The salaries of the partners constitute an operating expense of the business and do not represent "wages" as defined in the social security and income tax laws; hence, their salaries are not subject to the FICA tax imposed upon employers and employees. Neither are such salaries subject to withholding for employee's income tax.

Each payday the accountant is supplied with a report prepared by the payroll clerk showing the total amount of wages and salaries earned during the pay period, the amount of payroll deductions, and the net amount of cash needed for payroll purposes. The report for June 16 appears on page 539.

PAYROLL STATEMENT
Period Beginning June 1 and Ending June 16

Classification	Total Earnings	DEDUCTIONS		Net Amount Payable
		FICA Tax	Employee's Income Tax	
Store Clerks Wages	1,000.00	75.00	119.80	805.20
Truck Drivers Wages	1,104.00	82.80	154.50	866.70
Office Salaries	1,736.00	130.20	225.70	1,380.10
Partners' salaries:				
H. Spinner	1,200.00	None	None	1,200.00
C. Thomas	1,200.00	None	None	1,200.00
	6,240.00	288.00	500.00	5,452.00

Employer's payroll taxes:		
(a) FICA tax, 7.5% of $3,840.00		$288.00
(b) Unemployment compensation taxes—		
State unemployment compensation tax, 5.4% of $1,200	$64.80	
FUTA tax, 0.8% of $1,200	9.60	74.40
Total		$362.40

A check made payable to Payroll is issued for the net amount payable. This check is then cashed at the Federal National Bank to obtain currency in the denominations necessary to pay each employee. The accountant is instructed to deposit Spinner's and Thomas' salaries in their individual bank accounts and to furnish them with copies of the deposit tickets.

The payroll voucher was entered in the voucher register by debiting the proper salary accounts for the earnings, by crediting the proper liability accounts for the taxes withheld, and by crediting the vouchers payable account for the amount of the check to be subsequently issued. The payroll taxes imposed on the employer were entered in the general journal by debiting Operating Expenses in the Debit column, by debiting Payroll Taxes Expense in the Detail column, and by crediting the proper liability accounts for the taxes imposed.

Issued Checks Nos. 609 and 610 in payment of Vouchers Nos. 207 and 208.

Spinner reported that interest coupons amounting to $600 from government notes were deposited in the Federal National Bank. This transaction was entered in the cash receipts journal.

Cash sales for the day were $1,726 for Dept. A and $1,476 for Dept. B.

The white space appearing at this point in the illustrated records indicates omission of the transactions completed on the days between June 16 and 30.

Monday, June 30

Issued vouchers as follows:

Voucher No. 219 to Flowers Baking Co., Indianapolis, $4,044; pastries, $1,211; breads, $2,833.

Voucher No. 220 to Omar Bakeries, Indianapolis, pastries, $2,500.

Voucher No. 221 to U.S. Post Office for postage, $59.

Voucher No. 222 to Petty Cash to replenish the petty cash fund. The following report was submitted by the clerk responsible for the fund.

Statement of Petty Cash Payments for June

Acct. No.	Description	Amount
5409	Telephone Expense	$ 3.00
5422	Miscellaneous General Expense	79.00
5433	Advertising Expense	13.00
5441	Truck Gas & Oil Expense	12.00
5452	Miscellaneous Selling Expense	30.00
	Total Disbursements	$137.00

Issued Voucher No. 223 to Payroll for the semimonthly wages, $5,503, in accordance with the payroll statement for the period June 16-30, shown on page 541.

Issued Checks Nos. 638, 639, and 640 in payment of Vouchers Nos. 221, 222, 223.

Received checks from customers on account as follows:

Heritage House, $829, for merchandise sold on June 25.

The Tin Star, $714, for merchandise sold on June 25.

Cash sales for the day were $1,850 for Dept. A and $1,615 for Dept. B.

End-of-the-Month Work

(1) Footed the amount columns, proved the footings, entered the totals, and ruled each of the books of original entry. (2) Proved the cash balance in the following manner:

Cash balance, June 1	$ 26,122
Total receipts for June per cash receipts journal	103,790
Total	$129,912
Less total checks issued during June per check register	95,477
Cash balance, June 30	$ 34,435

PAYROLL STATEMENT
Period Beginning June 16 and Ending June 30

Classification	Total Earnings	DEDUCTIONS		Net Amount Payable
		FICA Tax	Employee's Income Tax	
Store Clerks Wages	1,023.00	76.78	122.40	823.82
Truck Drivers Wages	1,126.00	84.45	157.00	884.55
Office Salaries	1,757.00	131.77	230.60	1,394.63
Partners' Salaries:				
H. Spinner	1,200.00	None	None	1,200.00
C. Thomas	1,200.00	None	None	1,200.00
	6,306.00	293.00	510.00	5,503.00

Employer's payroll taxes:		
(a) FICA tax, 7.5% of $3,906.00		$293.00
(b) Unemployment compensation taxes—		
State unemployment compensation tax, 5.4% of $1,200	$64.80	
FUTA tax, 0.8% of $1,200	9.60	74.40
Total		$367.40

(The accounting procedure used is similar to that shown on pages 538-539 relating to payroll.)

(3) Completed the individual posting from the books of original entry to the general ledger and to the operating expense ledger accounts. (4) Completed the summary posting of the totals of the special columns of each of the books of original entry to the general ledger accounts. (5) Prepared a trial balance and schedules of accounts receivable, vouchers payable, and operating expenses.

Step (5) would be completed as a part of the normal routine at the end of each month. However, since the end of June is also the end of the fiscal year for Spinner & Thomas, the procedure is varied slightly. The preparation of the general ledger trial balance and the schedule of operating expenses is combined with the preparation of the end-of-year work sheets used to assist in producing the income statement for the year and the balance sheet as of June 30. This process is described and illustrated in the following chapter. (The schedule of accounts receivable is shown on page 586.)

VOUCHER REGISTER FOR MONTH OF *June* **19 --** **PAGE** 25

	Purchases Dr.		Operating Expenses Dr.			Sundry Accounts Dr.						Sundry Accounts Cr.			Vouchers Payable Cr.	Disposition		
	Dept. A	Dept. B	Acct. No.	Amount	√	Acct. No.	Amount	√	Day	Vou. No.	To Whom Issued	Acct. No.	Amount	√		Date	Ck. No.	
1											**AMOUNTS FORWARDED**							1
2									5/27	171	Walnut Paper				282 00	6/2	601	2
3									5/31	194	Flowers Baking Co.				5 130 00	6/4	603	3
4									5/31	195	Omar Bakeries				4 274 00	6/4	604	4
5															9 686 00			5
6			5443	1 500 00	√				2	196	Estate Leasing Co.				2 500 00	6/2	602	6
7			5406	1 000 00	√													7
8						151	201 00	√	4	197	Walnut Paper				201 00	6/11	605	8
9			5409	101 00	√				5	198	Indiana Bell				101 00	6/20	619	9
10	2 960 00	1 606 00							6	199	Flowers Baking Co.				4 566 00	6/11	606	10
11	2 136 00	2 237 00							6	200	International Bakers				4 373 00	6/11	607	11
12	4 460 00								6	201	Omar Bakeries				4 460 00	6/11	608	12
13	9 556 00	3 843 00	5408	2 601 00 239 00	√		201 00		12	202	Indianapolis Power & Light				16 201 00 239 00	6/26	627	13
14	1 256 00	2 604 00							13	203	Heileman Baking Co.				3 860 00	6/17	612	14
15	4 410 00								13	204	Omar Bakeries				4 410 00	6/17	613	15
16	1 459 00	2 777 00							13	205	Tri-Baking Co.				4 236 00	6/17	614	16
17			5408	172 00	√				14	206	Indianapolis Water Co.				172 00	6/27	631	17
18	16 681 00	9 224 00		3 012 00		211	201 00 1 138 00	√	16	207	Federal National Bank				29 118 00 2 258 00	6/16	609	18
19						214	1 120 00	√										19
20			5431	1 000 00	√				16	208	Payroll	211	288 00	√	5 452 00	6/16	610	20
21			5432	1 104 00	√							214	500 00	√				21
22			5401	1 736 00	√													22
23			5402	1 200 00	√													23
24			5434	1 200 00	√													24
48	1 211 00	2 833 00							30	219	Flowers Baking Co.				4 044 00			48
49	2 500 00								30	220	Omar Bakeries				2 500 00			49
50			5416	59 00	√				30	221	U.S. Post Office				59 00	6/30	638	50
51	62 720 00 62 720 00	41 256 00 41 256 00		6 056 00 6 056 00			5 444 00 5 444 00		30		Carried forward		788 00		114 688 00			51

Voucher Register—Spinner & Thomas

VOUCHER REGISTER FOR MONTH OF *June* **19 --** **PAGE** *26*

	PURCHASES DR.		OPERATING EXPENSES DR.			SUNDRY ACCOUNTS DR.						SUNDRY ACCOUNTS CR.			VOUCHERS PAYABLE CR.	DISPOSITION		
	DEPT. A	DEPT. B	ACCT. NO.	AMOUNT	√	ACCT. NO.	AMOUNT	√	DAY	VOU. NO.	TO WHOM ISSUED	ACCT. NO.	AMOUNT	√		DATE	CK. NO.	
1	62 720 00	41 256 00		6 056 00			5 444 00		30		AMOUNTS FORWARDED		788 00		114 688 00			1
2			5409	3 00	√				30	222	Petty Cash				137 00	6/30	639	2
3			5422	79 00	√													3
4			5433	13 00	√													4
5			5441	12 00	√													5
6			5452	30 00	√													6
7			5431	1 023 00	√				30	223	Payroll	211	293 00	√	5 503 00	6/30	640	7
8			5432	1 126 00	√							214	510 00	√				8
9			5401	1 757 00	√													9
10			5402	1 200 00	√													10
11			5434	1 200 00	√													11
12	62 720 00 62 720 00	41 256 00 41 256 00		12 499 00 12 499 00			5 444 00 5 444 00						1 591 00 1 591 00		120 328 00 120 328 00			28
13	(511)	(521)		(541)			(√)						(√)		(218)			13
14																		14
15																		15
16																		16
17																		17
18																		18
19																		19
20																		20
21																		21
22																		22
23																		23
24																		24
25																		25
26																		26
27																		27
28																		28
29																		29

Voucher Register—Spinner & Thomas *(concluded)*

SALES JOURNAL FOR MONTH OF *June* 19 -- PAGE *27*

	DEBIT								CREDIT					
	GENERAL LEDGER								SALES		GENERAL LEDGER			
	ACCT. NO.	AMOUNT	√	ACCOUNTS RECEIVABLE	√	DAY	NAME	SALE NO.	DEPT. A	DEPT. B	ACCT. NO.	AMOUNT	√	
1				1003 00	√	4	Bakemeier's Bakery	297	734 00	269 00				1
2				746 00	√	4	Heritage House	298	392 00	354 00				2
3				738 00	√	4	Sam's Deli	299	234 00	504 00				3
4				1188 00	√	6	Ayres Department Stores	300	767 00	421 00				4
5				602 00	√	6	Brother Juniper's	301	450 00	152 00				5
6				480 00	√	6	Houlihan's Place	302	332 00	148 00				6
7				4757 00 939 00	√	11	Bakemeier's Bakery	303	2909 00 631 00	1848 00 308 00				7
8				742 00	√	11	Methodist Hospital	304	236 00	506 00				8
9				527 00	√	11	The Tin Star	305	312 00	215 00				9
10				1245 00	√	13	Ayres Department Stores	306	763 00	482 00				10
11				581 00	√	13	Brother Juniper's	307	436 00	145 00				11
12				569 00	√	13	Houlihan's Place	308	342 00	227 00				12
13				9360 00					5629 00	3731 00				13
30														30
31				20323 00 20323 00					11453 00 11453 00	8870 00 8870 00				31
32				(131)					(411)	(421)				32

Sales Journal—Spinner & Thomas

CASH RECEIPTS JOURNAL FOR MONTH OF *June* 19 –

	DEBIT						CREDIT							
	GENERAL LEDGER								CASH SALES		GENERAL LEDGER			
	ACCT. NO.	AMOUNT	√	CASH NET AMOUNT	DAY	RECEIVED FROM—DESCRIPTION	ACCOUNTS RECEIVABLE	√	DEPT. A	DEPT. B	ACCT. NO.	AMOUNT	√	
1						**AMOUNTS FORWARDED**								1
2				3600 00	2	*Cash sales*			1882 00	1718 00				2
3				808 00	3	*Brother Juniper's*	808 00	√						3
4				514 00	3	*Houlihan's Place*	514 00	√						4
5				782 00	3	*The Tin Star*	782 00	√						5
6				3457 00	3	*Cash sales*			1782 00	1675 00				6
7				3205 00	4	*Cash sales*			1681 00	1524 00				7
8				1180 00	5	*Ayres Department Stores*	1180 00	√						8
9				983 00	5	*Bakemeier's Bakery*	983 00	√						9
10				605 00	5	*Methodist Hospital*	605 00	√						10
11				3210 00	5	*Cash sales*			1808 00	1402 00				11
12				2918 00	6	*Cash sales*			1582 00	1336 00				12
13				2927 00	7	*Cash sales*			1566 00	1361 00				13
14				24 189 00 3148 00	9	*Cash sales*			10 301 00 1715 00	9016 00 1433 00				14
15				1003 00	10	*Bakemeier's Bakery*	1003 00	√						15
16				746 00	10	*Heritage House*	746 00	√						16
17				738 00	10	*Sam's Deli*	738 00	√						17
18				3261 00	10	*Cash sales*			1777 00	1484 00				18
19				3184 00	11	*Cash sales*			1738 00	1446 00				19
20				1188 00	12	*Ayres Department Stores*	1188 00	√						20
21				595 00	12	*Brother Juniper's*	595 00	√						21
22				480 00	12	*Houlihan's Place*	480 00	√						22
23				3344 00	12	*Cash sales*			1812 00	1532 00				23
24				2725 00	13	*Cash sales*			1524 00	1201 00				24
25				2543 00	14	*Cash sales*			1423 00	1120 00				25
26				47 144 00 600 00	16	*Interest on Gov't Notes*	9622 00		20 290 00	17 232 00	431	600 00	√	26
27				3202 00	16	*Cash sales*			1726 00	1476 00				27
40				829 00	30	*Heritage House*	829 00	√						40
41				714 00	30	*The Tin Star*	714 00	√						41
42				3465 00	30	*Cash sales*			1850 00	1615 00				42
43				103 790 00 103 790 00			18 328 00 18 328 00		44 875 00 44 875 00	39 987 00 39 987 00		600 00 600 00		43
44				(111)			(131)		(411)	(421)		(√)		44

Cash Receipts Journal—Spinner & Thomas

CHECK REGISTER FOR MONTH OF *June* **19 --** **PAGE** *24*

	Vouchers Payable Dr. No.	Vouchers Payable Dr. Amount	Day	Drawn to the Order of	Cash Cr. Chk. No.	Cash Cr. Amount	
1				**AMOUNTS FORWARDED**			1
2	171	282 00	2	Walnut Paper	601	282 00	2
3	196	2500 00	2	Estate Leasing Co.	602	2500 00	3
4	194	5130 00	4	Flowers Baking Co.	603	5130 00	4
5	195	4274 00	4	Omar Bakeries	604	4274 00	5
6	197	12186 00 201 00	11	Walnut Paper	605	12186 00 201 00	6
7	199	4566 00	11	Flowers Baking Co.	606	4566 00	7
8	200	4373 00	11	International Bakers	607	4373 00	8
9	201	4460 00	11	Omar Bakeries	608	4460 00	9
10	207	25786 00 2258 00	16	Federal National Bank	609	25786 00 2258 00	10
11	208	5452 00	16	Payroll	610	5452 00	11
30	221	59 00	30	U.S. Post Office	638	59 00	30
31	222	137 00	30	Petty Cash	639	137 00	31
32	223	5503 00	30	Payroll	640	5503 00	32
33		95477 00 95477 00				95477 00 95477 00	33
34		(218)				(111)	34

Check Register—Spinner & Thomas

GENERAL JOURNAL

PAGE *41*

	DATE		DESCRIPTION	ACCT. NO.	DETAIL	√	DEBIT	√	CREDIT	√	
1	19-- June	9	Sales Returns and Allowances—Dept. A	411.1			7 00			√	1
2			Accounts Receivable	131					7 00	√	2
3			Brother Juniper's, CM7								3
4		16	Operating Expenses	541			362 40	√			4
5			Payroll Taxes Expense	5407	362 40	√					5
6			FICA Tax Payable	211					288 00	√	6
7			FUTA Tax Payable	212					9 60	√	7
8			State Unemployment Tax Payable	213					64 80	√	8
9			Payroll taxes—June 16 payroll								9
31		30	Operating Expenses	541			367 40	√			31
32			Payroll Taxes Expense	5407	367 40	√					32
33			FICA Tax Payable	211					293 00	√	33
34			FUTA Tax Payable	212					9 60	√	34
35			State Unemployment Tax Payable	213					64 80	√	35
36			Payroll taxes—June 30 payroll								36
37					729 80 729 80		754 00 754 00		754 00 754 00		37
38					(√)		(√)		(√)		38
39											39
40											40

General Journal—Spinner & Thomas

BUILDING YOUR ACCOUNTING KNOWLEDGE

1. What are the differences in the owner's equity accounts that are kept in a single proprietorship, a partnership, and a corporation?
2. Name five separate books of original entry and indicate the type of business transaction normally entered in each.
3. Give four advantages of a functional division of the accounting activity.
4. What kinds of equipment often are used to aid the accounting work in the modern office of a big business enterprise?
5. What special information requirement has led to the organization of specialized accounting departments in large firms?
6. Describe the function of each of the five books of original entry kept by Spinner & Thomas.
7. Describe the function of each of the two subsidiary ledgers kept by Spinner & Thomas.
8. What are the two major auxiliary records that Spinner & Thomas maintain? Name two other auxiliary records that are kept in files by Spinner & Thomas.

APPLYING ACCOUNTING CONCEPTS

Exercise 17-1. Given the following columnar totals from the Voucher Register of Bradshaw's Florist, what should be the total of the vouchers payable column? Identify the total as either a debit or credit balance.

Column	Debit	Credit
Purchases, Department A	$26,270	
Purchases, Department B	14,526	
Operating Expenses	1,656	
Sundry Accounts	4,544	$878
Vouchers Payable	?	?

Exercise 17-2. The following totals were taken from the Sales Journal of Computer Sales and Service. What should be the total of the accounts receivable column? Indicate whether the total is a debit or credit balance.

Column	Debit	Credit
General Ledger	$ 437	$ 250
Accounts Receivable	?	?
Sales, Hardware Department		8,543
Sales, Software Department		7,075

Exercise 17-3. The following are the columnar totals taken from the Cash Receipts Journal of Bay Area Pools. Determine the toal amount of cash sales for Department B. Will the balance be a debit or a credit?

Column	Debit	Credit
General Ledger	$27,123	$ 605
Cash	92,685	
Accounts Receivable		15,763
Cash Sales, Department A		34,015
Cash Sales, Department B	?	?

Exercise 17-4. If the total of the vouchers payable column of the Check Register for Austin's Antiques is $75,974, what should be the total of the Cash column?

Exercise 17-5. Identify the appropriate journal in which the following transactions would be entered:

1. Issued a voucher.
2. Issued a check in payment of a voucher.
3. Entered cash sales for the day.
4. Entered checks received from customers on account.
5. Made a charge sale.
6. Issued a credit memorandum to a customer.
7. Entered the liability for payroll taxes owed.
8. Issued a voucher for payment of payroll taxes.
9. Deposited interest coupons from government notes held by the bank.
10. Issued a voucher to replenish the petty cash fund.
11. Entered expenditures summarized in the Statement of Petty Cash Payments.

Exercise 17-6. In completing the end-of-the-week work on May 13, the following amounts were taken from the accounting records of Victory Home Builders Supply:

Cash balance, May 1	$37,145
Receipts for May 1-13 per cash debit column in the cash receipts journal	35,732
Checks issued May 1-13 per cash credit column in the check register	23,294

Prove the cash balance as of May 13.

Report No. 17-1

The study assignments contain an analysis test that should be completed at this time. Before beginning work on the test, this chapter should be reviewed thoroughly. The narrative of transactions for June should be compared with the illustrations to see how each transaction is recorded and to note the effect of each transaction on the accounts involved. Special attention should be given to the analysis following certain transactions. Unless the procedure involved in entering the transactions completed by Spinner & Thomas during the month of June is thoroughly understood, you cannot hope to make a satisfactory grade on the test.

EXPANDING YOUR BUSINESS VOCABULARY

What is the meaning of each of the following terms:

- **cash receipts journal** (p. 527)
- **Detail column** (p. 529)
- **operating expense ledger** (p. 531)
- **sales journal** (p. 526)

CHAPTER 18

Accounting Procedure At Year End

CHAPTER OBJECTIVES

Careful study of this chapter should enable you to:

- Prepare a ten-column, end-of-year summary work sheet supplemented by a three-column end-of-year operating expenses work sheet.
- Prepare end-of-year departmental summary accounts for cost of goods sold.
- Prepare adjustments that involve debits to accounts on the operating expenses work sheet (with a summary debit to the general ledger account, Operating Expenses) and credits to various general ledger accounts on the summary work sheet.
- Prepare the adjusting entries and the closing entries in the general journal (using the summary work sheet as a guide) and post to the general ledger end-of-period summary accounts (Expense and Revenue Summary, and the two departmental accounts for cost of goods sold).
- Prepare the post-closing trial balance.
- Prepare any reversing entries required in the general journal as of the first day of the new accounting period.

One of the several reasons for maintaining an accounting information system is to make it possible to prepare periodic financial reports, including an income statement for the fiscal year and a balance sheet as of the close of that year. Long experience has shown that one of the fastest ways to produce these financial statements is (1) to use the information provided by the accounts—as reflected by the year-end trial balance taken after the regular posting has been completed, (2) to determine the needed adjustments, and (3) to bring these amounts together in a manner that facilitates statement preparation. The device most commonly used for these purposes is the work sheet.

This chapter continues the use of the ten-column work sheet in summary form, and also introduces a three-column supplementary work sheet for operating expenses. The use of departmental summary accounts for cost of goods sold as partial substitutes for the expense and revenue summary account is introduced and illustrated. The adjusting and closing process is explained and illustrated for each type of work sheet. Finally, a post-closing trial balance and the one necessary reversing entry are described and illustrated.

SUMMARY AND SUPPLEMENTARY YEAR-END WORK SHEETS

A simple eight-column work sheet for a personal service enterprise was discussed and illustrated in Chapter 5. A ten-column work sheet for a retail merchandising business was introduced in Chapter 9. Following is a discussion and illustration of Spinner & Thomas's ten-column summary work sheet supplemented by a three-column operating expenses work sheet. In the preceding chapter, a partial narrative of transactions for this firm for the month of June, 19-- (the last month of the fiscal year) was given. These transactions were entered in the books of original entry. The books of original entry were reproduced as they would appear after both the individual and the summary posting had been completed. The general ledger accounts and the accounts in each of the two subsidiary ledgers (accounts receivable and operating expenses) were not reproduced. However, it may be assumed that trial balances of these ledgers were taken. The general ledger was found to be in balance and the total of the account balances in each subsidiary ledger was found to agree with the balance of the related control account in the general ledger.

Summary Year-End Work Sheet

The Spinner & Thomas work sheet is shown on pages 554 and 555. It is identical to that used for MicroWorld on page 282. The first step in its preparation was to place the proper heading at the top, to insert the proper heading in the space provided at the top of each of the five pairs of amount columns, and to list the general ledger account titles and numbers in the spaces provided at the left. Note that with one exception the title and number of each general ledger account was listed (refer to the chart of accounts given on page 530 for the complete list) even though some of the accounts had no balances at the time the trial balance was taken. The one exception is Expense and Revenue Summary, Account No. 331. This account is used in the formal process of closing the books but is not needed on the work sheet. Expense and Revenue Summary was included in the MicroWorld work sheet on page 282 because the account was used to adjust the beginning and ending inventories. These inventory adjustments in the Spinner & Thomas work sheet are made using two cost of goods sold accounts that MicroWorld did not maintain. Note also that for Cost of Goods Sold—Department A, Account No. 531, and Cost of Goods Sold—Department B, Account No. 532, two lines were allowed in each case to accommodate the several debits and credits that will be involved. (The purpose of the cost of goods sold account is to provide a means of bringing together all the elements that are involved in calculating the amount of this cost: (1) beginning inventory, (2) purchases, (3) purchases returns and allowances, and (4) ending inventory.) The account balances were entered in the first pair of columns (trial balance) and these columns were totaled to prove their equality.

Adjustment of the Merchandise Accounts. Eight entries (a-h), were made in the adjustments columns of the work sheet to show the calculation of the cost of goods sold for each department and to adjust the merchandise inventory accounts.

Entry (a): The amount of the beginning inventory for Department A, $1,714, was transferred to Cost of Goods Sold— Department A by a debit to that account (No. 531) and by a credit to Merchandise Inventory—Department A, Account No. 141.

Entry (b): The amount of the beginning inventory for Department B, $1,410, was transferred to Cost of Goods Sold— Department B by a debit to that account (No. 532) and by a credit to Merchandise Inventory—Department B, Account No. 142.

SPINNER & THOMAS

Work Sheet

For the Year Ended June 30, 19--

	ACCOUNT	ACCT. NO.	TRIAL BALANCE DEBIT	TRIAL BALANCE CREDIT	ADJUSTMENTS DEBIT	ADJUSTMENTS CREDIT	ADJ. TRIAL BALANCE DEBIT	ADJ. TRIAL BALANCE CREDIT	INCOME STATEMENT DEBIT	INCOME STATEMENT CREDIT	BALANCE SHEET DEBIT	BALANCE SHEET CREDIT	
1	Cash	111	34435 00				34435 00				34435 00		1
2	Petty Cash Fund	112	200 00				200 00				200 00		2
3	Government Notes	121	10000 00				10000 00				10000 00		3
4	Accrued Interest Receivable	122			(i) 50 00		50 00				50 00		4
5	Accounts Receivable	131	10978 00				10978 00				10978 00		5
6	Allowance for Doubtful Accounts	131.1		60 00		(p) 180 00		240 00				240 00	6
7	Merchandise Inventory—Dept. A	141	1714 00		(g) 1680 00	(a) 1714 00	1680 00				1680 00		7
8	Merchandise Inventory—Dept. B	142	1410 00		(h) 1500 00	(b) 1410 00	1500 00				1500 00		8
9	Store Supplies	151	8974 00			(m) 7724 00	1250 00				1250 00		9
10	Office Supplies	152	7896 00			(n) 7141 00	755 00				755 00		10
11	Prepaid Insurance	155	5532 00			(o) 4650 00	882 00				882 00		11
12	Store Equipment	181	19780 00				19780 00				19780 00		12
13	Accumulated Depr.—Store Equip.	181.1		1680 00		(j) 1978 00		3658 00				3658 00	13
14	Delivery Equipment	185	57100 00				57100 00				57100 00		14
15	Accumulated Depr.—Del. Equip.	185.1		42800 00		(k) 7138 00		49938 00				49938 00	15
16	Office Equipment	191	19001 00				19001 00				19001 00		16
17	Accumulated Depr.—Off. Equip.	191.1		1415 00		(l) 1848 00		3263 00				3263 00	17
18	FICA Tax Payable	211		1162 00				1162 00				1162 00	18
19	FUTA Tax Payable	212		28 00				28 00				28 00	19
20	State Unemployment Tax Pay.	213		389 00				389 00				389 00	20
21	Employees Income Tax Pay.	214		1010 00				1010 00				1010 00	21
22	Notes Payable	216		-0-				-0-				-0-	22

23	Accrued Interest Payable	217		-0-				-0-				-0-	23
24	Vouchers Payable	218		34375 00				34375 00				34375 00	24
25	Harlan Spinner, Capital	311		38731 00				38731 00				38731 00	25
26	Harlan Spinner, Drawing	311.1	10300 00				10300 00				10300 00		26
27	Carol Thomas, Capital	321		16599 00				16599 00				16599 00	27
28	Carol Thomas, Drawing	321.1	7800 00				7800 00				7800 00		28
29	Sales–Dept. A	411		734629 00				734629 00		734629 00			29
30	Sales Ret. & Allow.–Dept. A	411.1	376 00				376 00		376 00				30
31	Sales–Dept. B	421		620988 00				620988 00		620988 00			31
32	Sales Ret. & Allow.–Dept. B	421.1	338 00				338 00		338 00				32
33	Purchases–Dept. A	511	628785 00			(c) 628785 00							33
34	Purchases Ret. & Allow.–Dept. A	511.1		820 00	(e) 820 00								34
35	Purchases-Dept. B	521	466110 00			(d) 466110 00							35
36	Purchases Ret. & Allow.–Dept. B	521.1		460 00	(f) 460 00								36
37	Cost of Goods Sold–Dept. A	531			(a) 1714 00	(e) 820 00	627999 00		627999 00				37
38					(c) 628785 00	(g) 1680 00							38
39	Cost of Goods Sold–Dept. B	532			(b) 1410 00	(f) 460 00	465560 00		465560 00				39
40					(d) 466110 00	(h) 1500 00							40
41	Operating Expenses	541	205712 00		(j-p) 30659 00		236371 00		236371 00				41
42	Interest Earned	431		1295 00		(i) 50 00		1345 00		1345 00			42
43	Interest Expense	571	-0-				-0-		-0-				43
44			1496441 00	1496441 00	1133188 00	1133188 00	1506355 00	1506355 00	1330644 00	1356962 00	175711 00	149393 00	44
45	Net Income								26318 00			26318 00	45
46									1356962 00	1356962 00	175711 00	175711 00	46

Spinner & Thomas—Ten-Column Work Sheet

Entry (c): The amount of the purchases for the year by Department A, $628,785, was transferred to Cost of Goods Sold–Department A by a debit to that account (No. 531) and by a credit to Purchases–Department A, Account No. 511.

Entry (d): The amount of the purchases for the year by Department B, $466,110, was transferred to Cost of Goods Sold–Department B by a debit to that account (No. 532) and by a credit to Purchases–Department B, Account No. 521.

Entry (e): The amount of the purchases returns and allowances for the year for Department A, $820, was transferred to the proper cost of goods sold account by a debit to Purchases Returns and Allowances–Department A, Account No. 511.1 and by a credit to Cost of Goods Sold–Department A, Account No. 531.

Entry (f): The amount of the purchases returns and allowances for the year for Department B, $460, was transferred to the proper cost of goods sold account by a debit to Purchases Returns and Allowances–Department B, Account No. 521.1, and by a credit to Cost of Goods Sold–Department B, Account No. 532.

Entry (g): The cost assigned to the June 30 merchandise inventory for Department A, $1,680, was debited to that account (No. 141) with an offsetting credit to Cost of Goods Sold–Department A, Account No. 531. Spinner & Thomas uses the periodic method of accounting for inventory. A physical count of the goods on hand at the year's end had been made. Reference to recent purchase invoices provided unit costs for the various items. Each time a physical inventory is taken, the quantities found to be on hand are recorded on detailed physical inventory summary sheets, showing the quantity, unit price, and extension for each pastry and cake item in Department A, and the total extensions.

Entry (h): The cost assigned to the June 30 merchandise inventory of Department B, $1,500, was debited to that account (No. 142) with an offsetting credit to Cost of Goods Sold–Department B, Account No. 532. The procedure followed in determining the inventory cost in Department B was the same as that described above for Department A.

The amount of the cost of goods sold for each department was determined by subtracting the sum of the two credits from the sum of the two debits to each of the cost of goods sold accounts. The amounts, $627,999 for Department A and $465,560 for Department B, were extended to the Adjusted Trial Balance Debit column.

Adjustment of the Interest Accounts. On June 30, Spinner & Thomas owned $10,000 face value, 12% United States government notes. Semiannual interest totaling $600 had been collected on June 16. Since that date, interest for 15 days amounting to $50 had accrued. In order to have the calculation of the net income for the year reflect the correct amount of interest earned, this type of accrual had to be taken into consideration.

Entry (i): The interest receivable on June 30, $50, was entered on the work sheet by debiting Accrued Interest Receivable, Account No. 122, and by crediting Interest Earned, Account No. 431: (Because Spinner & Thomas have no notes payable outstanding on June 30, no adjustment for accrued interest expense or payable is required at this time.)

At this point, work on the summary end-of-year work sheet was suspended temporarily until certain information needed from the supplementary work sheet for operating expenses was determined.

Supplementary Work Sheet for Operating Expenses

To provide the desired information, the income statement that was prepared had to be supplemented by a schedule of operating expenses. The accounting system of Spinner & Thomas includes a subsidiary operating expenses ledger which is controlled by the account Operating Expenses (No. 541) in the general ledger. Many of the operating expense accounts required end-of-year debit adjustments (with, of course, a summary debit to the general ledger control account). These adjustments involved offsetting credits to various general ledger accounts.

SPINNER & THOMAS
Supplementary Operating Expenses Work Sheet
For the Year Ended June 30, 19--

ACCOUNT	ACCT. NO.	TRIAL BALANCE DEBIT	ADJUSTMENTS DEBIT	ADJ. TRIAL BALANCE DEBIT
Office Salaries Expense	5401	41920 00		41920 00
Harlan Spinner, Salary Expense	5402	28800 00		28800 00
Office Supplies Expense	5403		(n) 7141 00	7141 00
Depreciation of Office Equip.	5404		(l) 1848 00	1848 00
Office Equip.—Insurance Exp.	5405		(o) 1200 00	1200 00
Office Rent Expense	5406	12000 00		12000 00
Payroll Taxes Expense	5407	8758 00		8758 00
Heat, Light & Water Expense	5408	4528 00		4528 00
Telephone Expense	5409	1029 00		1029 00
Postage Expense	5416	549 00		549 00
Uncollectible Accounts Expense	5417		(p) 180 00	180 00
Misc. General Expense	5422	754 00		754 00
Store Clerks Wage Expense	5431	24418 00		24418 00
Truck Drivers Wage Expense	5432	26376 00		26376 00
Advertising Expense	5433	2502 00		2502 00
Carol Thomas, Salary Expense	5434	28800 00		28800 00
Depreciation of Delivery Equip.	5435		(k) 7138 00	7138 00
Delivery Equip.—Ins. Expense	5436		(o) 2300 00	2300 00
Depreciation of Store Equip.	5437		(j) 1978 00	1978 00
Store Equipment Ins. Expense	5438		(o) 1150 00	1150 00
Truck Gas & Oil Expense	5441	6228 00		6228 00
Truck Repairs & Maint. Exp.	5442	696 00		696 00
Store Rent Expense	5443	18000 00		18000 00
Store Supplies Expense	5444		(m) 7724 00	7724 00
Misc. Selling Expense	5452	354 00		354 00
		205712 00	30659 00	236371 00

Spinner & Thomas—Operating Expenses Work Sheet

To assemble all the information needed both for the income statement and for the supporting schedule of operating expenses, and to facilitate the entering of adjustments in the general ledger and subsidiary ledger accounts (which must be done later), a supplementary operating expenses work sheet was used. As will be seen, it is very closely tied in with the summary work sheet. The Spinner & Thomas operating expenses work sheet is reproduced on page 558. Note that it was given an appropriate heading that included the period involved. This work sheet needed only three amount columns: (1) to show the account balances when the trial balance was taken, (2) to provide space for certain adjustments, and (3) to show the adjusted amounts. In every case only debits were involved. The titles and numbers of all the accounts in the subsidiary operating expenses ledger were placed in the columns provided at the left. (Refer to the chart of accounts given on page 530 for the complete list.) Observe that many of the accounts had no balance when the trial balance was taken. The balance of each account was entered in the Trial Balance Debit column. That column was totaled. If the total, $205,712, did not agree with the balance shown on the summary work sheet for Operating Expenses, Account No. 541 (the control account), it would have been necessary to discover and correct the discrepancy before the preparation of either work sheet could proceed.

All the adjustments that follow (for depreciation, supplies used, insurance expired, and the doubtful accounts provision) involved both the summary work sheet and the supplementary work sheet. One or more operating expense accounts were debited on the operating expenses work sheet, and one or more general ledger accounts were credited on the summary work sheet.

Depreciation Expense. In the general ledger of Spinner & Thomas, there are three long-term asset accounts with related accumulated depreciation accounts: Store Equipment, Delivery Equipment, and Office Equipment. In the operating expenses ledger, there are three depreciation expense accounts that correspond to the asset classifications. The firm's policy is that no depreciation is taken on assets owned for less than six months. The schedule on page 560 was prepared to determine the estimated depreciation expense for the year.

Based on the calculations shown on the schedule, the following adjustments were made on the work sheets—the debits on the operating expenses work sheet and the credits on the summary work sheet:

Entry (j): Depreciation of Store Equipment, Account No. 5437, was debited and Accumulated Depreciation—Store Equipment, Account No. 181.1, was credited for $1,978.

Schedule of Depreciation Expense
For the Year Ended June 30, 19--

Asset	*Cost*	*Annual (Straight-Line) Rate of Depreciation*	*Depreciation For the Year*
Store Equipment	$19,780	10%	$1,978
Delivery Equipment	57,100	12½	7,138
Office Equipment	18,480*	10	1,848

*Note that the balance of the office equipment account shown on the work sheet on page 554 is $19,001. That is because the cost of an electronic desk calculator ($521) purchased on June 18 is included. Since this asset has been owned for less than six months, no depreciation is taken on it.

Entry (k): Depreciation of Delivery Equipment, Account No. 5435, was debited and Accumulated Depreciation–Delivery Equipment, Account No. 185.1, was credited for $7,138.

Entry (l): Depreciation of Office Equipment, Account No. 5404, was debited and Accumulated Depreciation–Office Equipment, Account No. 191.1, was credited for $1,848.

Supplies Expense. The general ledger of Spinner & Thomas includes two asset accounts for supplies–Store Supplies and Office Supplies. When purchased, the supplies are entered as assets by debiting the accounts, Store Supplies, Account No. 151, and Office Supplies, Account No. 152. An inventory of unused supplies is taken at the end of the year so that the cost of the supplies used can be calculated and charged to the proper operating expense accounts. The following schedule was prepared to determine the needed adjustments. The amount shown for each type of supplies was determined by a count of the unopened packages and boxes, which were assigned approximate costs of recent purchases.

Schedule of Supplies Used
For the Year Ended June 30, 19--

Asset	*Account Balance June 30, 19--*	*Amount on Hand June 30, 19--*	*Expense For Year*
Store Supplies	$8,974	$1,250	$7,724
Office Supplies	7,896	755	7,141

Based upon the calculation, the following adjustments were made on the work sheets:

Entry (m): Store Supplies Expense, Account No. 5444, was debited and Store Supplies, Account No. 151, was credited for $7,724.

Entry (n): Office Supplies Expense, Account No. 5403, was debited and Office Supplies, Account No. 152, was credited for $7,141.

Insurance Expense. Prepaid insurance premiums are entered by Spinner & Thomas in the same manner as supplies. At the time of payment of a premium, the amount paid is entered as an asset by debiting Prepaid Insurance, Account No. 155. At the end of the fiscal year, June 30, calculations are made to determine the fraction of the total term of each policy that elapsed during the year. Each amount thus determined is classified according to the type of asset insured and charged to the proper insurance expense account. The operating expenses ledger of Spinner & Thomas includes insurance expense accounts for the insurance on delivery equipment, store equipment, and office equipment.

The following schedule of insurance expense was prepared from a file of information relating to insurance policies.

Schedule of Insurance Expense
For the Year Ended June 30, 19--

Type of Property Insured	*Expense for Year*
Delivery Equipment	$2,300
Store Equipment	1,150
Office Equipment	1,200
Total	$4,650

Based upon this schedule, the following adjustment was made on the work sheets:

Entry (o): Delivery Equipment Insurance Expense, Account No. 5436, was debited for $2,300; Store Equipment Insurance Expense, Account No. 5438, was debited for $1,150; Office Equipment Insurance Expense, Account No. 5405, was debited for $1,200; and Prepaid Insurance, Account No. 155, was credited for $4,650.

Doubtful Accounts. Spinner & Thomas uses the allowance method of accounting for doubtful accounts. On the basis of "aging" the accounts receivable, it was estimated that $240 of such accounts will not be collected. Since there already is a $60 balance in the allowance for doubtful accounts, $180 more is needed to make the required $240. The following entry was made on the work sheets:

Entry (p): Uncollectible Accounts Expense, Account No. 5417, was debited and Allowance for Doubtful Accounts, Account No. 131.1, was credited for $180.

Completing The Operating Expenses Work Sheet

In order to complete this work sheet, the amount for each operating expense account was extended into the Adjusted Trial Balance column. Note that in every case, the extended amount was either the unadjusted amount or the amount of the adjustment. The Adjustments and Adjusted Trial Balance columns were then totaled. Since only debits were involved in this work sheet, the total of the Adjusted Trial Balance column, $236,371, had to be equal to the sum of the totals of the Trial Balance and Adjustments columns ($205,712 + $30,659). A double rule was placed below the three totals.

Completing The Summary Work Sheet

To complete the adjustments on the summary work sheet, the balance of the control account, Operating Expenses, had to be increased to reflect the total of all of the debits to the operating expenses that had been made on the supplementary work sheet. Accordingly, that total, $30,659, was entered on the line for Operating Expenses, Account No. 541, in the Adjustments Debit column. Note that the debit was identified as "(j-p)," since it was offset by credits to seven general ledger accounts made when adjustments (j) through (p) were entered on the work sheets to adjust the operating expense accounts.

The Adjustments columns were totaled to prove the equality of the debits and credits. The amounts in the Trial Balance columns, adjusted where indicated by amounts in the Adjustments columns, were extended to the Adjusted Trial Balance columns. The latter also were totaled to prove the equality of the debits and credits. Each amount in the Adjusted Trial Balance columns was extended to the proper Income Statement or Balance Sheet column. The last four columns were then totaled.

Note that the Income Statement Credit column exceeded the Debit column by $26,318, and that the Balance Sheet Debit column exceeded the Credit column by the same amount. This means that Spinner & Thomas had a profitable year. "Net Income" was written on the next line at the left, and the amount, $26,318, was placed in the two proper places (Income Statement debit column and Balance Sheet credit column). The Income Statement and Balance Sheet columns were then totaled to prove that each pair was in balance. Double rules were placed below the final totals in all ten columns.

The summary work sheet then can be used to prepare the income statement for the fiscal year (shown on page 579) and the balance sheet as of the last day of that year (shown on page 585). The supplementary work sheet provided the information for the schedule of operating expenses (shown on page 580).

BUILDING YOUR ACCOUNTING KNOWLEDGE

1. What three functions does a work sheet perform in the production of year-end (or other period-end) financial reports?
2. What was the first step in the preparation of the Spinner & Thomas summary work sheet?
3. Why was the Expense and Revenue Summary account omitted from the Spinner & Thomas work sheet when it was included in the MicroWorld work sheet?
4. What is the purpose of each of the cost of goods sold accounts maintained by Spinner & Thomas?
5. How many entries were made in the adjustments columns of the Spinner & Thomas summary work sheet to show the calculation of the cost of goods sold for each department and to adjust the departmental merchandise inventory accounts? Briefly explain the purpose of each of these adjustments.
6. What was the purpose of the only other adjustment made entirely in the summary work sheet?
7. What is the purpose of the supplementary work sheet for operating expenses? How many columns does it have and what is the purpose of each column?
8. How many entries were made both in the adjustments columns of the Spinner & Thomas summary work sheet and in the adjustments column of the supplementary operating expenses work sheet? Briefly explain the purpose of each of these adjustments.

APPLYING ACCOUNTING CONCEPTS

Exercise 18-1. The following amounts were taken from the accounts of Sewell and Cherry, partners of a small retail business. Determine the individual cost of goods sold for Departments A and B for the fiscal year ended June 30, 19--:

Merchandise Inventory, Department A, July 1	$ 1,613
Merchandise Inventory, Department B, July 1	1,309
Merchandise Inventory, Department A, June 30	1,579
Merchandise Inventory, Department B, June 30	1,499
Purchases, Department A	517,675
Purchases, Department B	355,100
Purchases Returns and Allowances, Department A	719
Purchases Returns and Allowances, Department B	359

Exercise 18-2. On June 30, Sewell and Cherry owned United States government notes, face value of $5,000, interest rate 12%. Semiannual interest totaling $300 had been collected on May 15.

Determine the amount of interest earned but not yet received that would be entered as an adjustment on the summary work sheet for the year ended June 30, 19--.

Exercise 18-3. Sewell and Cherry follow the policy of taking depreciation only on assets owned for six months or more. Complete the following schedule to determine the estimated depreciation expense for the year.

Assets	Cost	Annual Rate of Depreciation	Depreciation for the Year
Store Equipment	$14,866	10%	?
Delivery Equipment	34,100*	12 1/2%	?
Office Equipment	12,500	10%	?

*The balance of the delivery equipment account includes $7,800 for a vehicle purchased on September 15.

Exercise 18-4. Sewell and Cherry enter payments for supplies as assets when they are purchased. An inventory of unused supplies is taken at the end of the year so that the cost of the supplies used can be calculated and charged to the proper operating expense accounts.

Complete the following schedule to determine the needed adjustments for the fiscal year ended June 30, 19--.

Asset	Account Balance June 30, 19--	Amount on Hand June 30, 19--	Expense For Year
Store Supplies	$6,748	$750	?
Office Supplies	5,696	255	?

Exercise 18-5. At the time of payment of insurance premiums, Sewell and Cherry enter the amount paid as an asset by debiting Prepaid Insurance. Complete the following schedule to determine the adjustments needed for Insurance Expense for the year ended June 30, 19--.

Type of Property Insured	Account Balance June 30, 19--	Unexpired Insurance Premium	Expense For Year
Delivery Equipment	$1,374	$916	?
Store Equipment	936	468	?
Office Equipment	1,458	972	?

Exercise 18-6. Sewell and Cherry use the allowance method of accounting for doubtful accounts. On the basis of ''aging'' the accounts receivable, it was estimated that $1,425 of such accounts would not be collected. For each of the following situations, use a T account to show the beginning balance, amount of adjustment, and end-of-the-year balance in the Allowance for Doubtful Accounts.

(a) If the Allowance for Doubtful Accounts already has a credit balance of $75, what is the amount to be entered as an adjustment to Uncollectible Accounts Expense for the current year? **(b)** If the Allowance for Doubtful Accounts has an unadjusted debit balance of $55, what is the amount to be entered as an adjustment to Uncollectible Accounts Expense for the current year?

Report No. 18-1

Complete Report No. 18-1 in the study assignments. Do not submit the report at this time. Since Reports Nos. 18-1 and 18-2 are related, you should retain the working papers until you have completed both reports. Continue with the textbook discussion until Report No. 18-2 is required.

ADJUSTING, CLOSING, AND REVERSING ENTRIES

The most important function of the year-end work sheet is to facilitate the preparation of the income statement and the balance sheet as soon as possible after the end of the accounting period. Having completed the work sheets illustrated and discussed in the preceding pages, the accountant for Spinner & Thomas would next prepare the financial statements. A secondary function of the work sheets is to aid in the process of formally entering adjusting and closing entries in the books. For the purpose of the organization of subject matter in this textbook, adjusting, closing, and reversing entries will be considered next. The financial statements will be illustrated and discussed in Chapter 19.

Journalizing The Adjusting Entries

Adjusting entries as of June 30 were entered in the general journal reproduced on pages 568-569. The form of general journal used by Spinner & Thomas provided a special Detail column for charges to the accounts in the operating expenses subsidiary ledger. Journalizing the adjusting entries involved the use of this column as well as the Debit and Credit columns. Several features of these entries should be noted:

1. The general ledger accounts are debited or credited in the conventional form; each subsidiary ledger account and its detail are also entered. However, the account numbers were entered when the journalizing was done, *not* as a step in the posting.
2. The entries were made in the same order as shown alphabetically (a) through (p), on the work sheets (pages 554-555, and 558). While this order is not essential, the danger of omitting an entry is slightly reduced by using the work sheets as a guide in journalizing the entries.
3. To be sure that the total of the debits equaled the total of the credits, the Debit and Credit columns were footed. The Detail column was footed and found to agree with the total of the Adjustments Debit column on the operating expenses work sheet. Finally, the totals were entered and the usual rulings were supplied.

Posting The Adjusting Entries

As the individual amounts in the Debit and Credit columns were posted to the accounts (indicated by the account numbers), a check mark (√) was placed to the right of each amount in the column provided. A check mark also was placed in parentheses below the total of each of these two columns to indicate that the amount was *not* posted to any ledger. In the case of the entries in the Detail column, a check mark was placed to the right of each amount as it was posted. A check mark was also placed in parentheses below the total of that column to indicate that the amount was also *not* posted to any ledger. In both the general ledger and the operating expenses ledger, the page of the general journal (GJ42) was placed in the Posting Reference column as each posting was made.

Journalizing The Closing Entries

The page of the general journal showing the closing entries as of June 30, 19--, is reproduced on page 570. Certain features of these entries should be noted:

1. Each closing entry was made in conventional form—the names of the accounts to be debited or credited were given. The names of the accounts to be credited were slightly indented. As in the case of the adjusting entries, however, the numbers of the accounts were entered at the time of journalizing. The check marks were made later as the posting was completed.
2. The order of the closing entries follows a logical sequence. The revenue accounts are closed first, followed by the expense accounts. The third entry closes the expense and revenue summary account by dividing the income ($26,318) between Spinner & Thomas in a 60-40 ratio as their partnership agreement specifies. The last two closing entries transfer the amount of each partner's withdrawals to the related capital account. The amount columns were footed to prove the equality of the debits and credits.

Note that, while there was a credit of $236,371 to close Operating Expenses, Account No. 541, the individual credits to close the twenty-five accounts in the operating expenses subsidiary ledger were not shown. One reason is that the form of the journal page does not accommodate credits to the operating expenses accounts, because these accounts rarely are credited (except when they are closed). The occasional transaction that requires a credit to an operating expense account can be handled by noting *both* the number of the control account (No. 541) and the number of the subsidiary ledger account in the account number column provided just to the left of the Detail column. The amount of the credit will then be posted as a credit to both accounts.

The operating expense accounts in the subsidiary ledger *must be closed* at the end of the fiscal year. The manner of doing so is illustrated by the reproduction of the account for Advertising Expense, Account No. 5433, shown on page 571. When a general ledger control account is closed, all accounts in a ledger that is subsidiary to that

GENERAL JOURNAL

PAGE 42

	DATE		DESCRIPTION	ACCT. NO.	DETAIL	√	DEBIT	√	CREDIT	√	
1	19– June	30	*Adjusting Entries*								1
2			Cost of Goods Sold–Dept. A	531			1,714.00	√			2
3			Merchandise Inventory–Dept. A	141					1,714.00	√	3
4			Cost of Goods Sold–Dept. B	532			1,410.00	√			4
5			Merchandise Inventory–Dept. B	142					1,410.00	√	5
6			Cost of Goods Sold–Dept. A	531			62,878.00	√			6
7			Purchases–Dept. A	511					62,878.00	√	7
8			Cost of Goods Sold–Dept. B	532			46,611.00	√			8
9			Purchases–Dept. B	521					46,611.00	√	9
10			Purchases Returns and Allowances–Dept. A	511.1			820.00	√			10
11			Cost of Goods Sold–Dept. A	531					820.00	√	11
12			Purchases Returns and Allowances–Dept. B	521.1			460.00	√			12
13			Cost of Goods Sold–Dept. B	532					460.00	√	13
14			Merchandise Inventory–Dept. A	141			1,680.00	√			14
15			Cost of Goods Sold–Dept. A	531					1,680.00	√	15
16			Merchandise Inventory–Dept. B	142			1,500.00	√			16
17			Cost of Goods Sold–Dept. B	532					1,500.00	√	17
18			Accrued Interest Receivable	122			50.00	√			18
19			Interest Earned	431					50.00	√	19

20			Operating Expenses	541			3 0 6 5 9 00	√			20
21			Office Supplies Expense	5403	7 1 4 1 00	√					21
22			Office Supplies	152					7 1 4 1 00	√	22
23			Store Supplies Expense	5444	7 7 2 4 00	√					23
24			Store Supplies	151					7 7 2 4 00	√	24
25			Uncollectible Accounts Expense	5417	1 8 0 00	√					25
26			Allowance for Doubtful Accounts	131.1					1 8 0 00	√	26
27			Depreciation of Store Equipment	5437	1 9 7 8 00	√					27
28			Accumulated Depreciation—Store Equipment	181.1					1 9 7 8 00	√	28
29			Depreciation of Delivery Equipment	5435	7 1 3 8 00	√					29
30			Accumulated Depreciation—Delivery Equipment	185.1					7 1 3 8 00	√	30
31			Depreciation of Office Equipment	5404	1 8 4 8 00	√					31
32			Accumulated Depreciation—Office Equipment	191.1					1 8 4 8 00	√	32
33			Delivery Equipment—Insurance Expense	5436	2 3 0 0 00	√					33
34			Store Equipment—Insurance Expense	5438	1 1 5 0 00	√					34
35			Office Equipment—Insurance Expense	5405	1 2 0 0 00	√					35
36			Prepaid Insurance	155					4 6 5 0 00	√	36
37					3 0 6 5 9 00		113 3 1 8 8 00		113 3 1 8 8 00		37
38					(√)		(√)		(√)		38
39											39

Spinner & Thomas—Adjusting Entries

GENERAL JOURNAL

PAGE *43*

	DATE		DESCRIPTION	ACCT. NO.	DETAIL	√	DEBIT	√	CREDIT	√	
1	*19– June*	*30*	*Closing Entries*								1
2			*Sales—Department A*	*411*			*73 4 6 2 9 00*	√			2
3			*Sales—Department B*	*421*			*62 0 9 8 8 00*	√			3
4			*Interest Earned*	*431*			*1 3 4 5 00*	√			4
5			*Expense and Revenue Summary*	*331*					*135 6 9 6 2 00*	√	5
6			*Expense and Revenue Summary*	*331*			*133 0 6 4 4 00*	√			6
7			*Sales Returns and Allowances—Department A*	*411.1*					*3 7 6 00*	√	7
8			*Sales Returns and Allowances—Department B*	*421.1*					*3 3 8 00*	√	8
9			*Cost of Goods Sold—Department A*	*531*					*62 7 9 9 9 00*	√	9
10			*Cost of Goods Sold—Department B*	*532*					*46 5 5 6 0 00*	√	10
11			*Operating Expenses*	*541*					*23 6 3 7 1 00*	√	11
12			*Expense and Revenue Summary*	*331*			*2 6 3 1 8 00*	√			12
13			*Harlan Spinner, Capital*	*311*					*1 5 7 9 1 00*	√	13
14			*Carol Thomas, Capital*	*321*					*1 0 5 2 7 00*	√	14
15			*Harlan Spinner, Capital*	*311*			*1 0 3 0 0 00*	√			15
16			*Harlan Spinner, Drawing*	*311.1*					*1 0 3 0 0 00*	√	16
17			*Carol Thomas, Capital*	*321*			*7 8 0 0 00*	√			17
18			*Carol Thomas, Drawing*	*321.1*					*7 8 0 0 00*	√	18
19							*273 2 0 2 4 00*		*273 2 0 2 4 00*		19
20							(√)		(√)		20
21											21
22											22
23											23
24											24
25											25
26											26

Spinner & Thomas—Closing Entries

control account also must be closed. The space and time required to list all of the subsidiary ledger accounts, numbers, and balances (twenty-five in the present case) can be saved if all subsidiary ledger expense accounts are closed at the same time that the operating expenses account is closed.

Posting The Closing Entries

The postings were made to the general ledger accounts indicated. A check mark was placed in the column provided in the general journal as each posting was made. The page of the general journal (GJ43) was noted in the Posting Reference column of the account involved. As mentioned in the preceding paragraph, the balance of each account in the subsidiary operating expenses ledger was closed in the manner indicated by the entry on the last line of the illustration of the account for Advertising Expense shown below. (Note that "GJ43" was entered in the Posting Reference column, since that is the page of the general journal on which the closing entry for the operating expenses control account was made.) The other twenty-four operating expense accounts were closed in a similar fashion.

ACCOUNT *Advertising Expense* ACCOUNT NO. *5433*

DATE		ITEM	POST. REF.	DEBIT	CREDIT	BALANCE
19–						
June	*1*	*Dr. Balance*	√			*2 4 8 9 00*
	30		*VR26*	*1 3 00*		*2 5 0 2 00*
	30		*GJ43*		*2 5 0 2 00*	*- 0 -*

Closed Subsidiary Operating Expense Ledger Account

The expense and revenue summary account and the two cost of goods sold accounts after the adjusting and closing entries had been posted are reproduced on page 572. Note that these accounts are summarizing accounts that are used only at the end of the accounting period. In some accounting systems, cost of goods sold accounts are used throughout the year if such cost is known at the time of sale. This is possible if perpetual inventories are maintained. In the periodic inventory method of Spinner & Thomas, the cost of goods sold accounts are used only at the end of the fiscal year.

ACCOUNT *Expense and Revenue Summary* ACCOUNT NO. 331

DATE		ITEM	POST. REF.	DEBIT	CREDIT	BALANCE DEBIT	BALANCE CREDIT
19–							
June	30		GJ43		135696200		
	30		GJ43	133064400			2631800
	30	To Close	GJ43	2631800		-0-	-0-

ACCOUNT *Cost of Goods Sold - Department A* ACCOUNT NO. 531

DATE		ITEM	POST. REF.	DEBIT	CREDIT	BALANCE DEBIT	BALANCE CREDIT
19–							
June	30	Beg. Inventory	GJ42	171400			
	30	Purchases	GJ42	62878500			
	30	Purchases R & A	GJ42		82000		
	30	End. Inventory	GJ42		168000	62799900	
	30	Exp. & Rev. Summary	GJ43		62799900	-0-	-0-

ACCOUNT *Cost of Goods Sold - Department B* ACCOUNT NO. 532

DATE		ITEM	POST. REF.	DEBIT	CREDIT	BALANCE DEBIT	BALANCE CREDIT
19–							
June	30	Beg. Inventory	GJ42	141000			
	30	Purchases	GJ42	46611000			
	30	Purchases R & A	GJ42		46000		
	30	End. Inventory	GJ42		150000	46556000	
	30	Exp. & Rev. Summary	GJ43		46556000	-0-	-0-

Closed General Ledger Summary Accounts

Post-Closing Trial Balance

After the closing entries were posted, a trial balance of the general ledger accounts that remained open was taken to prove the equality of the debit and credit balances. The post-closing trial balance of the general ledger of Spinner & Thomas is reproduced on page 573.

Spinner & Thomas Post Closing Trial Balance June 30, 19--			
Account	Acct. No.	Dr. Balance	Cr. Balance
Cash	111	34 435 00	
Petty Cash Fund	112	200 00	
Government Notes	121	10 000 00	
Accrued Interest Receivable	122	50 00	
Accounts Receivable	131	10 978 00	
Allowance for Doubtful Accounts	131.1		240 00
Merchandise Inventory—Department A	141	1 680 00	
Merchandise Inventory—Department B	142	1 500 00	
Store Supplies	151	1 250 00	
Office Supplies	152	755 00	
Prepaid Insurance	155	882 00	
Store Equipment	181	19 780 00	
Accumulated Depreciation—Store Equip.	181.1		3 658 00
Delivery Equipment	185	57 100 00	
Accumulated Depreciation—Delivery Equip.	185.1		49 938 00
Office Equipment	191	19 059 00	
Accumulated Depreciation—Office Equip.	191.1		3 263 00
FICA Tax Payable	211		1 162 00
FUTA Tax Payable	212		86 00
State Unemployment Tax Payable	213		389 00
Employees Income Tax Payable	214		1 010 00
Vouchers Payable	218		34 375 00
Harlan Spinner, Capital	311		44 222 00
Carol Thomas, Capital	321		19 326 00
		157 669 00	157 669 00

Spinner & Thomas—Post Closing Trial Balance

Some accountants feel that it is necessary to prepare a post-closing trial balance in the form illustrated and file it with various other records. Others think that it is sufficient merely to use an adding machine tape to list and total (1) the amounts of the debit balances and (2) the amounts of the credit balances to be sure that the totals are the same. In the latter case, if the ledger was found not to be in balance, the cause of the discrepancy would have to be located and remedied. Then the tapes would be discarded.

Reversing Entries

One adjusting entry (entry (i)) of the accrual type, Accrued Interest Receivable, was made as of June 30 in the amount of $50. In order that interest collections may be entered in routine fashion in the new period, Spinner & Thomas follows the practice of reversing accrual adjustments. The first entries for the new period are the reversals of the previous accrual adjustments. The reversing entry made on July 1, 19--, is shown below.

GENERAL JOURNAL **PAGE 43**

	DATE		DESCRIPTION	ACCT. NO.	DETAIL	√	DEBIT	√	CREDIT	√	
21	July	1	*Reversing Entry*								21
22			*Interest Earned*	431			50 00	√			22
23			*Accrued Interest Receivable*	122					50 00	√	23

Spinner & Thomas—Reversing Entry

BUILDING YOUR ACCOUNTING KNOWLEDGE

1. What is the purpose of the Detail column in Spinner & Thomas' general journal?
2. In what two ways are the accounts identified in entering the adjusting entries in the general journal?
3. Why are the Debit and Credit columns of the general journal footed? Why is the Detail column footed?
4. In what two ways are the accounts identified in entering the closing entries in the general journal?
5. What is the purpose of each of the five closing entries made by Spinner & Thomas?
6. How is the posting of the individual amounts in the adjusting and closing entries indicated in the general journal? In the general and operating expenses ledgers?
7. What is the purpose of the post-closing trial balance? What do some accountants use as a substitute?
8. Why does the accountant for Spinner & Thomas reverse accrual adjustments?

APPLYING ACCOUNTING CONCEPTS

Exercise 18-7. Using a general journal with a special Detail column for charges to the accounts in the operating expenses subsidiary ledger, enter the adjusting entries for the following exercises. Foot and rule the Detail, Debit and Credit columns. (Omit account numbers.)

1. Exercise 18-1.
2. Exercise 18-2.

Exercise 18-8. Enter the adjusting entries for the following exercises in a general journal with a special Detail column for charges to the accounts in the operating expenses subsidiary ledger. Foot and rule the Detail, Debit and Credit columns. (Omit account numbers.)

1. Exercise 18-3.
2. Exercise 18-4.
3. Exercise 18-5.
4. Exercise 18-6 (a).

Exercise 18-9. The following are account balances taken from the accounting records of Sentinel Electronic Equipment.

Sales, Department A	$623,518
Sales, Department B	519,876
Interest Earned	234
Sales Returns and Allowances, Department A	265
Sales Returns and Allowances, Department B	227
Cost of Goods Sold, Department A	516,888
Cost of Goods Sold, Department B	354,450
Operating Expenses	125,260
Charlene Potts, Drawing	10,400
Carol Corley, Drawing	7,900

(a) Using a general journal with a special Detail column for charges to the accounts in the operating expenses subsidiary ledger, enter the necessary closing entries. Divide profits and losses equally. **(b)** Prepare a T account for the expense and revenue summary account. Post the closing entries to this account. **(c)** Foot and rule the columns.

Exercise 18-10. Refer to Exercises 18-7 and 18-8. Prepare in general journal form reversing entries for any accrual type adjustments so that transactions in the new period may be entered in routine fashion.

Report No. 18-2

Complete Report No. 18-2 in the study assignments and submit Reports Nos. 18-1 and 18-2 for approval. Continue with the textbook discussion in Chapter 19 until Report No. 19-1 is required.

EXPANDING YOUR BUSINESS VOCABULARY

What is the meaning of each of the following terms:

- adjusting entries **(p. 566)**
- closing entries **(p. 567)**
- post-closing trial balance **(p. 572)**
- reversing entries **(p. 574)**
- summary year-end work sheet **(p. 553)**
- supplementary work sheet for operating expenses **(p. 557))**

CHAPTER 19

The Annual Report

CHAPTER OBJECTIVES

Careful study of this chapter should enable you to:

- Describe and explain the nature of an annual report.
- Prepare a summarized income statement that shows the components and amounts of gross margin on sales by departments and in total, supplemented by schedules of cost of goods sold and of operating expenses.
- Analyze the income statement using percentage analysis, merchandise turnover analysis, and comparative analysis.
- Prepare a balance sheet for a partnership supplemented by a schedule of accounts receivable.
- Analyze the balance sheet using ratio analysis and comparative analysis.
- Perform an analysis of profitability of a business.
- Describe and prepare a statement of changes in financial position (working capital basis), including a supporting schedule of changes in working capital.

The term annual report as applied to a business usually refers to the financial statements and schedules relating to the accounting (fiscal) year of the enterprise. The report generally includes an income statement, a balance sheet, and a statement of changes in financial position. In business corporations with many stockholders (thousands, even hundreds of thousands, in some cases), the annual report may be a thirty- to sixty-page printed publication—sometimes in full color with numerous pictures of the company's products, plants, officers, and various graphs and statistics in addition to the financial statements.

Reports of this type usually include a letter addressed to the stockholders signed by the president of the corporation or by the chairman of the board of directors and sometimes by both. The letter is printed in the report booklet and is often described as "highlights" of the year. Such annual reports invariably include the **opinion** (sometimes referred to as the **Auditor's Report**) of the CPA firm that performed the audit of the company's financial statements.

Annual reports of the elaborate type just mentioned are not used if the business has few owners. In a partnership, it is probable that only the partners and, possibly, one or two of the officials at their bank see the reports. The annual report of Spinner & Thomas consists of the following statements and schedules:

Income Statement for the Year
- Schedule of Cost of Goods Sold
- Schedule of Operating Expenses

Balance Sheet as of June 30
- Schedule of Accounts Receivable

Statement of Changes in Financial Position for the Year (Working Capital Basis)
- Schedule of Changes in Working Capital

THE INCOME STATEMENT

The income statement and schedule of cost of goods sold for the year ended June 30, 19--, for Spinner & Thomas are reproduced on page 579. They were prepared from information provided by the Income Statement columns of the work sheet reproduced on pages 554 and 555. The income statement is arranged to show the sales, cost of goods sold, and the gross margin on sales for each department as well as in total. The schedule of cost of goods sold shows the components that made up the cost of goods sold for each department and the total.

The schedule of operating expenses reproduced on page 580 was prepared from information provided by the operating expenses work sheet shown on page 558. The schedule provides the detail of what makes up the total amount of operating expenses ($236,371) shown on the income statement. If there were only five or ten accounts for operating expenses, it is probable that (1) there would have been no subsidiary ledger for such expenses and (2) the accounts would have been included in the income statement, in which case no schedule would have been needed. There is wide variation in the form and content of financial statements. Some accountants, for example, may present the components of cost of goods sold in the income statement instead of in the "supporting" schedule as illustrated below.

Spinner & Thomas
Income Statement
For the Year Ended June 30, 19--

	Dept. A	Dept. B	Total
Sales	$734,629	$620,988	$1,355,617
Less sales returns and allowances	376	338	714
Net sales	$734,253	$620,650	$1,354,903
Cost of goods sold	627,999	465,560	1,093,559
Gross margin on sales	$106,254	$155,090	$ 261,344
Operating expenses			236,371
Operating income			$ 24,973
Other revenue:			
Interest earned			1,345
Net income			$ 26,318

Spinner & Thomas—Income Statement

Spinner & Thomas
Schedule of Cost of Goods Sold
For the Year Ended June 30, 19--

	Dept. A	Dept. B	Total
Merchandise inventory, July 1, 19--	$ 1,714	$ 1,410	$ 3,124
Purchases	$628,785	$466,110	$1,094,895
Less purchases returns and allowances	820	460	1,280
Net purchases	$627,965	$465,650	$1,093,615
Merchandise available for sale	$629,679	$467,060	$1,096,739
Less merchandise inventory, June 30, 19--	1,680	1,500	3,180
Cost of goods sold	$627,999	$465,560	$1,093,559

Spinner & Thomas—Schedule of Cost of Goods Sold

Spinner & Thomas
Schedule of Operating Expenses
For the Year Ended June 30, 19--

Administrative expenses:	
Office salaries expense	$ 41,920
Harlan Spinner, salary expense	28,800
Office supplies expense	7,141
Depreciation of office equipment	1,848
Office equipment insurance expense	1,200
Office rent expense	12,000
Payroll taxes expense	8,758
Heat, light, and water expense	4,528
Telephone expense	1,029
Postage expense	549
Uncollectible accounts expense	180
Miscellaneous general expense	754
Total administrative expenses	$108,707
Selling expenses:	
Store clerks wage expense	$ 24,418
Truck drivers wage expense	26,376
Advertising expense	2,502
Carol Thomas, salary expense	28,800
Depreciation of delivery equipment	7,138
Delivery equipment insurance expense	2,300
Depreciation of store equipment	1,978
Store equipment insurance expense	1,150
Truck, gas, and oil expense	6,228
Truck repairs and maintenance expense	696
Store rent expense	18,000
Store supplies expense	7,724
Miscellaneous selling expense	354
Total selling expenses	$127,664
Total operating expenses	$236,371

Spinner & Thomas—Schedule of Operating Expenses

Interpreting The Income Statement

There are numerous ways to analyze an income statement. Three types of analysis will be dealt with in this chapter: (1) percentage analysis, (2) merchandise turnover, and (3) comparative analysis.

Percentage Analysis. In order of importance, the most significant items shown by the annual income statement are the total amounts of (1) net income, (2) sales, (3) cost of goods sold and gross margin (considered together because of the interrelationship), and (4) operating expenses. The dollar amounts of these items take on added meaning if their proportionate relationship to each other is computed and compared. Using Spinner & Thomas's income statement as an example, the customary way of studying these relationships is by percentage analysis, using net sales as the base, 100%.

Net sales	$1,354,903	100.0%
Cost of goods sold	1,093,559	80.7
Gross margin	$ 261,344	19.3%
Operating expenses	236,371	17.5
Operating income	$ 24,973	1.8%
Other revenue	1,345	0.1
Net income	$ 26,318	1.9%

This analysis shows that net income is slightly less than 2% of net sales, with other revenue representing a relatively minor amount. In other words, each dollar of net sales resulted in about two cents of net profit.

Spinner & Thomas may compare these percentages with the same percentages for other similar wholesale/retail bakery businesses, or with their own percentages of operating results for prior years, to determine the relative profitability of their bakery operation.

The same type of analysis can be applied to the data for the net sales, cost of goods sold, and gross margin of each department, as shown below.

	Dept. A		Dept. B	
Net sales	$734,253	100.0%	$620,650	100%
Cost of goods sold	627,999	85.5	465,560	75
Gross margin	$106,254	14.5%	$155,090	25%

Spinner & Thomas might find this analysis useful in the determination of the relative emphasis to place on the output of each department, the possible expansion or contraction of either department, or the need for a review of the pricing policies in either department.

Merchandise Turnover. The data reported in the income statement and in the schedule of cost of goods sold make it possible to compute the merchandise turnover during the year. For the business as a whole, the average inventory was $3,152 ($3,124 beginning inventory plus $3,180 ending inventory, divided by two). Since the total cost of goods sold was $1,093,559, the turnover was almost 347 times ($1,093,559 ÷ $3,152). This means that, on the average, goods remained in stock for about a day, an obviously desirable condition for a bakery. Using the same calculation for each department reveals that the turnover in Department A was 370.1, and in Department B, 320.0. The turnover ratio can help Spinner & Thomas determine whether they are carrying significant amounts of slowmoving bakery products. Based on the departmental turnover ratios, Spinner & Thomas might want to examine in detail the turnover of selected products carried in Department B.

Comparative Analysis. Added meaning is given to the information supplied by an income statement if it is compared with statements for past periods. By using such comparative analysis, answers will be provided to such vital questions as: Are sales growing or shrinking? How much has net income increased or decreased (both absolutely and relatively)? Has the gross margin percentage become larger or smaller? It may be assumed that the first thing each partner did after looking at the income statement for the year just ended was to compare it with the statement for the preceding year—probably for several preceding years. Often, income statements and other financial statements are prepared in comparative form to aid in their interpretation.

BUILDING YOUR ACCOUNTING KNOWLEDGE

1. What three financial statements generally are included in the annual report of a business?
2. Who are likely to be the only users of the annual report of a partnership?
3. What three major items are shown for each department and in total on the Spinner & Thomas income statement?

4. What is the source of the information contained in the schedule of operating expenses?
5. What are the two major categories of expenses shown on the schedule of operating expenses of Spinner & Thomas?
6. What is the customary way of relating cost of goods sold, gross margin, operating expenses, and net income to net sales using percentage analysis? What use is made of such analysis?
7. How is the merchandise turnover for the year computed? What use is made of the turnover ratio?
8. How is the technique of comparative analysis applied to the information supplied by an income statement? What vital questions does comparative analysis help to answer?

APPLYING ACCOUNTING CONCEPTS

Exercise 19-1. The following account balances were taken from the income statement columns of the work sheet of Aztec Sales, a firm owned by Dennis Yee and Alvaro Yepez, partners. Aztec's fiscal year ends on December 31, 19--.

	Dept. A	Dept. B	Total
Sales	$823,518	$519,877	$1,343,395
Sales returns and allowances	265	277	492
Merchandise inventory, Jan. 1	1,903	1,309	3,212
Merchandise inventory, Dec. 31	1,579	1,499	3,078
Purchases	517,674	355,009	872,683
Purchases returns and allowances	719	359	1,078
Office salaries expense			30,800
Office supplies expense			6,030
Uncollectible accounts expense			179
Miscellaneous general expense			643
Sales salaries expense			1,491
Advertising expense			27,700
Depreciation of store equipment			867
Store rent expense			12,000
Miscellaneous selling expense			243

Prepare a schedule of cost of goods sold for each department and in total.

Exercise 19-2. Using the appropriate account balances from Exercise 19-1, prepare a schedule of operating expenses in total for Aztec Sales.

Exercise 19-3. Refer to Exercises 19-1 and 19-2 and prepare a summarized income statement. Show the components and amounts of gross margin on sales by department and in total for Aztec Sales.

Exercise 19-4. Refer to Exercise 19-3. Aztec Sales, using net sales as the base, studies the proportionate relationship between net income, sales, cost of goods sold, gross margin, and operating expenses by percentage analysis.

(a) Calculate these percentages in total. Each dollar of net sales resulted in approximately how many cents of net profit? **(b)** Calculate these percentages by department for net sales, cost of goods sold, and gross margin. Which department had a higher cost of goods sold percentage? Which department contributed a greater percentage of gross margin to the total? **(c)** Determine the merchandise turnover. Last year the turnover rate was 300. Is the merchandise selling faster or slower this year?

Report No. 19-1

Complete Report No. 19-1 in the study assignments. Do not submit the report at this time. Since Reports 19-1, 19-2, and 19-3 are related, you should retain the working papers until you have completed all three reports. Continue with the textbook discussion until Report No. 19-2 is required.

THE BALANCE SHEET

The following balance sheet of Spinner & Thomas as of June 30, 19--, is arranged in report form. It was prepared from information pro-

SPINNER & THOMAS
Balance Sheet
June 30, 19--

Assets

Current assets:				
Cash			$ 34,635	
Government notes			10,000	
Accrued interest receivable			50	
Accounts receivable		$10,978		
Less allowance for doubtful accounts		240	10,738	
Merchandise inventories:				
Department A		$ 1,680		
Department B		1,500	3,180	
Supplies and prepayments			2,887	
Total current assets				$ 61,490
Long-term assets:				
	Cost	Accum. Depr.	Undepr. Cost	
Store equipment	$19,780	$ 3,658	$ 16,122	
Delivery equipment	57,100	49,938	7,162	
Office equipment	19,001	3,263	15,738	
Total long-term assets	$95,881	$56,859		39,022
Total assets				$100,512

Liabilities

Current liabilities:			
Accounts payable		$ 34,375	
Accrued and withheld payroll taxes		2,589	
Total current liabilities			$ 36,964

Owners' Equity

	Harlan Spinner	Carol Thomas	
Capital, July 1, 19--	$ 38,731	$ 16,599	
Net income ($26,318, divided 60% – 40%)	15,791	10,527	
Less withdrawals	(10,300)	(7,800)	
Capital, June 30, 19--	$ 44,222	$19,326	63,548
Total liabilities and owners' equity			$100,512

Spinner & Thomas—Balance Sheet

vided by the Balance Sheet columns of the work sheet reproduced on pages 554 and 555. Note that the current assets were presented first and arrayed in their probable order of liquidity. Cash was shown first followed by government notes. These notes are regarded as temporary investments since they can be liquidated with relative ease if a shortage of cash should occur. Accrued interest receivable, accounts receivable (less the allowance for doubtful accounts) and merchandise inventories were shown next, and lastly supplies and prepayments. These latter items are included as current assets because their present ownership means that less money will have to be spent for such purposes in the near future. It is not expected that these items will be directly converted into cash. Long-term assets of Spinner & Thomas are the last assets listed. They are shown in columnar form, an approach not previously illustrated, for the purpose of condensing the report.

All of the liabilities of the firm are current liabilities. The owners' equity section is arranged to show the nature and amount of the change in each partner's equity during the year.

The balance sheet is supported by a schedule of accounts receivable as of June 30, 19--. This schedule is just a list of the subsidiary accounts receivable ledger accounts as of the close of the year. It is not an integral part of the balance sheet.

Spinner & Thomas
Schedule of Accounts Receivable
June 30, 19--

Ayres Department Stores	$ 1,915
Bakemeier's Bakery	1,610
Brother Juniper's	1,219
Heritage House	1,278
Houlihan's Place	1,150
Methodist Hospital	1,294
Sam's Deli	1,249
The Tin Star	1,263
	$10,978

Spinner & Thomas—Schedule of Accounts Receivable

Interpreting The Balance Sheet

In interpreting the balance sheet, it is important to remember that the amounts of certain assets as shown on a conventional balance sheet do not necessarily reflect their current values. For example, even though most of Spinner & Thomas's inventory is sold each day, there may be unsalable items in the inventory that remain on hand for another day or more. Also, the undepreciated cost of the long-term assets (the difference between the original cost of these assets and the depreciation so far charged off as expense) does not indicate what these assets would bring if they were to be sold nor does it indicate what it would cost to buy these assets. The difference ($39,022 in total) merely represents the amount, less any expected scrap or salvage value, that is to be charged against future revenues. With these considerations in mind, there are ways to analyze the balance sheet. Two commonly used types of analysis are discussed below: (1) ratio analysis and (2) comparative analysis.

Ratio Analysis. One use of the balance sheet is to aid in judging the liquidity of a business, that is, the ability of the enterprise to meet its current debt obligations. Besides the relative amounts of current assets and current liabilities, the composition of these resources and obligations must also be considered in judging liquidity. Two commonly used measures of liquidity are the current ratio and the quick ratio. The ratio of the current assets ($61,490) to current liabilities ($36,964) of Spinner & Thomas is 1.66 to 1. This is adequate, but of equal or greater significance is the fact that the "quick" assets (cash, temporary investments, and current receivables) total $55,423—1.5 times the current liabilities. This indicates that the firm more than passes the acid test (a ratio of quick assets to total current liabilities of at least 1 to 1).

Comparative Analysis. As in the case of income statements, a comparison of current and past balance sheets may be informative. Comparative balance sheets are often presented in stockholders' reports. In some cases, an analysis that involves expressing one amount as a percent of another may be helpful. In other cases, comparisons of ratios may be more meaningful.

This type of analysis can be illustrated by using the comparative balance sheet summary of Spinner & Thomas on page 596. Note that the current ratio has improved from 1.16 to 1 ($41,750 ÷ $35,885) to 1.66 to 1 ($61,490 ÷ $36,964) from the beginning to the end of the year. In addition, current assets amounted to 61% of total assets at the end of the year, compared with only about 46% at the beginning of the year.

These ratios and percentages indicate that Spinner & Thomas have strengthened their financial control of the business during the year. The percentages also suggest that Spinner & Thomas probably could afford to increase their investment in long-term assets.

Analysis of Profitability

Analysis of profitability involves the use of both income statement and balance sheet data. The amount of annual net income does not mean too much by itself. However, when this amount is contrasted with the volume of sales, the average total amount of the assets, or the average total of the owners' equity element of the business, a better indication of profitability is provided. It was noted on page 581 that Spinner & Thomas had net income equal to almost 2% of net sales. The relationship between Spinner & Thomas' net income and their assets and owners' equity will now be considered.

According to the comparative balance sheet summary on page 596, Spinner & Thomas had average total assets for the fiscal year of $95,863 [($91,215 + $100,512) ÷ 2]. The ratio of net income to average total assets, which is known as return on assets, was therefore 27.5% (net income of $26,318 ÷ average total assets of $95,863).

Spinner & Thomas' average total owners' equity for the fiscal year was $59,439 [($55,330 + $63,548) ÷ 2]. The ratio of net income to average owners' equity, which is known as return on equity, was therefore 44.3% (net income of $26,318 ÷ average owners' equity of $59,439).

Both the return on assets and the return on equity of Spinner & Thomas appear to be very favorable. In judging these relationships, however, it must be remembered that no income tax has been taken into consideration, since partnerships, as such, do not pay income taxes. In their individual income tax returns, Spinner & Thomas must include their shares of the partnership net income along with any "salary" payments or allowances. The amount of any cash or other assets received from the firm is not relevant to the calculation of each partner's taxable income. The amount of income tax that each partner must pay depends upon the total amount of income from various sources, the amount of various deductions and credits that may be taken, and the number of exemptions to which the partner is entitled.

BUILDING YOUR ACCOUNTING KNOWLEDGE

1. In what order are the current assets arrayed on the balance sheet of Spinner & Thomas?
2. Why are supplies and prepayments included among the current assets?
3. What group of assets is listed after the current assets?

4. What is the owner's equity section of the balance sheet arranged to show?
5. Give two examples of balance sheet assets that do not necessarily reflect their current values.
6. What are the current ratio and the quick ratio used to judge or measure?
7. What are the percentage of net income to sales, the return on assets, and the return on owner's equity, used to measure?

APPLYING ACCOUNTING CONCEPTS

Exercise 19-5. The following balances were taken from the balance sheet columns of the end-of-year work sheet of Blue Haven Supplies, a partnership owned by June Betes and Wendy Reed. The fiscal year ends December 31, 19--

Cash	$23,524
Government notes	9,000
Accrued interest receivable	150
Accounts receivable	9,867
Allowance for doubtful accounts	235
Merchandise inventory, Dept. A	1,579
Merchandise inventory, Dept. B	1,499
Supplies and prepayments	1,776
Store equipment	18,670
Accumulated depreciation on store equipment	3,547
Accounts payable	23,264
Accrued and withheld payroll taxes	1,479
June Betes, capital	27,620
Wendy Reed, capital	15,488

Net income for the year was $20,432; profits were split 50-50; and Betes withdrew $14,000 and Reed withdrew $12,000.

Prepare a classified balance sheet in report form for Blue Haven Supplies.

Exercise 19-6. Refer to Exercise 19-5. Make the following calculations related to the liquidity and profitability of Blue Haven Supplies: **(a)** current ratio, **(b)** quick ratio or acid test, **(c)** percent of current assets to total assets, **(d)** return on assets (total assets were $60,285 at the beginning of the current year), and **(e)** return on equity for each partner and for the partnership.

Report No. 19-2

Complete Report No. 19-2 in the study assignments. Do not submit the report at this time. Since Reports 19-1, 19-2, and 19-3 are related, you should retain the working papers until you have completed all three reports. Continue with the textbook discussion until Report No. 19-3 is required.

THE STATEMENT OF CHANGES IN FINANCIAL POSITION

The annual report of Spinner & Thomas includes a statement of changes in financial position for the year. Since this type of statement has not been discussed or illustrated in earlier chapters, its nature and purpose will be explained before the one for Spinner & Thomas is considered.

Nature and Purpose of the Statement

The managers of a business have the dual objective of generating net income (profitability) and of keeping the enterprise solvent (liquidity). It would seem that success in achievement of the first objective would automatically assure achievement of the second objective. Net income brings in cash—either at once, or as soon as receivables are collected. To assure solvency or liquidity is not that simple, however. The cash inflow resulting from profitable operations may be used to acquire long-term assets, to discharge long-term indebtedness, or it may be withdrawn by the owners. Many profitable and growing businesses suffer from a continual shortage of working capital (current assets minus current liabilities), or may suffer from a chronic *cash* shortage. Sometimes the reverse is the case. There may be little or no net income, and yet by occasional sales of long-term assets, by borrowing on a long-term basis, or by additional investments by the owners, the business maintains ample working capital, or may obtain a supply of ready cash. The increase or decrease in working capital or in cash is the result of the interplay of various management actions and outside influences.

In analyzing the affairs of a business, it is helpful to know the reasons for an increase or a decrease in working capital or in cash during the period under review. To provide this information, a special type of financial statement that explains the change in working capital or in cash has been developed. The preferred title for this financial statement is the statement of changes in financial position. However, it is sometimes called the fund-change statement, the statement of sources and uses of funds, or the statement of changes in working capital.

In ordinary usage, "funds" often is used as a synonym for cash. The term "fund" is used to describe cash or other assets set aside for a specified purpose such as a petty cash fund. In government finance and accounting, a fund is a segregated collection of cash and other assets (and, sometimes, related liabilities) held or used for a certain purpose, such as a highway construction fund. In connection with the Statement of Changes in Financial Position, the word "funds" usually means either working capital or cash. A number of slight variations from these meanings are used in practice, but these are the two basic definitions of "funds." A statement of changes in financial position is a statement explaining the increase or decrease in the working capital or cash of a business during a specified period of time.

At the present time, about an equal number of companies use cash and working capital to express their changes in financial position. Many accountants believe that a statement of sources and uses of cash better explains what is happening to the business. For many purposes, periodic statements of cash receipts and disbursements are needed. But the proper emphasis may be quite different in particular sets of circumstances. To illustrate, consider the following comparative statement of the current assets and current liabilities of a business at the beginning and end of a year:.

	Beginning of Year	End of Year
Current Assets:		
Cash	$ 20,000	$100,000
Temporary investments	40,000	10,000
Receivables (net)	80,000	60,000
Inventories and prepayments	60,000	70,000
Total	$200,000	$240,000
Current Liabilities:		
Notes, accounts, and taxes payable	50,000	160,000
Working capital	$150,000	$ 80,000

Cash increased 400% but the liquidity position of the company tightened considerably. The current ratio changed from 4 to 1 ($200,000:$50,000) to only 1.5 to 1 ($240,000:$160,000), and the quick (acid-test) ratio from 2.8 to 1 ($140,000:$50,000) to 1.06 to 1 ($170,000:$160,000). In analyzing what has happened in the business, the $70,000 decrease in working capital may prove to be of some future concern despite the increase in cash of $80,000. A statement of changes in financial position based on working capital would shed some light on such a potential problem in this set of circumstances. The working capital approach is explained and illustrated in this chapter. The cash approach will be explained and illustrated in Chapter 28.

Sources of Funds

Funds in the form of working capital may be secured or obtained in four ways:

Investments by Owners. When the owners invest cash or other current assets in the business, working capital is increased.

Profitable Operations. When there has been net income for an accounting period, the increase in cash and receivables due to sales and other revenue must have been more than the total of the decrease in inventory (because of goods sold) and either the decrease in cash or the increase in current payables that took place when expenses were incurred. (The special problem of depreciation and a few other expenses that do not reduce working capital when incurred will be discussed at a later point.)

Long-Term Borrowing. When money is borrowed and the promised date of repayment is two or more years in the future, working capital is increased as a result of a current asset increasing and a long-term liability increasing. (Short-term borrowing does not affect working capital because the increase in cash is exactly offset by the increase in a current liability—usually notes payable.)

Sale of Long-Term Assets. When long-term assets, such as land, buildings, equipment, or trucks are sold, usually either cash or current receivables is increased. In either case, working capital is increased.

Uses of Funds

Funds in the form of working capital may be used or applied in four ways:

Withdrawals by Owners. When the owners of a business take money out either because there has been a profit, or as a withdrawal of their capital investment, working capital is reduced. In corporations, the payment of cash dividends is an example of this type of use of funds.

Unprofitable Operations. When there has been a net loss for an accounting period, either the decrease in cash or the increase in current payables that took place when expenses were incurred plus the decrease in inventory (because of goods sold) must have been more than the increase in cash and receivables due to sales and other revenue.

Repayment of Long-Term Borrowing. When long-term liabilities, such as mortgages payable, are paid, cash and thus working capital are reduced. The discharge of short-term obligations does not affect working capital because the decrease in cash is offset by an equal decrease in a current liability.

Purchase of Long-Term Assets. When a long-term asset (land, building, equipment, etc.) is purchased, usually either cash is reduced or accounts payable is increased. In either case, working capital is diminished.

Direct Financing

There are some changes in financial position in the course of a year that affect only long-term assets and long-term liabilities. For example, buildings or equipment may be acquired in exchange for a mortgage payable over a period of years. In essence, the mortgage payable is a source of funds, and the acquisition of buildings or equipment is a use of funds, but since the source exactly offsets the use, there is no effect on working capital (or cash).

In spite of this, the accounting profession prefers, for purposes of adequate disclosure, that transactions of a direct financing nature (in which the use of funds exactly matches their source) be shown on the statement of changes in financial position. The mortgage payable in the example above may be shown under "Sources" (Long-term Borrowing) and the buildings (or equipment) acquired under "Uses" (Purchase of Long-term Assets).

Simplified Example of Statement of Changes in Financial Position

The statement of changes in financial position is prepared from information supplied by the balance sheets at the beginning and end of the accounting period involved, plus certain other data found in the income statement. To illustrate, the balance sheets of Mach & Mash at the beginning and end of the year 19-- are shown on page 594.

	Beginning of Year	End of Year
Assets:		
Cash	$120,000	$ 160,000
Receivables	360,000	320,000
Inventory	400,000	360,000
Total current assets	$880,000	$ 840,000
Land	80,000	80,000
Building		280,000
Equipment		200,000
	$960,000	$1,400,000
Liabilities and Owners' Equity:		
Notes payable	$ 80,000	$ 120,000
Accounts payable	360,000	240,000
Total current liabilities	$440,000	$ 360,000
Mortgage payable		280,000
Mach, capital	280,000	400,000
Mash, capital	240,000	360,000
	$960,000	$1,400,000

During the year, Mach and Mash each invested an additional $60,000 and each withdrew an additional $20,000. The net income for the year was $160,000.

The amount of working capital at the start of the year was $440,000 ($880,000 − $440,000). At the end of the year, the amount of working capital was $480,000 ($840,000 − $360,000). The change, then, was an increase of $40,000. The objective of the statement of changes in financial position is to explain how this happened.

Comparison of the two balance sheets reveals that the building increased from zero to $280,000 and the equipment increased from zero to $200,000. A building was constructed during the year and completed just before the year ended, directly financed with a $280,000 mortgage. At that time the equipment also was purchased for cash. Acquisition of this asset was a $200,000 use of funds. The owners' equity in the business increased from $520,000 ($280,000 + $240,000) to $760,000 ($400,000 + $360,000). This $240,000 increase in funds came from two sources: (1) the net income for the year, $160,000, and (2) the partners' additional investment of $120,000 in total, less one use: the partners' withdrawals of $40,000 in total. These findings can be classified to produce the statement shown on page 595.

Mach & Mash
Statement of Changes in Financial Position—Working Capital Basis
For the Year Ended December 31, 19--

Sources of funds:			
Net income for the year		$160,000	
Investments by partners:			
Mach	$60,000		
Mash	60,000	120,000	
Issuance of mortgage		280,000	$560,000
Uses of funds:			
Purchase of equipment		$200,000	
Partners' withdrawals:			
Mach	$20,000		
Mash	20,000	40,000	
Construction of building		280,000	520,000
Increase in working capital			$ 40,000

Mach & Mash—Statement of Changes in Financial Position

Assembling the Data for Statement of Changes in Financial Position

There are various techniques for assembling and organizing data to produce a statement of changes in financial position. If the calculations are likely to be complicated, it may be advisable to use a special work sheet, otherwise the use of a work sheet is not warranted. The first step is to summarize, in comparative form, the balance sheets at the beginning and end of the period. Spinner & Thomas used the balance sheet at the close of the preceding year (not reproduced in this textbook) and the balance sheet at the close of the year just ended (reproduced on page 585). The statements were summarized and the changes in each element were noted, as follows:

	Beginning of Year	End of Year	Increase (Decrease)
Cash	$30,602	$ 34,635	$ 4,033
Government notes	-0-	10,000	10,000
Receivables (net)	5,592	10,788	5,196
Merchandise inventories	3,124	3,180	56
Supplies and prepayments	2,432	2,887	455
Total current assets	$41,750	$ 61,490	$ 19,740
Long-term assets (less accumulated depreciation)	49,465	39,022	(10,443)
Total assets	$91,215	$100,512	$ 9,297
Notes and interest payable	$ 3,172	-0-	$ (3,172)
Accounts payable	30,263	$ 34,375	4,112
Accrued and withheld payroll taxes	2,450	2,589	139
Total current liabilities	$35,885	$ 36,964	$ 1,079
Owners' equity	55,330	63,548	8,218
Total liabilities and owners' equity	$91,215	$100,512	$ 9,297

The foregoing summary shows that working capital increased $18,661 (current assets increased $19,740 while current liabilities increased only $1,079). The purpose of the statement of changes in financial position is to explain this increase. Note that cash only increased $4,033. This was overshadowed by the increase in temporary investments, coupled with the increase in net receivables and the modest increase in the current liabilities. It was mentioned earlier that the change in the amount of cash might not be as significant as the change in working capital, especially when surplus cash is temporarily invested in high-return, relatively liquid securities.

The list of sources and uses of funds was enumerated on pages 592 and 593. The possible sources are: (1) investments by owners, (2) profitable operations, (3) long-term borrowing, and (4) sales of long-term assets. Spinner and Thomas made no investments during the year; there was no long-term borrowing or sale of long-term assets; hence, the only source of funds for the year under review was profitable operations.

The possible uses of funds are: (1) withdrawals by owners, (2) unprofitable operations, (3) repayment of long-term borrowing, and (4) purchase of long-term assets. Items (2) and (3) do not apply since the year had been profitable and there were no long-term debts to repay during the year. Since both partners made withdrawals during the year and a piece of equipment had been purchased, items (1) and (4) are to be considered as uses of funds.

The sources of funds and uses of funds for the Spinner & Thomas business will be explained in the following sections.

Sources of Funds: Operations

The income statement of Spinner & Thomas for the year ended June 30, 19--, revealed a net income of $26,318. This amount represented a source of working capital for the business, which can be explained as follows. There were two types of revenue: sales and interest earned. In both cases, either cash was collected or a current receivable (accounts receivable or accrued interest receivable) was increased, and accordingly, working capital was increased. Almost all expenses that were incurred caused working capital to be reduced. Cost of goods sold reduced the merchandise inventory—an important current asset. Prepaid Insurance, a current asset, was reduced by an amount equal to the cost of the insurance that expired during the period. The allowance for doubtful accounts was, in effect, a reduction of current receivables. Most of the expenses incurred caused either an immediate reduction in cash or an increase in a current payable of some sort. If the current assets are reduced or the current liabilities are increased, working capital is reduced.

The single exception to the above analysis of the effect of expenses upon working capital is depreciation expense. When the depreciation of the three types of long-term assets was entered (refer to adjustments (j), (k), and (l) in the work sheets on pages 554 and 555), the offset to the depreciation expense debit was a credit to the proper accumulated depreciation account. Accumulated depreciation represents the total amount of asset cost charged to operations. An addition to accumulated depreciation is a reduction in the undepreciated cost of the long-term asset—not a reduction in a current asset.

The total amount of Spinner & Thomas' depreciation expense for the year was $10,964 ($1,848 + $1,978 + $7,138). Since this expense did not reduce working capital (as funds are defined here), for purposes of the statement of changes in financial position, the amount of the net income for the year, $26,318, was increased by the amount of the depreciation expense for the year and reported as follows:

Funds provided by current operations:	
Net income (per income statement)	$26,318
Add expenses not requiring funds:	
Depreciation	10,964
Total funds provided by current operations	$37,282

Another method of showing "funds provided by current operations" would be to deduct expenses that reduced working capital from total revenue that increased working capital (sales and interest earned). The difference would be $37,282, the same amount as shown above. Depreciation expense is not mentioned in the statement if this method is used. In the Spinner & Thomas statement, the operating expenses excluding depreciation would total $225,407, and funds provided by current operations would be shown as follows:

Funds provided by current operations:		
Net sales	$1,354,903	
Other revenue	1,345	$1,356,248
Less expenses that reduced working capital:		
Cost of goods sold	$1,093,559	
Operating expense (excluding $10,964 of depreciation expense)	225,407	1,318,966
Funds provided by current operations		$ 37,282

The above method is not as widely used because it is considered desirable to have the statement of changes in financial position start with the amount shown as the net income in the income statement. This treatment serves to tie the financial statements together in a more professional manner.

A great deal of misunderstanding has arisen about depreciation in the statement of changes in financial position. The idea that "depreciation is a source of funds" is entirely incorrect. Depreciation, while difficult to measure on a periodic basis, is a very real expense. It differs from other expenses only in that most expenses reduce working capital, while depreciation expense is a reduction in certain long-term assets. With most other expenses, the payment of cash and recognition of the expense are closely related—money is paid in the same period that the expense is incurred. In a few cases, money was spent in the preceding period, such as payments for inventory and supplies that were not sold or used until the next period; and in some cases, money will not be paid until the next period, such as employer's payroll taxes that relate to one year but are not paid until the next year. Depreciation is considered an expense because cash was paid when the assets that are being depreciated were bought. Depreciation is too often misunderstood because the point in time that the money was spent for the depreciable asset and the point in time when the outlay becomes an expense may be far apart.

Another argument that may be used to show that depreciation is not a source of funds is as follows: Suppose that depreciation expense had been overlooked in calculating the net income for a period. Would the funds provided by current operations be any less? The answer clearly is "no." If Spinner & Thomas had failed to enter the depreciation expense totalling $10,964, the net income for the year would have been incorrectly calculated to be $37,282. In the statement of changes in financial position, that amount would be shown as funds provided by current operations, just as when the net income calculation includes the depreciation expense.

There are some other expenses that have the same characteristics as depreciation. These expenses arise whenever an asset is purchased and gradually written off as an expense over a number of succeeding years. A good example is a patent. Patents have a legal life of 17 years. A company may have purchased a patent soon after it was issued. The management of the acquiring company may not think that the patent will be valuable for 16 to 17 years, but may expect that ownership of the patent will be of benefit, perhaps, for 10 years. Accordingly, one tenth of the cost may be charged to an expense for each of the ten years, which is described as amortizing the cost. The portion written off each year is described as **amortization expense**. A patent is classified as a long-term asset. As portions of its cost are taken into expense, no decrease in working capital is involved. Accordingly, amortization expense, like depreciation expense, must be "added back" to determine the amount of funds provided by current operations.

Occasions may arise when the net income figure must be further modified to arrive at funds provided by current operations. If, for example, a piece of land that cost $30,000 some years before was sold for $36,000 and the $6,000 gain was reported in the income statement, that amount, $6,000, would have to be excluded from funds provided by current operations. Unless the business was engaged in buying and selling land, such a transaction would not be considered a part of regular operations. The $36,000 received from the sale of the land would be reported separately as a source of funds from the sale of long-term assets in the statement of changes in financial position.

Current operations were the only source of funds for Spinner & Thomas during the year ended June 30, 19--. The two uses of funds during that year will be considered next.

Uses of Funds: Owners' Withdrawals

The owners' equity section of the balance sheet for the year ended June 30, 19--, shown on page 585 indicates that during the year, Spinner withdrew $10,300 and Thomas, $7,800. These amounts are shown in the uses of funds section of the statement of changes in financial position.

Uses of Funds: Purchase of Long-Term Assets

The analysis of the changes in the balance sheets of Spinner & Thomas, shown on page 596, shows a decrease in the total undepreciated cost (cost less accumulated depreciation) of the long-term assets in the amount of $10,443. There was a decrease in the total undepreciated cost amounting to $10,964 caused by depreciation expense for the year. This amount of depreciation, $10,964, was taken into consideration in preparing the income statement. If the decrease in undepreciated cost due to depreciation for the year was $10,964, but the total decrease was only $10,443, there must have been a use of funds in the amount of $521 ($10,964 − $10,443) to purchase some new long-term assets. An examination of the long-term asset accounts revealed that on June 18, an electronic desk calculator was purchased at a cost of $521. Since the bill had been paid, the decrease in cash reduced working capital; hence the purchase of office equipment is a use of funds for the year. This acquisition was so reported in the statement of changes in financial position.

Statement of Changes in Financial Position with Supporting Schedule of Changes in Working Capital

The annual report of Spinner & Thomas includes a statement of changes in financial position with a supporting schedule of changes in working capital. These are reproduced on page 601. The statement of changes in financial position explains the net change in working capital that occurred between the start and the close of the fiscal year. The supporting schedule shows the amounts of the changes in the elements that comprise working capital (current assets and current liabilities). The balance sheets as of the beginning and end of the year provided the data for the schedule. Such a schedule is customarily provided when the working capital approach is used in preparing the statement of changes in financial position. It is important to note that the increase in working capital in the statement itself must agree with the increase in working capital shown in the schedule–$18,661 in this case.

Statements of changes in financial position are not always presented in the form illustrated. One form sometimes used begins with the amount of working capital at the beginning of the period (usually a year). To this are added the sources of funds, appropriately classified. The uses of funds are then shown and their total is subtracted to show the amount of working capital at the end of the period. As was noted earlier, titles other than "statement of changes in financial position" sometimes are used. By whatever name it is called, the inclusion of the statement in the annual report has now become standard practice.

Spinner & Thomas
Statement of Changes in Financial Position
For the Year Ended June 30, 19--

Sources of funds:		
Funds provided by current operations:		
Net income (per income statement)		$26,318
Add expenses not requiring funds:		
Depreciation		10,964
Total sources of funds		$37,282
Uses of funds:		
Partners' withdrawals:		
Harlan Spinner	$10,300	
Carol Thomas	7,800	
Purchase of office equipment	521	
Total uses of funds		18,621
Increase in working capital		$18,661

Spinner & Thomas—Statement of Changes in Financial Position

Spinner & Thomas
Schedule of Changes in Working Capital
For the Year Ended June 30, 19--

	Beginning of Year	End of Year	Working Capital Increase	Working Capital Decrease
Cash	$30,602	$34,635	$ 4,033	
Government notes	-0-	10,000	10,000	
Receivables (net)	5,592	10,788	5,196	
Merchandise inventories	3,124	3,180	56	
Supplies and prepayments	2,432	2,887	455	
Notes and interest payable	3,172	-0-	3,172	
Accounts payable	30,263	34,375		$ 4,112
Accrued and withheld payroll taxes	2,450	2,589		139
			$22,912	$ 4,251
Increase in working capital				18,661
			$22,912	$22,912

Spinner & Thomas—Schedule of Changes in Working Capital

BUILDING YOUR ACCOUNTING KNOWLEDGE

1. Why is solvency or liquidity not assured merely because a business is profitable?
2. Give three alternate titles for the statement of changes in financial position.
3. What two meanings does the term "funds" generally have as used in connection with the statement of changes in financial position?
4. What two approaches are used by most companies to express changes in financial position? Which approach is explained and illustrated in this chapter?
5. List four potential sources of funds. List four potential uses of funds.
6. What is the first step in assembling the data for the statement of changes in financial position.
7. What misconception about depreciation in the statement of changes in financial position has arisen? What frequently is the reason for this misunderstanding? Why is the alternative method of showing "funds provided by current operations," discussed on pages 597 and 598, not commonly used in practice?
8. What two types of uses of funds are shown on the Spinner & Thomas statement of changes in financial position?

APPLYING ACCOUNTING CONCEPTS

Exercise 19-7. The summary balance sheets of Kelley and Flanigan's Sporting Goods at the beginning and end of the current year are as follows:

	Beginning of Year	End of Year
Assets:		
Cash	$110,000	$ 130,000
Accounts receivable (net)	340,000	300,000
Merchandise inventory	350,000	380,000
Total current assets	$800,000	$ 810,000
Land	100,000	100,000
Building (book value)		185,000
Equipment (book value)		145,000
	$900,000	$1,240,000
Liabilities and Owners' Equity:		
Notes payable	$ 60,000	$ 110,000
Accounts payable	350,000	210,000
Total current liabilities	$410,000	$ 320,000
Mortgage payable		190,000
Roberta Kelley, capital	260,000	380,000
Cyndy Flanigan, capital	230,000	350,000
	$900,000	$1,240,000

During the year, Kelley and Flanigan each invested an additional $50,000 and each withdrew an additional $15,000. The net income for the year was $170,000. Depreciation on the building was $5,000 and depreciation on the equipment was also $5,000.

(a) Determine the working capital at the beginning and end of the year. **(b)** Determine the change in working capital from the beginning to the end of the year. **(c)** Prepare a statement of changes in financial position using working capital as a basis.

Exercise 19-8. Refer to Exercise 19-7. Prepare a supporting schedule of changes in working capital for Kelley and Flanigan's Sporting Goods.

Report No. 19-3

Complete Report No. 19-3 in the study assignments and submit your working papers for Reports Nos. 19-1, 19-2 and 19-3 for approval. Continue with the textbook discussion in Chapter 20 until Report No. 20-1 is required.

EXPANDING YOUR BUSINESS VOCABULARY

What is the meaning of each of the following terms?

acid test **(p. 587)**
amortization expense **(p. 599)**
annual report **(p. 577)**
Auditor's report **(p. 578)**
comparative analysis **(p. 582)**
direct financing **(p. 593)**
fund **(p. 591)**
fund-change statement **(p. 590)**
highway construction fund **(p. 591)**
liquidity **(p. 587)**
merchandise turnover **(p. 581)**
opinion **(p. 578)**
percentage analysis **(p. 581)**
petty cash fund **(p. 591)**
profitability **(p. 581)**
return on assets **(p. 588)**
return on equity **(p. 588)**
sources of funds **(p. 592)**
statement of changes in financial position **(pp. 590, 591)**
statement of changes in working capital **(p. 590)**
statement of sources and uses of funds **(p. 590)**
undepreciated cost **(p. 587)**
uses of funds **(p. 592)**
working capital **(p. 590)**

CHAPTER 20

Interim Financial Statements

CHAPTER OBJECTIVES

Careful study of this chapter should enable you to:

- Define and describe interim financial statements.
- Explain the reason for preparing interim statements.
- Explain the tentative nature and the limitations of interim financial statements.
- Prepare interim financial statements using the summary-work-sheet technique supplemented by the technique of deriving an interim income statement by the use of successive year-to-date income statements.
- Describe the special problem of accounting for property taxes on an interim basis.

In accounting for business operations, it is general practice to determine income or loss on an annual basis and to prepare balance sheets at annual intervals. While the calendar year is widely used as the fiscal year, many firms adopt the natural business year, which is a year that starts and ends at the time when business activity is at its lowest level. In any case, twelve months is the basic time interval. Interested parties, notably owners and managers, need more frequent reports of the affairs of a business. For this reason, it is common to prepare interim financial statements. Interim means "between." An income statement for a period of time shorter than, and within the limits of, the fiscal year is an interim income statement. A balance sheet as of a date other than the close of the fiscal year is an interim balance sheet.

Interim Statements

Interim statements may be prepared for any segment of a year. However, it is impractical to use a very short period such as a day or a week because of (1) the considerable amount of work involved in producing the statements, and (2) the fact that the shorter the period, the more unreliable the determination of income. Many of the problems of accounting (in contrast to pure data gathering, entering, and storing) arise because numerous items of value are acquired in one period, but are not sold or used entirely within that period. Two important examples are (1) the problem of allocating cost between goods sold (or used) and goods unsold (or unused) at the end of the period, and (2) in the case of most long-term assets, the problem of cost allocation by means of depreciation. The need to allocate inventory costs is a particularly good example of the difficulty of preparing interim statements. At the end of the fiscal year, physical inventories may be taken to determine (or, in some cases, to verify) the quantities of merchandise inventory and various supplies on hand. The procedure is likely to be time consuming and, thus, expensive. It cannot be done at the end of every interim period. Estimates generally have to be used for interim-statement purposes. The shorter the period, the greater the problem.

Because of constraints such as those just mentioned, the month is considered to be the smallest time segment generally feasible for interim-statement purposes. Monthly time segments have the advantage of being universally understood.

Interim statements may be prepared on a quarterly (three months) basis. Quarterly statements tend to be somewhat more reliable than monthly statements. This is because the estimation and allocation methods used for items such as uncollectible accounts, depreciation, and inventories do not have as significant an effect in determining the income for a quarter as they do for a period as short as a month. In addition, quarters are more comparable in length. Quarterly statements in a very condensed form commonly are furnished to the stockholders of large business corporations.

In the majority of cases, interim statements must be regarded as very provisional or tentative in nature. Despite their imperfections, these statements can be useful if they are carefully interpreted.

Using Work Sheets to Produce Interim Financial Statements

It has been demonstrated in previous chapters that the end-of-year work sheet is a useful device to (1) assist in the production of the annual income statement and the year-end balance sheet, and (2) aid in the year-end process of formally adjusting and closing the accounts. The same type of work sheet can materially assist in the production of interim statements. Adjustments are entered on the work sheet, but no formal adjusting or closing of the accounts is done at the end of interim periods.

The use of interim period work sheets is illustrated in this chapter for the preparation of interim financial statements of the Gribbins & Gribbins Wholesale Building Supply Company owned and operated as a partnership by Ronald E. Gribbins and his wife, Martha L. Gribbins. For purposes of this illustration, the business is not departmentalized and the general ledger contains comparatively few accounts. Assume that appropriate books of original entry and auxiliary records are used, and there is no subsidiary operating expenses ledger. The firm uses the calendar year as its fiscal year.

The partners share profits and losses in a 50-50 ratio. The determination of net income takes partners' salaries into account. The accountant for the company prepares monthly income statements and year-to-date income statements, as well as balance sheets, as of the last day of each month. A year-to-date income statement is one that covers a variable time period from the beginning of the fiscal year up to and including the last day of the most current month.

Work Sheet for the First Month of a Fiscal Year

Eight columns of a ten-column work sheet for the first month are reproduced on pages 608 and 609. To conserve space, the Adjusted Trial Balance columns are not shown. For purposes of simplicity, the amounts are rounded to the nearest dollar. The amounts in the Trial Balance columns were taken from the general ledger after the posting for the month of January had been completed. The reasons why some accounts have no balances will become apparent in the discussion that follows.

The following entries were made in the Adjustments amount columns.

Entry (a): The amount of the beginning inventory of merchandise, $3,074,756, was debited to Cost of Goods Sold, Account No. 531, and was credited to Merchandise Inventory, Account No. 141.

Entry (b): The amount of the purchases for the month, $1,882,769, was debited to Cost of Goods Sold, Account No. 531, and was credited to Purchases, Account No. 511.

Entry (c): The amount of the purchases returns and allowances for the month, $23,425, was debited to Purchases Returns and Allowances, Account No. 511.1, and was credited to Cost of Goods Sold, Account No. 531.

Entry (d): The amount of the purchases discount for the month, $40,846, was debited to Purchases Discount, Account No. 511.2, and was credited to Cost of Goods Sold, Account No. 531.

Entry (e): The amount assigned to the merchandise inventory at January 31, $3,066,000, was debited to Merchandise Inventory, Account No. 141, and was credited to Cost of Goods Sold, Account No. 531. The firm uses the perpetual method of inventory accounting and maintains stock records of certain high value items. The stock records indicate the quantities of these items that were presumed to be on hand at January 31. Since very little discrepancy had been found in prior years between these records and the physical counts, the records were considered reliable. Quantities of various low value items were estimated. All quantities were costed by reference to recent purchase invoices.

Entry (f): The interest accrued, $21,875, since January 1, on the $3,000,000 mortgage payable was debited to Interest Expense, Account No. 571, and was credited to Accrued Interest Payable, Account No. 217. Interest at 8¾% per annum is payable semiannually each January 1 and July 1. Interest for the six months ended last December 31 ($131,250) was paid on January 2 since January 1 was a holiday. The determination of net income or loss for January must take into account the interest that has accrued during the month.

Entry (g): The amount of the insurance expense for January, $5,526,

GRIBBINS & GRIBBINS
Work
For the Month Ended

Account	Acct. No.	TRIAL BALANCE Debit	Credit
Cash	111	81,500	
Accounts Receivable	131	399,232	
Allowance for Doubtful Accounts	131.1		3,992
Merchandise Inventory	141	3,074,756	
Store Supplies	151	16,046	
Prepaid Insurance	155	22,432	
Land	161	1,170,000	
Building	171	4,873,939	
Accumulated Depreciation—Building	171.1		2,452,486
Furniture and Equipment	181	542,131	
Accumulated Depreciation—Furniture and Equipment	181.1		180,558
Delivery Equipment	185	188,173	
Accumulated Depreciation—Delivery Equipment	185.1		92,536
FICA Tax Payable	211		18,932
FUTA Tax Payable	212		790
State Unemployment Tax Payable	213		4,260
Employees Income Tax Payable	214		22,336
Accrued Interest Payable	217		
Accounts Payable	218		469,788
Mortgage Payable	262		3,000,000
Ronald E. Gribbins, Capital	311		2,124,017
Ronald E. Gribbins, Drawing	311.1	11,984	
Martha L. Gribbins, Capital	321		1,749,264
Martha L. Gribbins, Drawing	321.1	9,070	
Sales	411		2,365,812
Sales Returns and Allowances	411.1	23,466	
Sales Discount	411.2	50,462	
Purchases	511	1,882,769	
Purchases Returns and Allowances	511.1		23,425
Purchases Discount	511.2		40,846
Cost of Goods Sold	531		
Partners' Salaries Expense	541	9,600	
Salaries and Commissions Expense	542	157,775	
Utilities Expense	543	4,327	
Telephone Expense	544	1,280	
Supplies Expense	545		
Delivery Expense	546	5,687	
Depreciation Expense	547		
Insurance Expense	548		
Payroll Taxes Expense	551	14,515	
Property Tax Expense	552		
Uncollectible Accounts Expense	553		
Miscellaneous Expense	562	9,898	
Interest Expense	571		
		12,549,042	12,549,042
Accrued Property Tax Payable			
Net Income			

Gribbins & Gribbins Wholesale Building Supply Company—

WHOLESALE BUILDING SUPPLY COMPANY
Sheet
January 31, 19--

ADJUSTMENTS		INCOME STATEMENT		BALANCE SHEET	
Debit	Credit	Debit	Credit	Debit	Credit
				81,500	
				399,232	
	(j) 11,459				15,451
(e) 3,066,000	(a) 3,074,756			3,066,000	
	(h) 4,814			11,232	
	(g) 5,526			16,906	
				1,170,000	
				4,873,939	
	(i) 10,154				2,462,640
				542,131	
	(i) 2,824				183,382
				188,173	
	(i) 3,920				96,456
					18,932
					790
					4,260
					22,336
	(f) 21,875				21,875
					469,788
					3,000,000
					2,124,017
				11,984	
					1,749,264
				9,070	
			2,365,812		
		23,466			
		50,462			
	(b) 1,882,769				
(c) 23,425					
(d) 40,846					
(a) 3,074,756	(c) 23,425	1,827,254			
(b) 1,882,769	(d) 40,846				
	(e) 3,066,000				
		9,600			
		157,775			
		4,327			
		1,280			
(h) 4,814		4,814			
		5,687			
(i) 16,898		16,898			
(g) 5,526		5,526			
		14,515			
(k) 11,730		11,730			
(j) 11,459		11,459			
		9,898			
(f) 21,875		21,875			
	(k) 11,730				11,730
8,160,098	8,160,098	2,176,566	2,365,812	10,370,167	10,180,921
		189,246			189,246
		2,365,812	2,365,812	10,370,167	10,370,167

Work Sheet for One-Month Period

was debited to Insurance Expense, Account No. 548, and was credited to Prepaid Insurance, Account No. 155. The insurance policy file provides the information needed to calculate the amount.

Entry (h): The estimated cost of store supplies used during the month, $4,814, was debited to Supplies Expense, Account No. 545, and was credited to Store Supplies, Account No. 151. This amount was determined by subtracting the estimated cost of the store supplies on hand, January 31, $11,232, from the balance of the store supplies account, $16,046. Note that the firm uses the asset method of accounting for supplies.

Entry (i): The depreciation for the month, $16,898, was debited to Depreciation Expense, Account No. 547, with credits to Accumulated Depreciation—Building, Account No. 171.1, $10,154, Accumulated Depreciation—Furniture and Equipment, Account No. 181.1, $2,824, and Accumulated Depreciation—Delivery Equipment, Account No. 185.1, $3,920. The firm uses straight line depreciation calculated at the following annual rates; building 2½%; furniture and equipment, 6¼% and delivery equipment, 25%. These rates were applied to the cost of the assets as shown in the trial balance, and 1/12 of each resulting amount was taken as the depreciation for January. No long-term assets were purchased during January.

Entry (j): The amount of the adjustment in the doubtful accounts provision for the month, $11,459, was debited to Uncollectible Accounts Expense, Account No. 553, and was credited to Allowance for Doubtful Accounts, Account No. 131.1. Experience has indicated that uncollectible account losses average ½ of 1% of net sales. Net sales for January amounted to $2,291,884 [$2,365,812 (gross sales) − $23,466 (sales returns and allowances) − $50,462 (sales discount)]. One half of 1% of $2,291,884 is $11,459. The January 31 trial balance shows the allowance account to have a credit balance of $3,992, which represents the remainder of an amount determined to be necessary based on a percentage of net sales in one or more previous months. At this time, the $11,459 adjustment for January is added to the balance in the allowance for doubtful accounts of $3,992 to produce a new balance of $15,451. However, this balance will be watched carefully in subsequent months to avoid having it become larger than necessary.

Entry (k): The property tax assignable to January, $11,730, was debited to Property Tax Expense, Account No. 552, and was credited to Accrued Property Tax Payable. Note that the latter title had to be added to the list and that no account number is shown. The reason is that there is no need for such an account in the general ledger. The account is used solely to produce interim financial statements.

Property taxes pose a special accounting problem. Such taxes do not accrue in the conventional sense. Usually the amount of the tax is not known until the tax bill is received several months after the assessment date. The tax may be paid in two installments: one half by a specified day late in the calendar year and the other half by a specified day in the following spring. Property tax expense commonly is accounted for on a cash basis; that is, no record is made until a payment occurs. By the end of the year, the property tax expense account shows the amount of tax actually paid during the year. Gribbins & Gribbins accounts for property taxes in their interim report in the following manner: In the year just ended they paid $67,572 in April, and $70,380 in December. Since another $70,380 must be paid in April of the current year, it seems reasonable to allocate one sixth of the amount to each of the first six months. This is accomplished by a debit to the expense account and a credit to the liability. The purpose of this entry is to give the month of January a reasonable share of the year's property tax expense. Not all accountants treat property tax expense in precisely this manner, but some procedure has to be followed to cause a reasonable amount to be included in the income determination for each interim period.

The work sheet was completed by (1) totaling the Adjustments columns to prove their equality, (2) extending the amounts as adjusted to the proper Income Statement or Balance Sheet columns, (3) footing the last four columns to determine the net income for the month and entering this amount, $189,246, in the Income Statement Debit and the Balance Sheet Credit columns, and (4) entering the totals and making the rulings.

The Interim Statements for January

The income statement for the month of January, 19--, for Gribbins & Gribbins Wholesale Building Supply Company is reproduced on page 612. The balance sheet as of January 31, 19-- is shown on page

613. Note that, in the owners' equity section, the net income for the month is apportioned between the partners in the agreed ratio: 50%-50%.

Gribbins & Gribbins Wholesale Building Supply Company
Income Statement
For the Month of January, 19--

Sales		$2,365,812
Less: Returns and allowances		(23,466)
Sales discounts		(50,462)
Net sales		$2,291,884
Cost of goods sold:		
Merchandise inventory, January 1	$3,074,756	
Purchases	1,882,769	
Less: Returns and allowances	(23,425)	
Purchases discounts	(40,846)	
Cost of merchandise available for sale	$4,893,254	
Less merchandise inventory, January 31	3,066,000	1,827,254
Gross margin on sales		$ 464,630
Operating expenses:		
Partners' salaries expense	$ 9,600	
Salaries and commissions expense	157,775	
Utilities expense	4,327	
Telephone expense	1,280	
Supplies expense	4,814	
Delivery expense	5,687	
Depreciation expense	16,898	
Insurance expense	5,526	
Payroll taxes expense	14,515	
Property tax expense	11,730	
Uncollectible accounts expense	11,459	
Miscellaneous expense	9,898	
Total operating expenses		253,509
Operating income		$ 211,121
Interest expense		21,875
Net income		$ 189,246

Gribbins & Gribbins Wholesale Building Supply Company—Income Statement

The procedure of preparing a work sheet and the interim financial statements is almost identical to the steps that normally are followed at the end of the year. At year-end, however, the work of the accountant will not cease with statement preparation. The adjusting entries

Gribbins & Gribbins Wholesale Building Supply Company
Balance Sheet
January 31, 19--

Assets			
Current assets:			
Cash		$ 81,500	
Accounts receivable	$ 399,232		
Less allowance for doubtful accounts	15,451	383,781	
Merchandise inventory		3,066,000	
Store supplies		11,232	
Prepaid insurance		16,906	
Total current assets			$3,559,419
Long-term assets:			
Land		$1,170,000	
Building	$4,873,939		
Less accumulated depreciation	2,462,640	2,411,299	
Furniture and equipment	$ 542,131		
Less accumulated depreciation	183,382	358,749	
Delivery equipment	$ 188,173		
Less accumulated depreciation	96,456	91,717	
Total long-term assets			4,031,765
Total assets			$7,591,184
Liabilities			
Current liabilities:			
FICA tax payable		$ 18,932	
FUTA tax payable		790	
State unemployment tax payable		4,260	
Employees income tax payable		22,336	
Accrued interest payable		21,875	
Accrued property tax payable		11,730	
Accounts payable		469,788	
Total current liabilities			$ 549,711
Long-term liability:			
Mortgage payable			3,000,000
Total liabilities			$3,549,711
Owners' Equity			
Ronald E. Gribbins, capital:			
Capital, January 1	$2,124,017		
Add net income (50% of $189,246)	94,623		
Less withdrawals	(11,984)		
Capital, January 31		$2,206,656	
Martha L. Gribbins, capital:			
Capital, January 1	$1,749,264		
Add net income (50% of $189,246)	94,623		
Less withdrawals	(9,070)		
Capital, January 31		1,834,817	
Total owners' equity			4,041,473
Total liabilities and owners' equity			$7,591,184

Gribbins & Gribbins Wholesale Building Supply Company—Balance Sheet

have to be journalized and posted, followed by the journalizing and posting of the needed closing entries. It is likely that a post-closing trial balance will have to be taken. In many cases certain reversing entries will have been journalized and posted. At the end of each interim period, however, none of these steps is involved.

Work Sheet for the First Two Months of a Fiscal Year

The work sheet for the first two months is reproduced on pages 616 and 617. The amounts in the Trial Balance columns were the balances of all of the general ledger accounts after the posting for the month of February had been completed. A comparison of the January 31 trial balance on page 608 with the trial balance for February 28 on page 616 reveals that there are no changes in the balances of several accounts. As explained previously, this is because the adjustments made in the work sheet for January were solely to produce interim financial statements for January, and are not made a formal part of the accounting records.

The balance of the merchandise inventory account (No. 141) remains unchanged until the accounts are adjusted at the end of the year. There are no changes in the balances of the land and delivery equipment accounts (Nos. 161 and 185) because no assets of these types were acquired or disposed of during February. None of the accumulated depreciation accounts (Nos. 171.1, 181.1, and 185.1) received any debits, since none of the related assets was retired or sold during February, and the accumulated depreciation accounts will receive no credits until the year-end adjustments are recorded.

Accrued Interest Payable, Account No. 217, has no balance at the end of either month since the accrual is not entered on a monthly basis. There was no transaction during February that affected the balance of Mortgage Payable, Account No. 262. The partners' capital accounts (Nos. 311 and 321) are unchanged, since neither partner made any additional investment in February. The accounts will be unaffected by withdrawals and net income or loss until the annual closing entries are posted at the end of the year. The accounts for Depreciation Expense (No. 547), Insurance Expense (No. 548), Supplies Expense, (No. 545), and Uncollectible Accounts Expense (No. 553), have no balances at the end of either month, since they normally are not debited until the year-end adjustments are made. Property Tax Expense, Account No. 552, and Interest Expense, Account No. 571, have no balances at the end of either month, since no payments of property taxes were made during either month, and the payment of mortgage interest on January 2 discharged the liability entered at the end of the previous year. Cost of Goods Sold, Account No. 531, and Expense and Revenue Summary, Account No. 331 (not shown), have no balances at either date, since these accounts are used solely in the end-of-year process of formally adjusting and closing the accounts.

The entries in the Adjustments columns of the work sheet for the two months ended February 28 involve exactly the same accounts as the entries on the work sheet for the month ended January 31.

Entry (a): Cost of Goods Sold, Account No. 531, was debited and Merchandise Inventory, Account No. 141, was credited for exactly the same amount, $3,074,756, as on the earlier work sheet, since the January 1 inventory was involved in the calculations of cost of goods sold both for January alone and for the two-month period ended February 28.

Entries (b), (c), and (d): The balances of Purchases, Account No. 511, $3,358,352, Purchases Returns and Allowances, Account No. 511.1, $44,507, and Purchases Discount, Account No. 511.2, $77,611, were transferred to Cost of Goods Sold, Account No. 531. In each case, the balance represents the amount for the two months.

Entry (e): Merchandise Inventory, Account No. 141, was debited and Cost of Goods Sold, Account No. 531, was credited for $2,838,000, the estimated amount of the inventory on February 28.

Entry (f): Interest Expense, Account No. 571, was debited and Accrued Interest Payable, Account No. 217, was credited for $43,750, the mortgage interest accrued for the two months.

Entry (g): Insurance Expense, Account No. 548, was debited and Prepaid Insurance, Account No. 155, was credited for $10,965, the

GRIBBINS & GRIBBINS WHOLESALE

Work

For the Two-Month Period Ended

Account	Acct. No.	TRIAL BALANCE Debit	Credit
Cash	111	122,326	
Accounts Receivable	131	488,853	
Allowance for Doubtful Accounts	131.1	7,836	
Merchandise Inventory	141	3,074,756	
Store Supplies	151	19,852	
Prepaid Insurance	155	23,333	
Land	161	1,170,000	
Building	171	4,877,168	
Accumulated Depreciation—Building	171.1		2,452,486
Furniture and Equipment	181	608,670	
Accumulated Depreciation—Furniture and Equipment	181.1		180,558
Delivery Equipment	185	188,173	
Accumulated Depreciation—Delivery Equipment	185.1		92,536
FICA Tax Payable	211		18,175
FUTA Tax Payable	212		1,546
State Unemployment Tax Payable	213		8,350
Employees Income Tax Payable	214		20,458
Accrued Interest Payable	217		
Accounts Payable	218		294,071
Mortgage Payable	262		3,000,000
Ronald E. Gribbins, Capital	311		2,124,017
Ronald E. Gribbins, Drawing	311.1	43,562	
Martha L. Gribbins, Capital	321		1,749,264
Martha L. Gribbins, Drawing	321.1	37,036	
Sales	411		4,494,594
Sales Returns and Allowances	411.1	44,584	
Sales Discount	411.2	95,887	
Purchases	511	3,358,352	
Purchases Returns and Allowances	511.1		44,507
Purchases Discount	511.2		77,611
Cost of Goods Sold	531		
Partners' Salaries Expense	541	19,200	
Salaries and Commissions Expense	542	309,239	
Utilities Expense	543	8,438	
Telephone Expense	544	2,503	
Supplies Expense	545		
Delivery Expense	546	11,144	
Depreciation Expense	547		
Insurance Expense	548		
Payroll Taxes Expense	551	28,450	
Property Tax Expense	552		
Uncollectible Accounts Expense	553		
Miscellaneous Expense	562	18,811	
Interest Expense	571		
		14,558,173	14,558,173
Accrued Property Tax Payable			
Net Income			

Gribbins & Gribbins Wholesale Building Supply Company

BUILDING SUPPLY COMPANY

Sheet
February 28, 19--

Adjustments Debit	Adjustments Credit	Income Statement Debit	Income Statement Credit	Balance Sheet Debit	Balance Sheet Credit
				122,326	
				488,853	
	(j) 21,771				13,935
(e) 2,838,000	(a) 3,074,756			2,838,000	
	(h) 9,244			10,608	
	(g) 10,965			12,368	
				1,170,000	
				4,877,168	
	(i) 20,308				2,472,794
				608,670	
	(i) 5,648				186,206
				188,173	
	(i) 7,840				100,376
					18,175
					1,546
					8,350
					20,458
	(f) 43,750				43,750
					294,071
					3,000,000
					2,124,017
				43,562	
					1,749,264
				37,036	
			4,494,594		
		44,584			
		95,887			
	(b) 3,358,352				
(c) 44,507					
(d) 77,611					
(a) 3,074,756	(c) 44,507	3,472,990			
(b) 3,358,352	(d) 77,611				
	(e) 2,838,000				
		19,200			
		309,239			
		8,438			
		2,503			
(h) 9,244		9,244			
		11,144			
(i) 33,796		33,796			
(g) 10,965		10,965			
		28,450			
(k) 23,460		23,460			
(j) 21,771		21,771			
		18,811			
(f) 43,750		43,750			
	(k) 23,460				23,460
9,536,212	9,536,212	4,154,232	4,494,594	10,396,764	10,056,402
		340,362			340,362
		4,494,594	4,494,594	10,396,764	10,396,764

—Work Sheet for Two-Month Period

share of insurance premiums applicable to the two months. (The amount is not exactly twice the amount for January because one policy expired early in February and was renewed at a slightly lower rate.)

Entry (h): Supplies Expense, Account No. 545, was debited and Store Supplies, Account No. 151, was credited for $9,244, which was the calculated cost of supplies used during the two months. This amount was determined by subtracting the estimated cost of supplies on hand February 28, $10,608, from the amount of the balance of the store supplies account on February 28, $19,852.

Entry (i): Depreciation Expense, Account No. 547, was debited for $33,796, and Accumulated Depreciation—Building, Account No. 171.1, was credited for $20,308, Accumulated Depreciation—Furniture and Equipment, Account No. 181.1, was credited for $5,648, and Accumulated Depreciation—Delivery Equipment, Account No. 185.1, was credited for $7,840. In each case, the amount is exactly twice that for January. During February, $66,539 was added to the furniture and equipment account and $3,229 to the building account. Since the partnership does not compute depreciation on assets owned for less than one month, no depreciation was taken on these newly acquired assets.

Entry (j): Uncollectible Accounts Expense, Account No. 553, was debited and Allowance for Doubtful Accounts, Account No. 131.1, was credited for $21,771. This amount was determined by taking ½ of 1% of the net sales for the two months, $4,354,123 ($4,494,594 − $44,584 − $95,887). Since the allowance for doubtful accounts had a debit balance of $7,836, an adjusting entry in the amount of $21,771 produced a credit balance in the allowance for doubtful accounts of $13,935 as of February 28.

Entry (k): Property Tax Expense, Account No. 552, was debited and Accrued Property Tax Payable was credited for $23,460. This amount represents the share of property tax expense for the two months. It is exactly twice the amount of the adjustment for January.

Note that in calculating the amounts of insurance expense, depreciation expense, interest expense and property tax expense, the fact that

January had more days than February was ignored. The month—not the number of days—was the unit of time used.

The work sheet was completed in the usual manner. Net income for the two-month period ended February 28, 19--, in the amount of $340,362 was calculated.

Interim Statements—Successive Periods

The work sheet reproduced on pages 616 and 617 assembled the data needed for an income statement covering the two-month period ended February 28, 19--, and a balance sheet as of the same date. The accountant for the partnership uses the same procedure to develop a succession of year-to-date income statements and month-end balance sheets. Income statements of this type are valuable for comparative purposes. Owners and managers are interested in learning how the progress in the current year compares with that of the preceding years.

In addition to the cumulative, year-to-date-income statement, an interim income statement is needed for each month by itself. Little effort is required to produce such statements using the year-to-date information. The technique is illustrated on page 620. At the left is the income statement of the company for the two-month period ended February 28, 19--. This was prepared from the Income Statement columns of the work sheet reproduced on pages 616 and 617. The income statement for January, 19-- is shown next. This statement is exactly the same as the one shown on page 612 developed from the Income Statement columns of the January work sheet on pages 608 and 609. At the right is the income statement for February, 19--, which was derived by subtracting the amounts in the January statement from those in the January-February statement, with the exception of the February merchandise inventory.

Since the income statements show the calculation of cost of goods sold, the amounts of the beginning and ending merchandise inventories shown in the February statement were not derived by subtraction. The beginning inventory for February, $3,066,000, was the ending inventory for January. The ending inventory for February, $2,838,000, is also the ending inventory for the two-month period.

GRIBBINS & GRIBBINS WHOLESALE BUILDING SUPPLY COMPANY
Income Statements

	For Two Months Ended February 28, 19--		For January, 19--		For February, 19--	
Sales		$4,494,594		$2,365,812		$2,128,782
Less: Returns and allowances		(44,584)		(23,466)		(21,118)
Sales discounts		(95,887)		(50,462)		(45,425)
Net sales		$4,354,123		$2,291,884		$2,062,239
Cost of goods sold:						
Merchandise inventory, beginning of period	$3,074,756		$3,074,756		$3,066,000	
Purchases	3,358,352		1,882,769		1,475,583	
Less: Returns and allowances	(44,507)		(23,425)		(21,082)	
Purchases discounts	(77,611)		(40,846)		(36,765)	
Cost of merchandise available for sale	$6,310,990		$4,893,254		$4,483,736	
Less merchandise inventory, end of period	2,838,000	3,472,990	3,066,000	1,827,254	2,838,000	1,645,736
Gross margin on sales		$ 881,133		$ 464,630		$ 416,503
Operating expenses:						
Partners' salaries expense	$ 19,200		$ 9,600		$ 9,600	
Salaries and commissions expense	309,239		157,775		151,464	
Utilities expense	8,438		4,327		4,111	
Telephone expense	2,503		1,280		1,223	
Supplies expense	9,244		4,814		4,430	
Delivery expense	11,144		5,687		5,457	
Depreciation expense	33,796		16,898		16,898	
Insurance expense	10,965		5,526		5,439	
Payroll taxes expense	28,450		14,515		13,935	
Property tax expense	23,460		11,730		11,730	
Uncollectible accounts expense	21,771		11,459		10,312	
Miscellaneous expense	18,811		9,898		8,913	
Total operating expenses		497,021		253,509		243,512
Operating income		$ 384,112		$ 211,121		$ 172,991
Interest expense		43,750		21,875		21,875
Net income		$ 340,362		$ 189,246		$ 151,116

Gribbins & Gribbins Wholesale Building Supply Company—Income Statements

The balance sheet as of February 28, 19--, is reproduced on page 622. This was prepared from the Balance Sheet columns of the work sheet on pages 616 and 617. Note that the owners' equity section shows each partner's equity as of January 1, plus the share of the net income for the two-month period less the withdrawals during the two-month period, to arrive at the amount of each partner's equity on February 28. An alternative would be: Partners' equity on January 31 (as shown in the balance sheet on page 613), plus the share of the February net income less the February withdrawals. The result would have been the same.

It should be evident that a similar procedure would have been employed if quarterly, rather than monthly, interim statements had been prepared.

BUILDING YOUR ACCOUNTING KNOWLEDGE

1. What two circumstances make it impractical to use a very short period for the preparation of interim statements (such as a day or a week)?
2. What advantage do monthly time segments have for interim statement preparation?
3. Why are interim statements which are prepared on a quarterly basis generally more reliable than interim statements prepared on a monthly basis?
4. Why is it unnecessary for an interim-statement work sheet to provide aid in formally adjusting and closing the accounts?
5. Describe how Gribbins & Gribbins determines its ending merchandise inventory for interim statement purposes.
6. Briefly describe the special accounting problem posed by the assessment and collection of property taxes.
7. How did the firm of Gribbins & Gribbins derive the amounts for its February, 19-- income statements?

Gribbins & Gribbins Wholesale Building Supply Company

Balance Sheet

February 28, 19--

Assets			
Current assets:			
Cash		$ 122,326	
Accounts receivable	$ 488,853		
Less allowance for doubtful accounts	13,935	474,918	
Merchandise inventory		2,838,000	
Store supplies		10,608	
Prepaid insurance		12,368	
Total current assets			$3,458,220
Long-term assets:			
Land		$1,170,000	
Building	$ 4,877,168		
Less accumulated depreciation	2,472,794	2,404,374	
Furniture and equipment	$ 608,670		
Less accumulated depreciation	186,206	422,464	
Delivery equipment	$ 188,173		
Less accumulated depreciation	100,376	87,797	
Total long-term assets			4,084,635
Total assets			$7,542,855
Liabilities			
Current liabilities:			
FICA tax payable		$ 18,175	
FUTA tax payable		1,546	
State unemployment tax payable		8,350	
Employees income tax payable		20,458	
Accrued interest payable		43,750	
Accrued property tax payable		23,460	
Accounts payable		294,071	
Total current liabilities			$ 409,810
Long-term liability:			
Mortgage payable			3,000,000
Total liabilities			$3,409,810
Owners' Equity			
Ronald E. Gribbins, capital:			
Capital, January 1	$2,124,017		
Add net income (50% of $340,362)	170,181		
Less withdrawals	(43,562)		
Capital, February 28		$2,250,636	
Martha L. Gribbins, capital:			
Capital, January 1	$1,749,264		
Add net income (50% of $340,362)	170,181		
Less withdrawals	(37,036)		
Capital, February 28		1,882,409	
Total owners' equity			4,133,045
Total liabilities and owners' equity			$7,542,855

Gribbins & Gribbins Wholesale Building Supply Company—Balance Sheet

APPLYING ACCOUNTING CONCEPTS

Exercise 20-1. The following are the account balances taken from the February 28 trial balance of Tate's Frame and Supplies.

Cash	$17,025
Accounts receivable	16,886
Merchandise inventory	37,456
Prepaid insurance	600
Accounts payable	45,626
A.J. Tate, capital	17,200
A.J. Tate, drawing	9,000
Sales	55,035
Sales returns and allowances	1,500
Purchases	33,520
Purchases returns and allowances	2,100
Utilities expense	2,215
Miscellaneous expense	1,759

(a) Enter the trial balance on a work sheet for the two-month period ended February 28. Include the insurance expense and cost of goods sold accounts. Leave one line blank after cost of goods sold. **(b)** Enter the adjusting entries based on the following: (1) Merchandise inventory, February 28, $35,235, (2) Transfer the Purchases and Purchases returns and allowances to cost of goods sold, (3) Insurance expired, $200. **(c)** Complete the work sheet.

Exercise 20-2. Refer to Exercise 20-1. Prepare a succession of year-to-date income statements: for the two-month period, for January, and for February. Additional amounts related to January 2 are as follows:

Sales	$29,231
Sales returns and allowances	475
Purchases	17,834
Purchases returns and allowances	605
Utilities expense	1,130
Insurance expense	100
Miscellaneous expense	840
Merchandise inventory, January 31	32,026

Report No. 20-1

Complete Report No. 20-1 in the study assignments and submit your working papers to the instructor for approval. The instructor will then give directions as to the work to be done next.

EXPANDING YOUR BUSINESS VOCABULARY

What is the meaning of each of the following terms?

- interim balance sheet **(p. 605)**
- interim income statement **(p. 605)**
- natural business year **(p. 604)**
- year-to-date income statement **(p. 606)**

CHAPTERS 16-20

Supplementary Practical Accounting Problems

PROBLEM 16-A Opening entry—Proprietorship

On September 1, Brad Basham organized a photographic equipment and supplies enterprise and opened a new set of books. Following is a list of the assets that were invested in the business.

Cash	$17,235
Office equipment	8,437
Store equipment	4,398
Delivery truck	5,156
Total	$35,226

Basham owed $2,026 on the delivery truck that was purchased on account.

Required: Prepare the opening entry in general journal form.

PROBLEM 16-B Opening entry—proprietorship

Robin Clerman, who has been conducting a wholesale wallpaper and paint enterprise, decides to install a formal set of books as of January 2. The balance sheet prepared as of December 31 is shown below.

Robin Clerman
Balance Sheet
December 31, 19--

Assets			**Liabilities**		
Cash		$ 4,907	FICA tax payable	$ 213	
Accounts receivable	$9,034		Employees income tax payable	247	
Less allowance for doubtful accounts	1,127	7,907	Accounts payable	6,011	
Merchandise inventory		17,211	Total liabilities		$ 6,471
Prepaid insurance		690	**Owner's Equity**		
Store equipment	$8,475		Robin Clerman, capital		25,244
Less accumulated depreciation	7,475	1,000	Total liabilities and owner's equity		$31,715
Total assets		$31,715			

Required: Prepare the opening entry in general journal form.

PROBLEM 16-C Capital account—proprietorship

R. J. Whippet is engaged in the wholesale leather goods business. After closing the revenue and expense accounts for the calendar year ended December 31, the expense and revenue summary account, No. 331, had a credit balance of $36,219. At the same time Whippet's capital account, No. 311, had a credit balance of $80,911, and the drawing account, No. 311.1, had a debit balance of $27,000.

Required: **(1)** Open Whippet's capital account, drawing account, and expense and revenue summary account, using the four-column account form of ledger paper. Enter the December 31 balances. **(2)** Assuming that Whippet wishes to have the balances of both the expense and revenue summary and drawing accounts transferred to the capital account, journalize and post the required entries. After posting, account Nos. 331 and 311.1 should show "zero" balances, and account No. 311 should show Whippet's present equity.

PROBLEM 16-D Opening entries—partnership

Bob Russell has been operating a wholesale hardware business as a single proprietor. The balance sheet prepared as of September 30 is shown below.

Bob Russell
Balance Sheet
September 30, 19--

Assets			Liabilities		
Cash		$ 9,270	FICA tax payable	$ 290	
Accounts receivable	$11,490		Employees income tax payable	360	
Less allowance for doubtful accounts	860	10,630	Notes payable	8,000	
Merchandise inventory		17,560	Accounts payable	4,320	
Store equipment	$ 8,100		Total liabilities		$12,970
Less accumulated depreciation	600	7,500	**Owner's Equity**		
			Bob Russell, capital		31,990
Total assets		$44,960	Total liabilities and owner's equity		$44,960

The fair market value of the equipment on September 30 is $7,900. The book values of the other assets are equal to their approximate fair market values. On October 1 of the current year, Frank Russell is admitted as a partner in the business to be conducted under the firm name of Russell & Russell Hardware. Under the partnership agreement, Frank Russell invests $32,390 in cash. The assets of Bob Russell become the property of the partnership and the liabilities are assumed by the partnership.

Required: Prepare the necessary opening entries in general journal form for the investments of the partners, assuming that a new set of books is installed by the partnership.

PROBLEM 16-E Opening entries—partnership

Barbara Conan and Jane Shanna are competitors in the wholesale drug business. On July 1 of the current year, they form a partnership to be operated under the firm name of Conan & Shanna. Their balance sheets as of June 30 are shown at the top of page 628.

Barbara Conan

Balance Sheet

June 30, 19--

Assets			Liabilities		
Cash		$16,927	FICA tax payable	$ 682	
Accounts receivable	$23,460		Employees income tax payable	940	
Less allowance for doubtful accounts	1,147	22,313	Notes payable	27,500	
Merchandise inventory		29,436	Accounts payable	15,643	
Delivery equipment	$12,468		Total liabilities		$44,765
Less accumulated depreciation	3,600	8,868	**Owner's Equity**		
Office equipment	$12,387		Barbara Conan, capital		41,966
Less accumulated depreciation	3,200	9,187	Total liabilities and owner's equity		$86,731
Total assets		$86,731			

Jane Shanna

Balance Sheet

June 30, 19--

Assets			Liabilities		
Cash		$16,437	FICA tax payable	$ 497	
Accounts receivable	$24,210		Employees income payable tax	655	
Less allowance for doubtful accounts	1,456	22,754	Accounts payable	20,411	
Merchandise inventory		28,469	Total liabilities		$21,563
Delivery equipment	$11,500				
Less accumulated depreciation	2,400	9,100	**Owner's Equity**		
Office equipment	$11,667		Jane Shanna, capital		65,197
Less accumulated depreciation	1,667	10,000	Total liabilities and owner's equity		$86,760
Total assets		$86,760			

The partnership agreement provides that the assets are to be taken over at their fair market values and that the liabilities are to be assumed by the partnership. Shanna's balance sheet has already been adjusted to recognize fair market values. The fair market values of Conan's delivery equipment and office equipment are $11,900 and $10,000, respectively. The agreement also provides that to equal Shanna's investment, Conan is to contribute a sufficient amount of additional cash. It is also agreed that the partners will share profits and losses equally.

Required: Prepare the necessary opening entries in general journal form for the investments of the partners, assuming that a new set of books is installed by the partnership.

PROBLEM 16-F Distribution of partner's share

The Natural Upholstering Co., a partnership, is engaged in the wholesale upholstering business. Ownership of the firm is vested in C. Weaver, J. Cutter, W. Evenden and B. Liester. Profits and losses are shared equally.

Cutter died on July 5. In the distribution of the partnership assets, the remaining partners agreed to buy Cutter's widow's interest at 110% of its book value. When the books were closed on July 5, Cutter's capital account had a credit balance of $22,975. On August 15, a partnership check was issued to the widow in final settlement.

Required: Compute the amount to be paid to Cutter's widow under the agreement, and prepare the general journal entry required to enter the check on the books of the partnership.

PROBLEM 16-G Subscriptions Receivable; Capital Stock

On January 2, The Computer Bytes Man Co. was incorporated with an authorized issue of 50,000 shares of common capital stock, par value $20 per share. Subscriptions were received from the following:

J. McCarty	12,000 shares, $240,000
J. Keller......................	10,000 shares, $200,000
D. Hagerup	15,000 shares, $300,000
E. Korhanen	13,000 shares, $260,000

On January 6, all subscribers paid the amounts due. The stock certificates were issued on January 10.

Following is a list of the corporate accounts to be kept:

Capital Stock
Subscriptions Receivable
Capital Stock Subscribed

Required: Prepare the general journal entries required for (1) the stock subscriptions received, (2) the cash received to apply on subscriptions, and (3) the capital stock issued.

PROBLEM 16-H Cash dividend

The following transactions relate to payment of cash dividends by The Gourmet Restaurant Co.:

Mar. 28 The board of directors declared a cash dividend of $6.50 per share, payable May 16, to holders of record April 15. There were 43,980 shares of stock outstanding.

May 16 The company mailed dividend checks amounting to $285,870 to stockholders.

Required: Enter **(1)** the dividend declaration on March 28 and **(2)** the dividend payment on May 16, using standard two-column general journal paper.

PROBLEM 16-I New set of books for a corporation

L. Larson, F. Somes, and L. Bowler are partners under the firm name of Larson, Somes, and Bowler. On January 2, The Emerald City Distributing Co., with an authorized capital of $300,000, consisting of 6,000 shares of common stock, par value $50 per share, was organized to take over the business formerly conducted by the partnership. The following balance sheet of the partnership was prepared at the time of incorporating the business. It has already been adjusted to reflect the fair market values of the inventory and long-term assets as of December 31.

Larson, Somes & Bowler
Balance Sheet
December 31, 19--

Assets			Liabilities		
Cash		$ 27,890	FICA tax payable	$ 980	
Accounts receivable	$46,270		Employees income tax payable	1,215	
Less allowance for doubtful accounts	4,085	42,185	Accounts payable	30,495	
Merchandise inventory		59,843	Total liabilities		$ 32,690
Office equipment	$18,435		**Owners' Equity**		
Less accumulated depreciation	4,980	13,455	L. Larson, capital	$50,000	
Delivery equipment	$21,260		F. Somes, capital	36,000	
Less accumulated depreciation	5,600	15,660	L. Bowler, capital	40,343	126,343
Total assets		$159,033	Total liabilities and owners' equity		$159,033

The partners subscribed for capital stock of the corporation as follows:

L. Larson	2,500 shares @ $50, $125,000
F. Somes	1,500 shares @ $50, $ 75,000
L. Bowler	2,000 shares @ $50, $100,000

The partners, as individuals, received credit toward their subscriptions for their respective equities in the assets of the partnership, and gave their personal checks for the balance of their respective subscriptions. A new set of books is to be installed by the corporation.

Required: Prepare entries in general journal form on the corporation books for the following: **(1)** the subscriptions to the capital stock of the corporation, **(2)** the transfer of the assets and liabilities of the partnership to the corporation, **(3)** the receipt of cash in settlement of the balances due on the respective subscriptions, and **(4)** the issuance of stock certificates.

PROBLEM 18-A Summary work sheet; supplementary work sheet

Rose & Thorn are partners in a wholesale mercantile business. Their accounts are kept on a fiscal year basis, with the year ending on May 31. The accounts with customers and operating expenses are kept in subsidiary ledgers with control accounts in the general ledger. Any necessary adjustments in the operating expense accounts are made at the end of each year after a trial balance is taken. Since annual financial statements must be prepared, the accountant prepares a ten-column summary work sheet and a three-column supplementary operating expenses work sheet at the end of each year as a means of compiling and classifying the information needed in financial statement preparation.

The following accounts in the operating expense ledger require adjustment as of May 31:

Office Supplies Expense	5403	
Depreciation of Office Equipment	5404	
Postage Expense	5416	$ 926.89
Uncollectible Accounts Expense	5417	
Depreciation of Delivery Equipment	5435	
Insurance Expense	5436	
Depreciation of Store Equipment	5437	
Store Supplies Expense	5444	
All Others (to balance)		187,371.32
		$188,298.21

The following data provide information needed in adjusting the general ledger accounts and the operating expenses ledger accounts.

Merchandise inventory, May 31	$79,402.65
Insurance expense	1,621.18
Store supplies inventory, May 31	291.40
Postage inventory, May 31	89.95
Depreciation of store equipment	621.16
Depreciation of delivery equipment	2,149.20
Estimated uncollectible accounts expense	396.50
Office supplies inventory, May 31	256.70
Depreciation of office equipment	1,256.90
Interest accrued on government notes, May 31	220.00
Interest accrued on notes payable, May 31	364.00

The trial balance of the general ledger taken as of May 31 is shown on page 633. To conserve space, the accounts primarily involved in the adjusting and closing process are given. To make it possible to complete the work sheet, in two cases the balances of several accounts are shown as one amount.

Required: Prepare a ten-column summary work sheet for the year ended May 31, 19--, and a supplementary work sheet for operating expenses. Use as a guide the work sheets reproduced on pages 554-555 and 558. Allow 2 lines for Cost of Goods Sold on the summary work sheet.

Retain the solution to this problem for use in Problems 18-B, 19A, and 19B.

Rose & Thorn
Trial Balance
May 31, 19--

Cash	111	21,497.68	
Government Notes	121	12,000.00	
Accrued Interest Receivable	122		
Accounts Receivable	131	20,163.18	
Allowance for Doubtful Accounts	131.1		563.80
Merchandise Inventory	141	56,062.98	
Store Supplies	151	1,821.30	
Office Supplies	152	1,615.95	
Postage Stamps	153	592.11	
Prepaid Insurance	155	2,857.57	
Long-Term Assets (cost)		26,216.52	
Accumulated Depreciation-Store Equipment	181.1		1,256.36
Accumulated Depreciation-Delivery Equipment	185.1		2,088.37
Accumulated Depreciation-Office Equipment	191.1		1,186.55
Accrued Interest Payable	217		
Other Current Liabilities			16,421.11
W. Rose, Capital	311		82,265.13
W. Rose, Drawing	311.1	17,500.00	
P. Thorn, Capital	321		85,721.61
P. Thorn, Drawing	321.1	18,400.00	
Sales	411		692,117.23
Sales Returns and Allowances	411.1	4,211.18	
Purchases	511	513,674.51	
Purchases Returns and Allowances	511.1		3,961.03
Cost of Goods Sold	531		
Operating Expenses	541	188,298.21	
Interest Earned	431		692.80
Interest Expense	571	1,362.80	
		886,273.99	886,273.99

PROBLEM 18-B Adjusting entries; closing entries; and reversing entries

The work sheets for Rose & Thorn for the year ended May 31, 19--, completed in Problem 18-A, will be used to solve this problem.

Required: **(1)** Prepare the entries necessary to adjust the general ledger accounts and the operating expense ledger accounts as of May 31, 19--. Use the general journal illustration reproduced on pages 568-569 as a guide. **(2)** After making the required entries, foot the amount columns of each general journal page to prove the footings. **(3)** Prepare the entries required to close the following types of accounts in the general ledger: revenue accounts, expense accounts, the expense and revenue summary account, No. 331, and the partners' drawing accounts. Distribute the balance of the expense and revenue summary account equally between the two partners. Use the general journal illustration reproduced on page 570 as a guide. **(4)** Prepare the necessary entries to reverse the accrual adjustments as of June 1, 19--. Use the general journal illustration reproduced on page 574 as a guide. **(5)** After making the required entries, foot the amount columns of each general journal page to prove the footings. **(6)** Assuming that the individual posting to the general ledger accounts and the operating expense ledger accounts has been completed, insert the necessary check marks in the general journal. Enter the totals of the amount columns on each page and rule each page of the general journal. Assuming that the summary posting has been completed, make the necessary notations in the general journal.

PROBLEM 19-A Income statement; balance sheet

The summary work sheet for Rose & Thorn for the year ended May 31, 19--, completed in Problem 18-A, will be used to solve this problem. Presented below is some detail regarding the summary amounts that were shown on the work sheet:

Long-term assets (cost):	
Store equipment	$ 6,863.52
Delivery equipment	8,432.00
Office equipment	10,921.00
	$26,216.52
Other current liabilities:	
Notes payable	$ 7,000.00
Accounts payable	8,400.10
Accrued and withheld payroll taxes	1,021.01
	$16,421.11

Required: (1) Prepare an income statement for the year ended May 31, 19--. Since the business is not departmentalized, a separate schedule of cost of goods sold is not needed. Use as a guide the statement for MicroWorld illustrated on page 293. However, insufficient data are available either to itemize the operating expenses or to prepare a separate schedule of them. Round all amounts to the nearest dollar. (2) Prepare a balance sheet as of May 31, 19--. Use as a guide the balance sheet illustrated on page 585. While the firm maintains subsidiary ledgers of accounts receivable and accounts payable, trial balances of these are not provided and, thus, the preparation of schedules is not possible. Round all amounts to the nearest dollar.

Retain the solution to this problem for use in Problem 19-B.

PROBLEM 19-B Statement of changes in financial position; schedule of changes in working capital

Use the work sheets of Rose & Thorn from Problem 18-A or the balance sheet from 19-A. Additional information is given below:

Beginning of Year Balance Sheet Information

Cash	$ 32,437
Government notes and accrued interest	32,072
Accounts receivable (net)	30,209
Merchandise inventory	56,063
Supplies and prepayments	1,180
Total current assets	$151,961
Long-term assets (less accumulated depreciation)	21,685
Total assets	$173,646
Notes and accrued interest payable	$ 2,087
Accounts payable	2,625
Accrued and withheld payroll taxes	947
Total current liabilities	$ 5,659
Owners' equity	167,987
Total liabilities and owners' equity	$173,646

Required: Prepare (1) a statement of changes in financial position for the year ended May 31, 19--, supplemented by (2) a schedule of changes in working capital for that year. Use as a guide the statement and schedule illustrated on page 601.

PROBLEM 20-A Completing the work sheet

The Heicks are partners in the wholesale grocery business. They share profits and losses in the following ratio: D. Heick, senior partner, 60%; R. Heick, junior partner, 40%. Salaries are included in the profit shares. The calendar year is used as a fiscal year.

The partnership's accountant prepares quarterly and year-to-date income statements, as well as balance sheets, as of the last day of each quarter. The completed trial balance for Heick & Heick for the quarter ended March 31, 19--, is shown on the next page.

Required: **(1)** Prepare a ten-column work sheet for the quarter ended March 31, 19--. Use as your guide the sample work sheet on pages 608 and 609 except that in the ten-column work sheet, you will have the Adjusted Trial Balance columns. Enter the trial balance in the trial balance columns of the work sheet. From the following data and information, enter the necessary adjustments in the adjustments columns of the ten-column work sheet:

a. Transfer the beginning merchandise inventory to Cost of Goods Sold.
b. Transfer the purchases for the quarter to Cost of Goods Sold.
c. Transfer the purchases returns and allowances for the quarter to Cost of Goods Sold.
d. Amount of ending merchandise inventory, $334,988.
e. Interest accrued on mortgage since January 1, $4,200.
f. Insurance expense for quarter, $564.
g. Store supplies used during quarter, $743.
h. Depreciation of building, $1,050.
Depreciation of furniture and equipment, $318.
i. Estimated uncollectible accounts expense for quarter, $912.
j. Property tax assignable to quarter, $1,350.

(2) Extend the adjusted amounts to the adjusted trial balance columns and foot the columns as a means of proof. **(3)** Complete the work sheet, determine the amount of net income or net loss, and foot the income statement and balance sheet columns as a means of proof.

The solution to this problem will be needed in solving Problem 20-C.

Heick & Heick

Trial Balance

For the Quarter Ended March 31, 19--

	Acct. No.	Debit	Credit
Cash	111	31,343	
Accounts Receivable	131	44,212	
Allowance for Doubtful Accounts	131.1	224	
Merchandise Inventory	141	381,422	
Store Supplies	151	2,477	
Prepaid Insurance	155	3,866	
Land	161	120,000	
Building	171	390,477	
Accum. Depreciation - Building	171.1		186,659
Furniture and Equipment	181	55,767	
Accum. Depreciation-Furniture & Equip.	181.1		20,913
FICA Tax Payable	211		1,280
FUTA Tax Payable	212		58
State Unemployment Tax Payable	213		380
Employees' Income Tax Payable	214		2,188
Accrued Interest Payable	217		—
Accounts Payable	218		53,897
Mortgage Payable	262		226,000
D. Heick, Capital	311		267,690
D. Heick, Drawing	311.1	3,900	
R. Heick, Capital	321		212,460
R. Heick, Drawing	321.1	3,000	
Sales	411		255,060
Sales Returns and Allowances	411.1	1,815	
Purchases	511	165,290	
Purchases Returns and Allowances	511.1		1,518
Cost of Goods Sold (allow 2 lines)	531		
Partners' Salaries Expense	541	7,500	
Salaries and Commissions Expense	542	14,299	
Utilities Expense	543	416	
Supplies Expense	545	—	
Delivery Expense	546	509	
Depreciation Expense	547	—	
Insurance Expense	548	—	
Payroll Taxes Expense	551	1,040	
Property Tax Expense	552	—	
Uncollectible Accounts Expense	553	—	
Miscellaneous Expense	562	546	
Interest Expense	571	—	
		1,228,103	1,228,103

Accrued Property Tax Payable

PROBLEM 20-B Completing the work sheet

This is a continuation of Problem 20-A. The completed trial balance for Heick & Heick for the six-month period ended June 30, 19--, is shown on page 639.

Required: (1) Prepare a ten-column work sheet for the six-month period ended June 30, 19--. Use as your guide the sample work sheet on pages 616 and 617, except that in the ten-column work sheet, you will have the Adjusted Trial Balance columns. Enter the trial balance on page 639 in the trial balance columns of the work sheet. From the following data and information, enter the necessary adjustments in the adjustments columns of the ten-column work sheet:

a. Transfer the beginning merchandise inventory to Cost of Goods Sold.

b. Transfer the purchases for the six-month period to Cost of Goods Sold.

c. Transfer the purchases returns and allowances for the six-month period to Cost of Goods Sold.

d. Amount of ending merchandise inventory, $342,695.

e. Interest accrued on mortgage since January 1, $8,400.

f. Insurance expense for six-month period, $1,128.

g. Store supplies used during period, $1,327.

h. Depreciation of building, $2,100.
Depreciation of furniture and equipment, $636.

i. Estimated uncollectible accounts expense for period, $1,950.

j. Property tax assignable to period, $2,700.

(2) Extend the adjusted amounts to the adjusted trial balance columns and foot the columns as a means of proof. (3) Complete the work sheet, determine the amount of net income or net loss, and foot the income statement and balance sheet columns as a means of proof.

The solution to this problem will be needed in solving Problem 20-C.

Heick & Heick

Trial Balance

For the Six-Month Period Ended June 30, 19--

	Acct. No.	Debit	Credit
Cash	111	26,297	
Accounts Receivable	131	56,243	
Allowance for Doubtful Accounts	131.1	478	
Merchandise Inventory	141	381,422	
Store Supplies	151	3,162	
Prepaid Insurance	155	4,213	
Land	161	120,000	
Building	171	390,477	
Accum. Depreciation-Building	171.1		186,659
Furniture and Equipment	181	55,767	
Accum. Depreciation-Furniture and Equip.	181.1		20,913
FICA Tax Payable	211		1,314
FUTA Tax Payable	212		107
State Unemployment Tax Payable	213		707
Employees' Income Tax Payable	214		2,134
Accrued Interest Payable	217		—
Accounts Payable	218		45,263
Mortgage Payable	262		226,000
D. Heick, Capital	311		267,690
D. Heick, Drawing	311.1	6,000	
R. Heick, Capital	321		212,460
R. Heick, Drawing	321.1	4,700	
Sales	411		505,006
Sales Returns and Allowances	411.1	3,473	
Purchases	511	370,374	
Purchases Returns and Allowances	511.1		3,843
Cost of Goods Sold (allow 2 lines)	531		
Partners' Salaries Expense	541	15,000	
Salaries and Commissions Expense	542	29,236	
Utilities Expense	543	913	
Supplies Expense	545	—	
Delivery Expense	546	931	
Depreciation Expense	547	—	
Insurance Expense	548	—	
Payroll Taxes Expense	551	2,167	
Property Tax Expense	552	—	
Uncollectible Accounts Expense	553	—	
Miscellaneous Expense	562	1,243	
Interest Expense	571	—	
		1,472,096	1,472,096

Accrued Property Tax Payable

PROBLEM 20-C Interim statements

This is a continuation of Problems 20-A and 20-B. The ten-column work sheets completed in these two previous problems will be used here.

Required: **(1)** Prepare a year-to-date income statement for the six-month period ended June 30, 19--, an income statement for the quarter ended March 31, 19--, and an income statement for the quarter ended June 30, 19--. Use as your guide the sample comparative income statements on page 620. **(2)** Prepare a balance sheet in report form as of June 30, 19--, using as your guide the sample balance sheet on page 622.

INDEX

-A-

-B-

-C-

-D-

-R-

-S-

-T-

-U-

-V-

-W-

X-Y-Z